# Re-examining
# *PAUL'S*
# *LETTERS*

# Re-examining
# PAUL'S
# LETTERS

The History of the
Pauline Correspondence

# BO REICKE
edited by David P. Moessner
and Ingalisa Reicke

TRINITY PRESS INTERNATIONAL

The editors offer special thanks to Geoff Snook for preparing the indexes and to Jim Gunn for proofreading the page proofs.

Trinity Press International, P.O. Box 1321, Harrisburg, PA 17105
Trinity Press International is a division of the Morehouse Group.

Cover Design: Corey Kent

**Library of Congress Cataloging-in-Publication Data**

Reicke, Bo Ivar, 1914-1987
    Re-examining Paul's letters : the history of the Pauline correspondence / Bo Reicke ; edited by David Moessner and Ingalisa Reicke.
        p.   cm.
    ISBN 1-56338-350-0 (alk. paper)
    1. Bible. N.T. Epistles of Paul – Criticism, interpretation, etc.   I. Moessner, David P., 1949-  II. Reicke, Ingalisa.   III. Title.

BS2650.52 R45 2001
277'.066 – dc21

                                                                          2001027251

*Printed in the United States of America*

01    02    03    04    05    06              10   9   8   7   6   5   4   3   2   1

# Contents

– III –
DISPUTED SETTINGS OF
THE PAULINE CORRESPONDENCE

# Abbreviations

| | |
|---|---|
| AB | Anchor Bible |
| AJ | Josephus, *Antiquitates judaicae* |
| ATANT | Abhandlungen zur Theologie des Alten und Neuen Testaments |
| BHH | B. Reicke and L. Rost, eds., *Biblisch-Historisches Handwörterbuch* |
| BJ | Josephus, *Bellum judaicum* |
| BZ | *Biblische Zeitschrift* |
| CIL | *Corpus inscriptionum latinarum* |
| HE | Eusebius, *Historia Ecclesiastica* |
| HThR | *Harvard Theological Review* |
| JBL | *Journal of Biblical Literature* |
| JQR | *Jewish Quarterly Review* |
| NedThT | *Nederlands Theologisch Tijdschrift* |
| NovT | *Novum Testamentum* |
| RSR | *Recherches de science religieuse* |
| SEÅ | *Svensk Exegetisk Årsbok* |
| SNTS | Society for New Testament Studies |
| StTh | *Studia Theologica* |
| TLZ | *Theologische Literaturzeitung* |
| TR | *Theologische Rundschau* |
| TZ | *Theologische Zeitschrift* |
| ZKTh | *Zeitschrift für katholische Theologie* |
| ZNW | *Zeitschrift für die neutestamentliche Wissenschaft* |

# Foreword

When my husband, in early May 1987, finished the text for a planned series of lectures titled "The History of the Pauline Correspondence"—which, as it turned out, was to be his last manuscript—he expressed his desire to have it published. After his sudden death about two weeks later, I began to nurture the hope of fulfilling his wish.

Now as the completed volume, *Re-examining Paul's Letters,* is presented to the publisher, I must first express my gratitude to those who over these few long years have been so instrumental in helping me see this wish come to fruition.

The readers of the Introduction, which is a penetrating analysis of my husband's thinking, will understand my deep gratitude to David Moessner, one of the last of my husband's doctoral students. He and his wife, Dr. Jeanne Stevenson Moessner, remained friends of ours after they had completed their doctorates here in Basel and returned to the United States. On two memorable visits to their home in Decatur, Georgia, in 1985 and 1986, following my husband's retirement, my husband shared with his young New Testament colleague his plan to publish in English a volume of all his essays on Paul and Pauline theology (see Appendix 3). Thus, after my husband's death, when Dr. Moessner heard of this last manuscript on Paul, he was prepared to take up the challenge. He has given advice and help in the process of finding a publisher, has selected the additional essays on the settings of the letters, and through continuing contacts with me has edited the whole of *Re-examining Paul's Letters.*

I would also like to thank Dr. Bruce Metzger, a longtime friend whom my husband and I got to know through the international Society for New Testament Studies (SNTS), for expressing his unbiased conviction regarding the value of publishing the lectures on Paul. I am grateful that for years I was able to accompany my husband in attending the SNTS meetings, and most especially, as a widow, to be encouraged to continue attending these gatherings and thus keep in contact with developments in NT research, but especially to stay in touch with old friends. It was during a visit to the Metzger home in Princeton on New Year's Day, 1994, that I told Dr. Metzger of my husband's manuscript, and his enthusiastic response encouraged me to take action.

The first step was the working over of my husband's uncorrected English. In this respect it was a great joy to be able to work with my friend Rebecca Reese, American musician and music teacher in Basel, whom we had first met in the Lutheran Church there. She not only corrected the English of the manuscript, discussing every sentence with me, but also translated two of the German essays included here.

There followed further conferences with Dr. Moessner, either when he came to Europe for the SNTS or when I visited my daughter in New York. On one occasion Dr. Moessner's students in Decatur read parts of the manuscript. Confronted with the text, they contributed valuable and helpful questions. In his Introduction Dr. Moessner calls me my husband's "amanuensis." Both Bo Reicke and I were students in Uppsala (Sweden) when we met in the late thirties. Soon after our marriage in 1941 and after finishing my Master's degree in Latin, History, and Comparative Literature, I took over this role of an academic secretary. I never studied theology, nor ever had the intention to do so. It was because of my own training in the humanities that my husband first engaged me as his assistant in editing the *Swedish Bible Encyclopedia*, a job he had taken over in the midst of preparing for his doctoral thesis. Throughout our life together, he appreciated my help both in typing and in retyping his handwritten manuscripts, as well as my critical remarks on the texts themselves. He used to call me his "catalyst," because my questions would often spark the process of his thinking further about certain issues.

If the story of the present volume following upon the author's death is rather lengthy, the story of Bo Reicke's occupation with the apostle Paul is even longer and goes back to the beginnings of his studies at the Faculty of Theology in 1938. (On Reicke's academic career, see Appendices 2 and 3.) As was the rule, he first followed the courses in Old Testament and in the fall took up New Testament, joining the seminar led by Dr. Olof Linton, later professor of New Testament in Copenhagen. The topic was Acts. Because of illness, one of the fellow students failed to meet the deadline for his paper. Dr. Linton asked for a volunteer to present a paper on the apostolic council. With just one week's time, Bo Reicke took up the challenge and during that week was totally absorbed by this topic. For the next meeting, he presented some twenty tightly handwritten pages, which remained in our files for many years. Many of these ideas were developed for his first contribution to an international Festschrift (J. De Zwaan, 1952), an essay included in the present volume.

After his graduation and ordination in 1941, Bo Reicke spent four and a half years preparing for his doctoral degree in New Testament; a substantial part of this time was given to studies of the Old Testament, including courses in Syriac and Aramaic. His thesis, *The Disobedient Spirits and Christian Baptism: A Study of 1 Pet. III, 19* (1946), was followed by a series of papers and books, many of which deal with the history of the early church and Acts, but also with the newly found texts from Qumran. Already as a student at the "gymnasium" in Stockholm, he had been especially keen on history. No other teacher of his school days was so often remembered as was his history teacher, who, as was not unusual in Sweden of those days, was also a university professor and author of scholarly books.

It was therefore something very typical of Bo Reicke's thinking when he called the manuscript, which would be his last writing, "The History of the Pauline Correspondence." Reicke regarded the biblical texts as historical documents, products of human beings in historical settings.

As always, he had written the first draft of his Pauline lectures by hand. Some three years earlier we had bought our first word processor and used it for the English manuscript of *The Roots of the Synoptic Gospels* (Fortress Press, 1986), which had originally been written in German. As with the *The Roots*, he now dictated the text, often pausing, searching for a better expression, asking if I could follow.

It was thrilling to follow his dictation. It seemed to me that my husband was putting together a complex puzzle. One after another the pieces fell into place. Many of them I recognized; they had been prepared in short papers or used in other connections. Now he was presenting the whole picture that he had carried in his mind for years. When the manuscript was finished, he knew from the advice of his doctor that the journey to the United States could not be undertaken. He left out the last Pauline letter according to his chronology, Philippians, saying that two lectures on this letter, one included in this volume and another held in a seminar group of the SNTS meeting in Atlanta in 1986, could fill the gap. He certainly meant that he had written a manuscript that he would like to see published.

He died peacefully at home on the Sunday morning of May 17, 1987.

Because the handwritten draft on the history of the Pauline correspondence (Part II) was written for a series of lectures, it is natural that it contains no footnotes. References to other scholars are general; only a few titles on archaeology are explicitly mentioned. However, earlier in his book on the Synoptic Gospels there had been scarcely any footnotes referring to modern exegetical literature. In the Introduction to *The Roots,* this uncommon habit is explained with the following words: "Since the study does not follow the general trend of modern scholarship, there has not been great reason for references to literature." When I asked him about this, he responded, smiling with the Latin phrase *"sat sapienti"* ("a word to the wise is sufficient," as Benjamin Franklin translated the well-known adage); that is, "those who

know modern research will know who I mean, and those who know me will
know that I am not uninformed."

Bo Reicke regarded the research on the historico-cultural and philological
aspects of the New Testament, for which he had been so well trained, as his
special charism. Although he never published a book specifically on New
Testament theology, the theological dimensions of the text were always of
paramount interest to him. He believed the *euangelion* of the living Christ to
be the center of biblical theology, to which the books of the New Testament
give witness, each in its own individual way.

Already in 1943, Reicke's first published scholarly article dealt with Paul
and the law (Swedish, 1943; English, 1951 [*JBL* 70]). At the end of this
article, he deplores that he had to refrain from a thorough investigation of
the contradictory aspects in Paul's view of the law. One of his last major
articles gives his own solution to this much disputed problem ("Paulus über
das Gesetz," 1985 [*TZ* 41]. I dare say that the problem had never been
absent from his thinking. The present volume, *Re-examining Paul's Letters,*
along with other articles of his on the theology of Paul (see Appendix 3), are
parts of the same image of the apostle, consistently developed throughout
his life as a New Testament scholar.

One could give many examples of my husband's conviction that careful
listening to the texts and historical research on their language and "Umwelt"
again and again would give renewed insight into their theological meaning.
Let me quote here from the foreword to his Swedish commentary *First and
Second Peter and Jude,* "If the reader is surprised by the strange actuality in
the . . . warnings of the letters against materialistic and anarchic rebels . . . this
is not due to any attempt to 'modernize' the translation and commentary. It
has always been my intention to let the biblical texts speak for themselves
from within their own historical situation. It is instructive, however, to see
that this historical way of interpretation makes the biblical message come
alive in each new historical setting."[1] It was his conviction that biblical
exegesis is a never-ending science. Toward the end of his life, in a speech to
a group of his former doctoral students (Atlanta, August 1986), he expressed
his gratitude and joy that he had been allowed to serve in this most sublime
science.[2]

INGALISA REICKE

# Introduction

*David P. Moessner*

It is a special joy to see Bo Reicke's manuscript on the historical settings of the Pauline correspondence come to publication. Professor Reicke had just completed a series of lectures on the thirteen Pauline letters of the New Testament for presentation in the United States before his untimely death in the spring of 1987. Now through the gracious efforts of his widow and lifelong "amanuensis," Ingalisa Reicke, and the directors of Trinity Press International, Hal Rast and Henry Carrigan, this last of Bo Reicke's many writings can take its rightful place on the stage of seminal biblical scholarship.

Back in the early 1980s at the University of Basel, I was privileged to attend Reicke's lectures on the "Smaller Pauline Epistles" as well as "Paul's Captivity Epistles." Similar to the way Mrs. Reicke was witnessing a great mind gently and resolutely solve the enormous puzzle of the interrelationships of the canonical letters of Paul (see Foreword), I, too, experienced an uncanny feeling as I heard his expositions. Professor Reicke had struck upon insights never before conceived nor aligned with other historical data in quite the same way. It was indeed, as Mrs. Reicke describes, as if Professor Reicke had, at last, been able to locate the final, critical pieces of a seemingly impossible jigsaw puzzle and put them into "place" to transform the entire portrait of Paul's literary career. Unlike many previous attempts that require a "second career" of Paul after an initial imprisonment in Rome (post *c.* A.D. 60/61–62/63), *Re-examining Paul's Letters* weaves a whole new tapestry of Paul's priorities and endeavors for the gospel. Bo Reicke provides here nothing less than a solution to the riddle of the Pastorals and "deutero-Paulines" by fitting them seamlessly—to borrow a phrase from Raymond Brown— "into Paul's 'original career' known from Acts and the undisputed Pauline letters."[1] Whether or not the reader is persuaded by every argument, there is no doubt that, to date, Professor Reicke presents the most comprehensive and creative historical mosaic of the thirteen Pauline letters of the New Testament.

There is also no doubt that Professor Reicke would graciously resist

1

this characterization of his lifelong preoccupation with the life and contributions of the great apostle. Ever the Christian and true "doctor of the
church,"Reicke never exhibited the slightest motivation to force Paul into
a doctrinal straitjacket or require all thirteen of the traditional "Pauline"
letters to be written—in the modern sense—"by Paul himself." Nor did he
ever feel obligated to show where other schemes had got it wrong. Indeed,
Reicke pursued the historical settings of each letter out of the sheer thrill
of exploring and discovering the world of Paul. Thus one of the most re-
warding aspects of *Re-examining Paul's Letters* is to follow Reicke's own
forays into the winding contours of the apostle to light upon new sightings
of the deutero-Paulines and Pastorals from angles and vantage points often
far above and beyond the well-worn paths of investigation. Precisely because
his career-long research into the Greco-Roman and Jewish social and literary worlds could not fit most of the details of these "secondary Paulines"
into a setting after Paul's death, Reicke did not relent in his search for the
authentic settings of each letter. He came to new conclusions because, ultimately, the evidence had led him to new horizons—not because ideological
pressures or "theologically correct" impulses had urged him to shift. In fact,
his conviction that even the Pastorals must be integrated fully into the active
mission of Paul was so wholly unmotivated by any theological or confes-
sional bias that he never felt compelled to explain his new dating of the
Pastorals in his standard-setting *Neutestamentliche Zeitgeschichte.* In his
third (and final) German edition of 1982, treating the postapostolic period
in Chapter 7, he simply deletes the word *Pastorals* and changes the number
of NT books from 10/11 to 7/8 of those that most likely reflect the last third
of the first Christian century.[2] Instead of setting out to "solve a problem"
or "resolve an issue," Reicke was exhilarated by the historical terrain itself,
letting the evidence fall where it may and making adjustments only when
new discoveries so warranted.

Two outstanding features of Reicke's contribution bear highlighting:

1. From first to last, Reicke's method was thoroughly historical, precision-
tuned by one steeped in the classical, critical approaches to the ancient world.
Due to both the depth and breadth of this background, he thought it necessarily counterproductive to exclude a priori any dimension of evidence that
could have conceivably influenced the rhetoric of a given text. Both external
historico-cultural forces and internal human dynamics combine to produce
texts, and thus both spheres of evidence must be given their due. Reicke
therefore adopted what we can term generally a "dialectical" approach to
evidence, allowing each bit of information to interact, be scrutinized, and
adjudicated with all the other evidence in sifting and assigning each piece its
proper weight and relationship to a new whole taking shape. As became char-

acteristic of all of Reicke's scholarship, questions of historical background and theological milieu were settled by such balancing of all the evidence rather than the privileging of one dimension over another—even when engaging such time-honored perspectives as 'progressive schemes of history' or 'logical developments' of an author's ideas. Reicke was convinced that any attempt from the outset to limit or skew the evidence would lead inevitably to *circulus in probando*.

This open-ended approach explains why Reicke was never enamored of attempts to settle the sequence of Paul's letters by reconstructing Paul's inner theological development, or by restricting the only reliable chronological evidence to the "authentic" letters of Paul, or by favoring some inherent linear (textual) progression of external factors such as the collection for the saints in Jerusalem. All of these sets and subsets of information are important and need to be factored into the dynamic equation that must be derived from all the available external evidence, as well as from the undisputed letters of Paul. Otherwise, circular argumentation becomes unavoidable.

Perhaps Reicke's way of working can best be illustrated by his use of Acts in addressing Pauline chronology.

(a) *The Apostolic Council.* Rather than force a decision whether Paul's own description of his encounter with the "pillars" in Jerusalem (Gal. 2:1–10) should be correlated with one of Act's accounts of Paul's visits to Jerusalem, Reicke took his cue from the common judaizing pressure in both texts and consistently compared Paul and Acts with other depictions of this phenomenon in Greco-Roman authors. Josephus quickly became an important partner in this conversation, along with other historians and historical data of the imperial period (see esp. below, "Judeo-Christianity and the Jewish Establishment" [1984]). An epiphenomenon of this comparison took form, namely, that on the whole, Luke's portrayals of larger movements and consequences were reliable and could contribute in their own right to an emerging historical profile. Much fruit, in fact, was born in Reicke's research when Acts was appreciated alongside other Greco-Roman sources, and especially when Luke was perceived as part of a larger Pauline school rather than an unreliable or even negative foil to Paul. Even as a younger scholar, Reicke was impressed with the potential of Acts in this dialogical role, without, however, succumbing to the collateral pressure of harmonizing every theme or date common to both writers (see esp. below, "The Historical Background of the Apostolic Council and the Episode in Antioch" [1953]).

(b) *Ephesian Imprisonment.* Reicke's quest for the settings of the captivity epistles led him to conclude the "total lack of evidence for a Pauline imprisonment in Ephesus."[3] To be sure, Paul might well have been incarcerated overnight at Ephesus, as he undoubtedly was in a number of locations, à la Paul's own declamations;[4] but Reicke could find no concrete evidence for an extended captivity that would allow sufficient time for correspondence such as his letter to the Philippians. Reicke pointed out that the inscriptions discovered near Ephesus incorporating the word *praetorium*—which proponents for an Ephesian origin of Philippians have claimed for the presence there of the praetorian guard—referred in all three instances to a single veteran *praetorian*, assigned in his retirement to the duties of constable or highway patrolman (*CIL*, 6085, 7135, and 7136; cf. Gk. *praitorion* in Phil. 1:13—in the environs of Paul's imprisonment). (As Reicke put it in his characteristic humor, "One can hardly create an entire force out of one policeman!").[5] Thus failing direct data in any ancient source for either an Ephesian imprisonment or, for that matter, any active stationing of Caesar's elite guard *outside of Italy*, Reicke turned to Acts' description of Paul's mission in Ephesus, which now took on considerable importance. Even if Acts were silent about a captivity in Ephesus but intimated or even allowed the inference that Paul was imprisoned there for some time, then one would still have to entertain Ephesus as a possible provenance for at least one of Paul's captivity letters. But for Reicke, Acts seemed to slam the door shut. Not only, like Paul himself, did Acts summarize Paul's whole time in the province of Asia as one of great distress and suffering and yet remain silent about any imprisonment;[6] Acts also presents Paul right at the height of this mounting tension as escaping his enemies and leaving Ephesus under a cloak of secrecy.[7] All the movement in Acts leads the reader away from an assumption of imprisonment, and Acts, therefore, must also tip the scale away from making such an assumption a point of departure or even *modus operandi* in determining the order of Paul's letters. Rather than an Ephesian imprisonment or early Macedonian mission, etc., functioning as an anchor for Paul's epistolary enterprise, Reicke found the widespread, multi-attested zeal for the law and Paul's corresponding responses to his congregations a far more reliable chassis for mounting Pauline chronology. An important methodological axis, of course, was also established. It was now illegitimate procedure to ignore or even exclude evidence from any of the captivity epistles that did not square with an alleged early incarceration of Paul (see esp. below, "Caesarea, Rome, and the Captivity Epistles" [1970]).

The upshot of Reicke's historical approach to Pauline chronology can best be expressed by his overall finding: neither the deutero-Paulines (Ephesians, Colossians [2 Thessalonians]) nor the Pastorals reflect the post-Pauline *Sitz im Leben* of the church. What is remarkably absent from both groups of correspondence is precisely the two closely pressed concerns that stamp the subapostolic literature (A.D. 70–100), namely: (1) growing martyrdom among the larger church, and (2) the church's response to the burgeoning imperialistic pressure of Roman rule.

2. The second feature follows from the first. *Re-examining Paul's Letters* presents a richly developed, nuanced appreciation of a Pauline school. Reicke became persuaded that the primary evidence for such a school had not been taken seriously enough. Particularly in a contemporary climate of research that was confirming the ancient practice of co-writers—writers or "secretaries" expressing in their own idioms the thought communicated to them by the "author" or authority behind the text—Reicke was not satisfied that much of Pauline scholarship was subjecting pertinent biographical-chronological data from the "secondary" Paulines to rigorous scrutiny.[8] He became convinced that the hundreds of names, greetings, geographical details, requests, prayers, directives, and so forth in the "deutero-Paulines" and Pastorals were too quickly relegated to the "virtual reality" of post-Pauline pseudepigraphy and thereby dismissed as irrelevant to the usual historical-dialectical processes of investigation. How could it have come about that evidence which purported to relate the very information that modern scholars were seeking could be met with such indifference or skepticism? In response, Reicke turned to the conventions of ancient pseudepigraphy, as well as to the handbooks of ancient epistolary style.

Of the many insights gleaned from these studies, the most telling convention of ancient letter writing underscored by Reicke was the widespread use of personal or biographical details. The fact that such details could be laced throughout both public and private communications, appear spontaneously formulated and yet remain rhetorically stereotyped, and be conventionally fabricated as well as straightforwardly factual meant, for Reicke, that nothing about the factuality or origin of the deutero-Paulines and Pastorals was necessarily revealed through these details. But this meant, then, that the greater density of such "personal" information in these two groups than in the "undisputed" Paulines could no longer form the point of departure for pseudepigraphal theories. Each letter would have to be judged in its own right. The line of questioning for each Pauline letter then became: Do the stylized personal notices, instructions to colleagues, greetings from individuals, and so forth, make more "sense" in the overall rhetoric of the letter as ostensibly true and integral to the primary message(s) to be communicated to their intended recipients? Or are these details present to create an aura of verisimilitude as stemming from Paul but in actuality are second-level rhetoric, genuine knowledge of which is far removed for later post-Pauline generations? Are the deutero-Paulines and Pastorals more coherent—historically and rhetorically speaking—when the author(s) expect(s) immediate recognition of the names and direct responses to the instructions and greetings contained in them? Or, on the other hand, are these details clear rhetorical markers, discernible immediately as epistolary pretension and appreciated for the atmosphere of the Pauline legacy they compose, but not to be taken seriously as first level communication?

One of the more intriguing trails of *Re-examining Paul's Letters* is Reicke's own charting of these trajectories for each of these secondary Paulines. Yet because he set out to explore the whole world of Paul and was intending to write an introduction to the New Testament in order to place all of Paul's legacy in proper context, the reader is not handed the typical fare of "group" tours. Instead, Reicke makes all of Paul's correspondence strangely relevant by evaluating each set of circumstances in the illumination of the rest. Undoubtedly Professor Reicke would have refined even more the distinct theological and ethical contributions of each of the Paulines had he lived to see the realization of his goal. But as his own circumstances would dictate, Reicke deemed the first order of importance the determination of historical setting for each of the thirteen Paulines and the exigencies that sparked the particular style, content, and amplitude of each of Paul's "addresses" to his beloved churches (see "The Chronology of the Pastoral Epistles" [1976]).[9]

The brilliance of Reicke's approach is nowhere more transparent than in his treatment of 2 Timothy. Rather than rehearse the usual arguments "for" or "against" the "possibilities" of authenticity, or coerce its unique information and character into a preconceived mold, Reicke shows how this personal yet public letter becomes a window into the whole of Paul's achievement, an epitome of his "school." From such instructions as "bring the coat and the books ... " (2 Tim. 4:13), Reicke pulls out from this small missive "treasures both old and new" to compose a coherent, finely hued portrait of the whole of Paul's mission and its legacy of letters. By taking Paul's colleagues seriously as "co-compositionists," Reicke breathes life into the moribund Paul of the "pseudepigraphal present" to produce the flesh-and-blood Paul of his own generation. Indeed, Reicke's achievement of taking full account of the diversity, versatility, and adaptability of Paul and his cohorts in producing a variety of epistolary styles and subgenres, is no less than to revive Paul from his archival past and to make him come alive for every new generation.[10]

# – I –

# Roman Rule
# and the Settings of
# the Pauline Correspondence

# Judeo-Christianity and
# the Jewish Establishment, A.D. 33–66

During the middle third of the first Christian century—that is, between the crucifixion of Jesus, c. A.D. 33, and the outbreak of the first Jewish war, A.D. 66—the centre of Christianity acknowledged by all was constituted by the Jewish Christians in Palestine (Matt. 24:16 with par.; Acts 15:2; 1 Thess. 2:14; Rom. 15:26f; Acts 21:18). Our understanding of the political attitude adopted by the church in the days of the apostles—including the question whether the disciples of Jesus had connections with Jewish zealotism—must depend on what can be observed about the relations of the Jewish Christians in Palestine with the Jewish authorities of the period. Because the country was controlled by the Romans, the Jewish establishment represented by the high priest and Sanhedrin was supposed to maintain good relations with the Roman establishment represented by the prefect in Caesarea and the governor in Antioch, and indirectly with the *princeps* and senate of the empire. For the same reason the positive or negative relations between the Jewish Christians of the Holy Land and the Jewish rulers and leaders were of importance for the political attitude of the entire church during the apostolic period, A.D. 33–66.

## I

The story of the passion told by the evangelists implies that Jesus was accused of two different crimes before the Sanhedrin and the prefect: *(a)* of false teaching and *(b)* of rebellion. Since the forensic context was in each case a different one, there had to be this double charge. *(a)* Before the Jewish Sanhedrin, the high priest referred to Jewish legislation and accused Jesus of religious false teaching, here called blasphemy (Matt. 26:65 with par.).[1] *(b)* Before the Roman prefect, the high priest referred to Roman interests, and presented Jesus as a political troublemaker (Luke 23:2) who claimed

First published with the same title in *Jesus and the Politics of His Day*, ed. E. Bammel and C. F. D. Moule (Cambridge: Cambridge University Press, 1984), 145–52; reprinted by permission.

to be the King of the Jews (Matt. 27:37 with par.). Thus the Nazarene was 'reckoned with transgressors' (Luke 22:37), sacrificed by the populace instead of a revolutionary assassin (Mark 15:7), and crucified together with two bandits (Matt. 27:38 with par.).

After the death of Jesus, *c.* A.D. 33, until the exodus of the Jewish church shortly before the outbreak of the first Jewish war, A.D. 66 (Eusebius, *HE* iii. 5.3), the Palestinian Christians were repeatedly molested by the Jewish establishment or by the mob. Several prophecies were also quoted in order to show that Jesus had already foreseen this analogy between himself and the believers (for instance, Matt. 10:17–25; 24:9–22 with par.). But the historical evidence available implies that his disciples were in fact only accused of false teaching or blasphemy *(a)*, and there is no trace of their having been accused of rebellion *(b)*. This is certainly an important circumstance with regard to the question whether the Palestinian Christians had connections with so-called Zealots, those Jewish nationalists who, during the period in question, fought desperately against Greek influence and Roman sovereignty.

## II

Disciples of Jesus were in fact merely accused of (*a*) false teaching or even blasphemy in connection with different persecutions ascribed to the apostolic period, but never of (*b*) rebellion.

In three cases the charge was blasphemy, which had to be punished by stoning (Lev. 24:16): (1) at the trial of Stephen, A.D. 36 (Acts 6:14; the blasphemy was his statement that Jesus is superior to Moses and the Temple); (2) at the arrest of Paul, A.D. 58 (Acts 21:28; 24:6; Paul was alleged to have polluted the Temple); and (3) of James the brother of Jesus, A.D. 62 (according to Josephus, *AJ* xx. 200, he was accused of transgression of the law; according to Hegesippus in Eus. *HE* ii. 23.4, it was the scribes who stoned James because his confession of Jesus as the messiah irritated them).

In connection with two other persecutions of Christians in Palestine during the apostolic period, the charge was false teaching (below, 1 and 2); in two further cases there is no hint of any denunciation or incrimination (below, 3 and 4).

(1) The arrest of Peter and John in the Temple, *c.* A.D. 34, was said to have been arranged by the captain of the Temple together with other priests, and by the Sadducees (Acts 4:1). They were embarrassed by the great success the apostles experienced among the people, who had seen them heal a lame man and heard them preach a gospel of resurrection which the Sadducees

rejected as false teaching (4:2). For the moment, however, the Sanhedrin was not able to find them guilty of any crime (4:14–16).

(2) Some time afterward, *c.* A.D. 35—according to a parallel tradition also used by Luke, and presented by him in similar terms—the high priest arrested the apostles since he was jealous of the enormous interest Peter aroused among the people because of the signs he did (Acts 5:17), but also since he was afraid of being accused of having caused the death of Jesus (5:28). This time, it was reported, the Pharisaic Rabbi Gamaliel I declared before the Sanhedrin that if there were any reason for it God himself would destroy the community as he dissolved the infamous movements of Theudas and Judas the Galilaean, the pioneer of zealotism (Jos. *AJ* xviii. 23; *BJ* vii. 253); but otherwise he would protect the Christians against every human attack (Acts 5:36–39). Luke wanted to make clear that Gamaliel and the Sanhedrin left the question open whether the apostolic community led by Peter was comparable to the rebellious movements led by Theudas and Judas, or quite different from them. The subsequent development of the Nazarene movement was supposed to be the criterion, for if Christianity did involve anarchy, it would certainly be destroyed by God like the insurrections of Theudas and Judas. Every reader of Acts knew that the church was flourishing, and the famous Pharisaic scholar had therefore given Christianity a double testimony confirmed by historical facts; the gospel was not comparable to any propaganda of the Jewish revolutionaries, but inspired by God.[2]

(3) Judaea became a kingdom again for the years 41–44 under Agrippa I, the grandson of Herod I. It was this snobbish Herod who, around A.D. 42, gave orders to kill James the son of Zebedee, and later to arrest Peter (Acts 12:2–4). The execution of James was said to have pleased the Jews, and Luke saw here the reason why the persecution was continued by the arrest of Peter (12:3). This explanation is quite in harmony with the pro-Jewish and pro-Pharisaic policy that Agrippa I began to practise as soon as Claudius had made him king of Judaea (Jos. *AJ* xix. 293–302, 327, 330–34). During the years 37–40, when Caligula had favoured Hellenism in the empire, Christianity had rapidly been spread over the whole of Palestine and even to Phoenicia, Cyprus and Syria, reaching Hellenistic areas of great importance (Acts 8:4–11:30). As was evident at the persecution of Stephen in the year 36 (Acts 6:1, 9), the success of the Gospel among the Hellenists irritated orthodox Jews. Though he favoured Hellenism abroad, Agrippa I arranged the persecution of James and Peter around the year 42 in order to confirm that he was the great protector of Judaism in Palestine. It was for the same political reason that he neglected the interests of the Hellenistic centers, Caesarea and Samaria, the population of which rejoiced when he died in the year 44 (Jos. *AJ* xix. 356–9).[3]

(4) Though the famine around A.D. 46 and the apostolic council of the year 49 reduced the Judaistic opposition to Hellenism and thus also to Christianity (Acts 11:28–30; 15:19–20; Gal. 2:9f), the years 50–52 brought about violent quarrels between legalistic Jews and their neighbours in Rome, Alexandria, and Palestine. Indirectly the Christians had to suffer from this *Kulturkampf*. By an edict of A.D. 50, Claudius expelled the Jews from Rome because of constant rioting among them in connection with the messiah (Suetonius, *Divus Claudius*, xxv.4, speaks of a man called Chrestus), and for this reason Aquila and Priscilla came to Corinth (Acts 18:2). Between the Greeks and Jews of Alexandria there had been violent struggles in A.D. 38, and they began again *c.* A.D. 50, when both groups had to send delegates to Rome. Claudius, in the year 52, and under the influence of Agrippa II, decided the issue in favour of the Jews (*Acta Alexandrinorum* IVA, ii. 16f; IVC, ii. 21–24; ed. H. Musurillo; [Oxford, 1954] *The Acts of the Pagan Martyrs; Acta Alexandrinorum* [Lipsiae, 1961]). At the same time, a real war took place in Palestine. First the Jews were irritated by the soldiers of the Roman procurator Cumanus, then they went to war against the Samaritans, well knowing that Cumanus protected the population of Hellenistic *poleis*, Caesarea and Sebaste. Their attacks were especially carried on by demagogic anarchists under the leadership of a famous Zealot, Eleasar Dinaei, but also supported by aristocratic patriots under the leadership of the former High Priest Jonathan. Like the Alexandrian struggle, this Palestinian war led to a trial before the Emperor in A.D. 52, and since Agrippa II was successful in his defence of the Jews, Cumanus and the Samaritans were condemned (Jos. *BJ* ii. 223–46; *AJ* xv. 105–36). The same revival of Judaism was the background of the Jewish abuse of Christians in Judaea, of which Paul complained in a letter written in A.D. 52 (1 Thess. 2:14–16). Paul did not refer to any details and Luke avoided the story with regard to Agrippa II, but in different ways Jewish Christians of Palestine must be understood to have become the victims of the reinforced Jewish patriotism and zealotism, which triumphed in the trials of A.D. 52.

Thus the historical evidence available shows that the double charge preferred against Jesus, implying *(a)* false teaching and *(b)* rebellion, was extended to Jewish Christians in Palestine only with regard to *(a)* religious heresy, but never with regard to *(b)* social or political rebellion. Some persecutions took place without any legal trial, and no accusation is referred to. Generally the Christians were exposed to Jewish zeal for the law. The trials of the years 34 to 36 were led by two high priests belonging to the family of Annas, and the charge implied preaching the gospel of resurrection (Acts 4:1f; 5:17, 28) or criticism of Moses and the Temple (6:11–14; 7:1; 9:1); in *c.* A.D. 42 the persecution was organized by Herod's grandson

Agrippa I simply in order to please the Jews (12:1); in *c.* A.D. 52 the Zealot movement involved the Christians in the general terror (1 Thess. 2:14); in A.D. 58 Paul was nearly lynched by the mob because of their zeal for the Temple (Acts 21:28, 24:6), and made the Sadducees furious because of belief in the resurrection (23:6); eventually, the trial of the year 62 was caused by another high priest of Annas's family who accused James the Lord's brother of transgressing the Jewish law (Jos. *AJ* xx. 200). In all these contexts the Christians are represented as the victims of the Jewish establishment which fostered patriotism and zealotism.

# III

The history of the church during the years 33–66 is known only from Luke in Acts and Paul in his letters, and it must be admitted that both authors might have left out details which they found embarrassing. Luke and Paul adopted an optimistic attitude to the Roman establishment (Acts 28:30f; Phil. 1:13; 4:22). Is it not possible that some of the Jewish Christians shared the antagonism of the Jewish Zealots against Rome, although Luke and Paul did not describe any movement of that kind?

Here one has to observe the difference between the first and last half of the apostolic era, that is, between (1) the period 33–54 when Tiberius, Caligula, and Claudius governed the empire and Peter was the leader of the Jewish believers (Gal. 2:7), and (2) the period 54–66 when Nero was emperor, when Jewish zealotism became more and more predominant in Palestine, and James, the Lord's brother, was the leader of the Judaean churches (Acts 21:18).[4]

(1) There is not the slightest hint of any connection between Jewish insurgents and Christian believers during the years 33–54. On the contrary, the Christians were repeatedly the victims of Jewish patriotism and zealotism during this period. An *argumentum e silentio* is here inevitable, for the only alternative is the illogical conclusion that members of the churches led by Peter were Zealots because the sources do not mention it.

(2) But indications of a certain Christian zeal for the law are in fact given by Luke in Acts and Paul in his letters with regard to the years 54–66. This was the period when the notorious Hellenism of Nero caused a reaction of Judaism which became more and more violent, and then led to the first Jewish war, A.D. 66–70. If the Zealot troubles had already imposed severe difficulties upon the Christians of Judaea around A.D. 52 (1 Thess. 2:14), they grew into a veritable terror after Nero's enthronement in A.D. 54. This terror compelled Jewish Christians to combine their belief with a zeal for

the law, but it cannot be proved that they ever took part in revolution and violence.

Josephus was seventeen years old when Nero became emperor in A.D. 54, so his description of the reaction in Palestine was based on personal recollections. He had been an eager student of law under the guidance of Pharisees, Sadducees, and Essenes, but then suddenly left Jerusalem, and spent the years 54–56 with a Baptist community in the desert (Jos. *Vita* 9–12). Bearing in mind his remarkable opportunism, one understands that Josephus seized the opportunity to avoid the political terror which broke out in the first years of Nero's pronouncedly Hellenistic government. In his works on the Jewish war, he gave dramatic reports of the violent resistance characteristic of this period (Jos. *BJ* ii. 254–65; *AJ* xv 160–72). Just after Nero's enthronement bandits of a new kind came up in Jerusalem, the assassins called *sicarii*, because they carried a curved dagger (*sica*) under their clothes. With this Parthian weapon they secretly killed people supposed to collaborate with the Romans. Throughout the country they set fire to the houses of those who refused to support the resistance. Josephus said that everybody expected death any moment as one might in time of war (*BJ* ii. 256).[5]

Under the pressure of this political terror, Judaean Christians began to ask themselves whether it would not be advisable to accept the Jewish zeal for the law, and so be able to avoid the mortal danger. This led to a development of Judaism within Christianity during the years 54–61, and the spread of the zeal for the law can be followed in Paul's opposition to it.

Although the apostolic council of A.D. 49 had guaranteed equal rights to Jewish and Greek believers, supporters of James, the Lord's brother, made Peter and Barnabas uncertain some years later, and they withdrew from intercommunion with the uncircumcised. Paul was obliged to criticise Peter for this when he met him in Antioch after his second journey, A.D. 54 (Gal. 2:11–14). He had earlier been a Jewish Zealot who fought violently against the Christians to defend the traditions of the fathers (1:14), and knew the destructive effects of any zeal for the law (2:18f). Having left Antioch for his third journey, Paul was shocked to see the same exclusive Zealot movement dominating the Christians of Galatia (4:17). Then he was confronted with the Judaistic movement at Ephesus in 55 (Acts 18:25), and finally at Corinth in 56 (1 Cor. 1:12). Writing from the capital of Greece in 58, Paul warned the Roman Christians against unlawful behaviour and zealotism (Rom. 13:1, 13). He came back to Jerusalem a few months later, and there found thousands of Christians who had become Zealots for the law (Acts 21:20). To avoid troubles, the friends of James, the Lord's brother, advised him to demonstrate a certain solidarity with Moses in the Temple (21:23f). It did not help, for the mob accused Paul of sacrilege, and only the Roman garrison saved him from being stoned (21:27–32). Just as Paul had earlier been a zealous enemy of the Christians, so he was now exposed to severe Jewish fanaticism. Luke indicated this analogy in a speech ascribed to Paul (Acts 22:3). Paul himself referred to it while he was still in captivity after the Zealot riot in Jerusalem, and in very sharp language warned the Philippians against the influence of Judaistic materialism (Phil. 3:2, 6, 19). In the capital of the empire the danger of zealotism was especially great, as was later confirmed by Clement of Rome when he found zeal to have been the reason for persecution of several Christians as well as for the catastrophe of Israel (1 Clem. 5:1 to 6:4).

It is thus evident from Luke's narrative in Acts and from Paul's opposition in his letters that a certain zeal for the law was developed by Jewish Christians during the years 54–61. But it can be said only of this limited period. The zeal was caused by a desire to avoid the dangers of the Jewish reaction against the pro-Hellenistic emperor Nero. For this very reason the documents seem to give a reliable picture when they do not indicate the slightest Christian participation in the Jewish activities whether these activities were led by patriots or Zealots. On the contrary, Christians who did not join the extreme nationalists in Judea were probably exposed to pressure or persecution, as emphasised by Josephus with regard to his countrymen in general (Jos. *BJ* ii. 264f; *AJ* xx. 192). Paul experienced this in Jerusalem and Caesarea, A.D. 58 to 60 (Acts 21:28; 23:12; 25:3). James, the Lord's brother, although the leading authority of those Christians who recommended concentration on Mosaic traditions (Gal. 2:12; Acts 21:18, 20), was made the victim of Jewish nationalism in A.D. 62. He was accused of transgression of the law and stoned by the High Priest Ananus, then leader of the aristocratic patriots who, during the years 62–66, competed in rebellion with the demagogic Zealots (Jos. *AJ* xx. 185–214).

The trial of James, the Lord's brother, implies that he no longer represented that zeal for the law characteristic of his supporters in the years 54 and 58—at least not so definitely that it satisfied the Jewish establishment. It is probable that James as well as Peter, although both represented pronounced Jewish-Christian points of view in A.D. 54 (Gal. 2:12), were driven to change their policy around A.D. 60, and desist from Jewish nationalism. At any rate the Epistles which carry their names reject inclinations to isolation and zealotism (James 4:2; 1 Pet. 3:13). It must also be observed that many Christians left Jerusalem and Palestine during the years before the war began in 66 (Eus. *HE* iii. 5:3). While there may have been some contacts between Jewish Zealots and Christians in the period 54–60, this possibility is reduced to a minimum in the subsequent years.

# The Historical Background
# of the Apostolic Council and the
# Episode in Antioch (Gal. 2:1–14)

## 1

(a) At the beginning of the second chapter of his letter to the Galatians, Paul states that he attended a council in Jerusalem, a gathering generally referred to as the apostolic council. There Paul's gospel of justification by faith was discussed and in particular the question whether Gentiles could be admitted to the church without being circumcised.

Galatians 2:1–10, slightly abridged, reads as follows:[1]

> [1]Then after fourteen years I went up again to Jerusalem with Barnabas, taking Titus along with me. [2]...I laid before them (but privately before those who were of repute) the gospel which I preach among the Gentiles lest somehow I should be running or had run in vain [7]...when they saw that I had been entrusted with the gospel to the uncircumcised, just as Peter had been entrusted with the gospel to the circumcised [8-9]....James and Cephas and John, who were reputed to be pillars, gave to me and Barnabas the right hand of fellowship, that we should go to the Gentiles and they to the circumcised. [10]Only they would have us remember the poor, which very thing I was eager to do.

According to Paul, the council decided to apportion the missionary field and to require of Paul, as missionary to the Gentiles, no additional duties apart from helping with the economic support of the Jerusalem congregation (referred to as "the poor" in verse 10). In this way, in Paul's opinion at least, the leaders of the church accepted—without any conditions—Jewish and Gentile Christians as equals.

The Book of Acts offers an apparent parallel to this account (Acts 15:1–35), but the proceedings are depicted somewhat differently. The most

First published as "Der geschichtliche Hintergrund des Apostelkonzils und der Antiochia-Episode, Gal. 2.1–14," in *Studia Paulina in honorem Johannis de Zwaan septuagenarii* (Haarlem: J. Bohn, 1953), 172–87. Translated by Rebecca Reese and by the editors.

important variation concerns the so-called apostolic decree, the requirement that Gentile Christians at the minimum abstain from food offered to idols (Acts 15:10, 29). Whether the decisions of Acts 15 reflect the same council of Galatians 2 is, of course, a well-known matter of disagreement,[2] the details of which fall outside the bounds of this article.[3] Most scholars, however, agree that the two accounts, and perhaps also that in Acts 11:27–30, do concern the same assembly,[4] despite the differing details.[5] For the moment, however, we will concern ourselves only with Paul's account in Galatians, supported occasionally by parallel passages in Acts, because it is clear that the two accounts basically agree.

According to both sources, Peter, whom Paul often referred to by his Aramaic name *Cephas* (Acts 15:7; Gal. 2:9), was among the leaders of the Jerusalem church who took part in the apostolic council and extended to Paul the "right hand of fellowship." On this occasion he is described as the person primarily responsible for the mission to the Jews (Acts 15:7–11; Gal. 2:7–8), whereas James, the brother of the Lord, now appears as the leader of the Jerusalem congregation (Acts 15:13–21; Gal. 2:9, 12).[6] In neither context is Peter presented as an advocate of the judaizers. On the contrary, Paul mentions Peter's unqualified support of the Gentile mission, and the Book of Acts even portrays him at an early stage as a convinced protagonist of the universal mission, not just in Caesarea (Acts 10:1–11:18), but at the apostolic council as well (Acts 15:7–11).

(b) For this reason, Paul must have been greatly disappointed when he heard later in Antioch that Peter no longer risked association with Gentile Christians but rather withdrew from the sacred meal fellowship with them. The description of this episode, which forms the second focus of this study, follows immediately upon the text cited above (Gal. 2:11–14):[7]

> [11]But when Cephas came to Antioch I opposed him to his face, because he stood condemned. [12]For before certain men came from James, he ate with the Gentiles; but when they came, he drew back and separated himself, fearing the circumcision party. [13]And with him the rest of the Jewish Christians acted insincerely, so that even Barnabas was carried away by their insincerity. [14]But when I saw that they were not straightforward about the truth of the gospel, I said to Cephas before them all: If you, though a Jew, live like a Gentile and not like a Jew, how can you compel the Gentile Christians to adhere to Jewish customs?

Paul deals with the same subject in the seven following verses, but here the "Antioch episode" serves only as a springboard. What begins as a report of the confrontation between Peter and Paul develops into a theological discussion with the recipients of the letter. We will leave these verses out of our discussion; the present study will restrict itself to the Antioch episode.

What is of particular interest to us is that while Peter was in Antioch, after a period of time he is alleged to have abandoned the principles of the council. Even Barnabas, who at the council also defended the admission of Gentiles to the church without submission to the Jewish law, was soon carried away with this "hypocrisy," as Paul was not hesitant to call it. Exactly how long after the council these events occurred is not reported. However, for social-psychological reasons, we may assume that the two missionary leaders did not discard the council's decisions immediately, but only some years later. It is therefore more logical to connect the Antioch episode with Acts 18:22, rather than with the mention of Antioch already in 15:35. This earlier reference describes the success of Paul and Barnabas in Antioch after the council, before the second missionary journey; the latter passage mentions only briefly that Paul visited this city after the second missionary journey. Together these references allow a closer estimate of the date of the Antioch episode. Because Paul's second journey took place from approximately A.D. 50–53, as determined by collating the Gallio inscription[8] with Acts 18:12–17, the Antioch episode most likely occurred in the year 53 or 54. It can further be observed that the relapse of Peter and Barnabas into the legal observances of the judaizers was due to agitation from the circle around James, as Paul makes clear in Gal. 2:12.

# 2

The argument developed here sheds light on the historical background of the two events described in Gal. 2:1–14. Why did the church leaders at the Jerusalem council at first agree that Gentile converts need not conform to Jewish law, and why at a later point did the circle around James pressure Peter and even Barnabas to distance themselves from the uncircumcised?

The historical-political climate of the young church at that time helps explain this peculiar change in their way of acting. The fact that under one set of circumstances the leaders in Jerusalem could reverse their way of behaving becomes understandable when the dynamics of the external situation are examined. We will see that Peter's behavior and that of the church leaders no longer appear as inconsistent and unfounded as they generally do when attributed to theological or psychological vacillation.[9] Our explanation does not mean that Paul's criticism was unjustified. If his description is correct, which in its essentials can hardly be doubted, then the church leaders did not act straightforwardly (*ouk orthopodousin*, Gal. 2:14). Their actions become explicable, however, when the surrounding circumstances are taken into account.

One important clue to these circumstances appears in Gal. 2:12, where Peter is described as withdrawing from the Gentiles "fearing those of the circumcision." "Those of the circumcision" must refer to Jews who zealously advocated circumcision, and not to Jewish Christians in general—the latter in this context always referred to as "Jews"—whom Peter had no reason to fear, being one himself. "Those of the circumcision" must designate those Jews zealous for the law who persecuted and oppressed Christians whenever they made contact with Gentiles. Paul himself had formerly belonged to this fanatical group. To be sure, individual Jewish Christians could be included among those posing danger, whether as informants or provocators of unrest. But by far the greater danger stemmed from the fanatics within Judaism itself.

In fact, it appears that the noticeable reversion to legalism on the part of some of the apostles in Antioch was connected to the rising advance of Jewish zealotism. Earlier, at the apostolic council, this movement had not posed a threat. Instead, there were perhaps other problems that necessitated better relations with the Gentile Christians. How and why this change took place is elucidated by the following historical overview of the church's relationship with these legalistic Jewish Zealots.

(a) According to the Book of Acts, the young church during the thirties was attacked from two sides, from Jewish public officials and from "zionistic" Diaspora Jews.

The priests and Sadducees were the source of the first two persecutions (Acts 4:1–22; 5:17–42), which were instigated by the authorities' fears of messianic insurrections (Acts 5:36–39).[10]

Acts 6:8–8:3 describes a persecution incited by Stephen's confrontation with Jews from Rome (where the "Freedmen" probably lived), Cyrene, Alexandria, Cilicia, and Asia. The charges involved an alleged disregard for the Mosaic law and the Temple in Jerusalem (Acts 6:11, 13–14). These Diaspora Jews were, so to speak, ardent "zionists,"[11] not surprisingly, for their relative freedom and independence from the Gentiles depended upon the unquestioned stability of the Jewish Temple and the law of Moses. These "palladia" were important above all for the Jews' own right of jurisdiction in Greco-Roman cities. This campaign of zionistic-oriented Diaspora Jews soon grew into a general persecution of Christians in Palestine and even as far as Damascus where, among others, Saul/Paul took part. The various forms of persecution became so violent that one is reminded of the tactics of the Zealots. Although Josephus places the emergence of the Zealots generally in the decade of the fifties, he nevertheless pushes back their founding to the beginnings of the century. For a variety of reasons it is probable that the group was also active in the intervening years. It is striking, for example, that Paul, when referring to himself as a former persecutor of the church, chooses the designation "zealot" (Acts 22:3; Gal. 1:14). Although this term need not imply his direct involvement with the movement, its use no doubt connotes the well-known zealot movement. In any event, an intensive zeal for the law was underfoot during this time. Moreover, during the thirties a violent *Kulturkampf* raged between Jews and Greeks in Alexandria, as is known from the accounts in Philo's *In Flaccum* and *Legatio ad Gaium,* and the *Acts* of the Alexandrian martyrs (*Acta Alexandrinorum*). It was precisely in the thirties when a strong Jewish sentiment began to play a dominant role.

In light of prevailing Jewish influence, it is remarkable that immediately after the death of Stephen the church could undertake a direct mission to the Gentiles. In fact, according to Acts, the missionaries were expelled from Jerusalem during the subsequent persecution and, as a consequence, proceeded to carry out successful evangelization in Hellenistic areas (Acts 8:1–40; 10:1–11:18). Some, including Paul (Acts 11:25–26), even worked in Antioch for the conversion of Greeks (Hellenes) (Acts 11:19–26). At that time there seem to have been no further persecutions by the Jews.

(b) In the early forties, however, the leaders of the church of Jerusalem underwent severe persecution through the hand of Herod Agrippa, who reigned over all of Palestine from A.D. 41 to 44. Acts 12:1–19 describes his execution of James the son of Zebedee and his imprisonment of Peter, although the latter would be miraculously released. Both Josephus and the Mishna recount how keen Herod Agrippa was to court the favor of Torah-zealous Jews;[12] in all probability this "judaizing" disposition was a key factor in these persecutions.

After Herod's death in 44 the land was again placed under the rule of a Roman procurator, which for a time caused the extremist movement to subside. The picture that emerges when reading Josephus is that life was relatively peaceful under the first three procurators who reigned in Caesarea from A.D. 44 to 52: Cuspius Felix, Tiberius Alexander, and Ventidius Cumanus. Josephus mentions only a few disturbances during this period, which forms a striking contrast to the dramatic treatment he affords the Zealots during the later procurators. To be sure, major insurrections did occur under Cumanus (48–52), but these "were only single instances provoked by individuals."[13] Claudius, who was elevated to Emperor in A.D. 41, probably contributed to this general peace through his *Epistula Claudiana* in the fall of 41, which publicly admonished the Jews of Alexandria to live in concord with the Greeks.[14] Apparently, Claudius' decree was effectual for a time,[15] which must have indirectly influenced Jewish life in Palestine.

In the second half of the forties, then, a relatively stable situation reigned in Palestine. Extreme Jewish nationalism was somewhat subdued, and the Zealots had not yet achieved any dominant influence.

The apostolic council probably took place at this time of relative security. The question of dating, of course, remains controversial. But because Paul appeals at the council to his success among the Gentiles (Gal. 2:7–8), it may be assumed that he had already completed his first missionary journey (Acts 13–14). Therefore the gathering described in Acts 15:1–35 is probably in fact the apostolic council, despite differences in the accounts.[16] Paul's second missionary journey took place after this council in the years A.D. 50–53, as sketched above. In this way the year 48 comes to the fore as the likely date of the council. As already argued, this date falls during the period of relatively peaceful inner-political relations, when Jewish Christianity would have been positively oriented to Gentile Christianity.

One particular circumstance may have contributed to the church leaders' acceptance of the stance of Barnabas and Paul, notwithstanding the misgiving of some believers toward the uncircumcised. As is known from ancient historians,[17] the eastern provinces of the Roman empire suffered a severe famine around the year A.D. 48, which is also alluded to in Acts 11:27–30.[18] In Judaea, the famine may also have been exacerbated by the occurrence of a Sabbath year in 47–48. At any rate, it is apparent that "the poor" of the Jerusalem congregation and Jewish Christians in Judaea in general must have experienced the effect of the famine precisely at the time of the apostolic council, assuming the usual dating of it is correct. In order to receive economic support from the Gentile Christians, the early church would have been inclined to accept the uncircumcised as equal partners (see Acts 11:29; 12:25). This historical background also makes understandable the stipulation under which Barnabas and Paul were allowed to carry out the mission to the Gentiles (Gal. 2:10): that they remember "the poor," namely, that they continue as before to collect offerings for Jerusalem from the Gentile Christians. The plight of the Jerusalem congregation, then, was critical in building the consensus of the council's decision.[19]

(c) However, in the decade of the fifties the congregation in Jerusalem was threatened by new developments that made open acceptance of the uncircumcised increasingly difficult. During this time, the Zealots grew in power and influence and began a reign of terror over the Jewish people that lasted until the end of the Roman-Jewish war around A.D. 70. Anyone who had anything to do with Greeks or Romans was subjected to ghastly persecution. Isolated rebellions of the Jewish people had already occurred under the procurator Ventidius Cumanus (A.D. 48–52), but it was not until the rule of Antonius Felix (52–60) that the chauvinistic terror became relentless, only to increase to unbelievable proportions during succeeding procuratorships. Among other things, Josephus and Tacitus relate that during the time of Felix the chauvinists, or "bandits," ratcheted up their violence and appeared as *sicarii* ("dagger-carriers") or would hire such assassins to eliminate all suspected "collaborators."[20] This zealotism was also at home in the Diaspora. According to Acts 21:38, it was an Egyptian Jew who led the four thousand *sicarii* (assassins); Acts 21:27 mentions Jews from the province of Asia who violently threatened Paul for entering the Temple. On the whole, it was Jews in Greece and Asia Minor who repeatedly used violent means to thwart Paul's Gentile mission. These tactics amount to nothing other than zealotism when understood in the broadest sense of the word, and not solely as the organized political movement upon which Josephus diplomatically focuses his attention in order to avoid casting suspicion on his own people. Nevertheless, despite this widespread engagement, the center of this terror certainly emanated from within Palestine.

Given such inner-political intrigue in the fifties, it is not surprising that Christians in Judaea and elsewhere were threatened and persecuted by Jewish zealots. An apostle such as Peter had every good reason to fear "those of the circumcision," and, in fact, Gal. 2:12 states explicitly that it was out of this fear that he separated himself from the uncircumcised. Paul, of course, is also clear that Peter had made a calculated mistake. But even a cursory glance at the church's inner-political situation reveals that Peter and the leaders of the Jerusalem church had concrete reasons for their renewed caution. As previously described, the Antioch episode probably occurred in A.D. 53 or 54, namely, during the procuratorship of Antonius Felix, which was seething with zealotic outbreaks of violence.

Moreover, Paul himself mentions in 1 Thessalonians (2:14–16) (probably written in A.D. 51 or 53), that a persecution of Jewish Christians took place precisely at this time:

> [14]For you, brethren, became imitators of the churches of God in Christ Jesus which are in Judaea; for you suffered the same things from your own compatriots as they did from the Jews, . . . [16]by hindering us from speaking to the Gentiles that they may be saved—so as always to fill up the measure of their sins. But the (God's) wrath has come upon them for their end.

That is to say, the Thessalonians were persecuted by the Greeks just as the Jewish Christians were persecuted by the Jews. This persecution belongs in the same period as the resurgence of zealotism and the Antioch episode.

One should recognize, then, that Peter withdrew from the Gentile Christians out of well-founded fears of reprisal that threatened not only him but also the congregation. That Paul so severely condemned his colleague's action was not due to ignorance of the situation; according to 1 Thessalonians, Paul was well aware of the impending persecution. Rather, Paul's severe condemnation was due to his unflinching love for the Gentile mission and his willingness to suffer for Christ. But given the enormous pressure they were experiencing, the leaders of the church in Jerusalem felt differently. As the historical documents attest, the Palestinian Jewish Christians were in danger of persecution by the Zealots, and the church leaders would have come to something like the following conclusion: There is only one effective solution to this crisis; for the time being, break off relations with all Gentiles or uncircumcised and agree as much as possible to the demands of the judaizers regarding the law and circumcision.

This understanding of the situation is undoubtedly the purely substantive reason why Peter, Barnabas, and other Jewish Christians in Antioch found themselves under the influence of James and his circle and subsequently broke off relations with the Gentile Christians. From their vantage point, the very existence of the early church was at stake.

3

The specific historical reasons for this "judaizing" of church politics in Jerusalem must, moreover, be viewed in conjunction with the appearance of the Lord's brother, James, as the main leader of the congregation during the same time that Peter is engaged with mission primarily outside Palestine (following his persecution in Acts 12). With his judaizing sympathies, James was the person best suited to emerge as head of the church in this time of nationalistic fervor. His words at the apostolic council are representative of this judaizing orientation as they stress the special position of the chosen people and the Davidic royal line (Acts 15:14–18). James declares to Paul upon the latter's return to Jerusalem around A.D. 58 (Acts 21:20): "You see, brother, how many thousands there are among the Jews of those who have become believers, and they are all zealots (*zelotai*) for the law." Zealots in this phrase is used without its negative connotation; but it cannot be denied that, at some level, the word here itself smacks of the self-designated sense for the Zealot movement. The highest authority in the Jerusalem congregation is now advising Paul to adapt to the fact that there are many thousands of Christian zealots in the church. Even though these converted Jews did not resort to the violent tactics of the (Jewish) Zealots and the *sicarii* (assassins), nevertheless, they—by all appearances—were able to monitor compliance to ritual purity. Because of this enforcement and the zeal of the Jewish Christians for the law, the Christian "presbytery" under the leadership of James found it expedient to advise Paul to take the greatest of precautions (cf. Paul's compulsory circumcision of Timothy in Acts 16:3).

James served as leader of the church in Jerusalem until his death in A.D. 62, and his relations with the judaizers in the congregation must have been close, though not with the warring Zealots, or *sicarii*. Eusebius[21] cites the much-traveled Hegesippus (d. *c.* A.D. 180), who relates that James bore the messianic title "the righteous one," that he presented himself as a Nazirite, and that he spent much time in the Temple, where he would pray so persistently for his people that his knees became as calloused as a camel's. It was for this reason that he was also much loved by the Jews, not least by the strict Rechabites. In A.D. 62 James fell victim to a horrible "judicial murder," instigated by the Sadducean high priest Ananus the Younger, who used the riot-filled interregnum between the procurators Felix and Albinus "to do away" with his own as well as Rome's alleged enemies. Yet even at the moment of his death James did not cease to pray for Israel. His death caused such outrage in the Jewish community that many saw the destruction of Jerusalem some years later as the punishment for the execution of this "righteous one." Finally, James' claims to Davidic lineage should be mentioned, claims upon which both his family and his successors placed such great importance. The details in Hegesippus should not be challenged in their essentials; they are, moreover, confirmed by Josephus, whose short description can certainly not be a secondary interpolation.[22] In fact, everything that can be known about James speaks in favor of his close connections with the judaizing movement—apparently, however, without succumbing to the more violent tactics of some in the broader Torah-zealous movement.[23]

It was obviously quite valuable, therefore, during the time of a strong judaizing thrust to have as leader of the Jerusalem congregation one as blameless and upright in the eyes of the Jews as James. That this one known by all to be the "righteous" brother of the Lord was placed at the head of the church was probably even a conscious accommodation to the nationalistic fervor of Judaism during this time.

Fundamentally, therefore, it was no accident that the episode that unfolded in Antioch according to Gal. 2:11–14 was successful in enabling "the people around James" to segregate Jewish Christians from their uncircumcised brethren. This development was, in fact, the result of a programmatic and ever-increasing judaizing of the church, influenced by leading circles of the Jerusalem congregation.

It was not long before this Jerusalem-centered judaizing movement extended its influence to more remote Christian congregations, and it was for this reason that Paul wrote, among other correspondence, his letter to the Galatians. Those behind the judaizing of the Galatian congregations appealed vigorously to Jerusalem for their authority, as can be gathered indirectly from the polemic of Gal. 1:10–24 and 4:24–25. But in response, Paul stresses that Christians should never strive to "please human beings" (Gal. 1:10; cf. 1 Thess. 2:4). That he, nevertheless—in the face of this opposition—continued to prove himself faithful to the task of collecting alms for the Jerusalem community, demonstrates, more than anything else, the magnanimity, as well as magnitude, of his Christian stature.

# – II –

# History of
# the Pauline Correspondence

# 1. Introduction

In the New Testament, the church has preserved thirteen letters written by Paul or published under his name. Hebrews is not among them, because it neither contains the name of Paul nor represents the same literary genre as the Pauline correspondence. Hebrews is an extended homily, overlapping only marginally with features characteristic of letters.

In contrast, the thirteen letters of the Pauline correspondence exhibit the essential elements of Greek letters, including the names of the author(s) and recipients, blessings (or wishes of good fortune), and greetings. Moreover, Paul's letters combine features of both private letters and public communications, or so-called "epistles." Pauline letters appear, in fact, to be hybrids of these two epistolary types, and thus each of the letters or epistles will be treated below without concern for any formal distinction between the two terms.

Nine of the Pauline letters were directed to churches of special importance to Paul:

- Galatians, Colossians, Ephesians: Asia Minor
- 1–2 Thessalonians, Philippians: Macedonia
- 1–2 Corinthians: Greece
- Romans: Italy

Four of the epistles were sent to personal friends of the apostle:

- Philemon to a friend in Colossae
- 1 Timothy to a collaborator in Ephesus
- 2 Timothy to a collaborator in Troas
- Titus to a collaborator in Crete

# 2. Questions of Method and Procedure

Paul also wrote other letters that are not included in the New Testament. Explicit references to such letters, however, make it clear that they were known to Paul's contemporaries, only sometime later to be lost for posterity (2 Thess. 2:2, 15, indications of letters spread in the vicinity; 1 Cor. 5:9, a predecessor of 1 Corinthians; 2 Cor. 2:3, 4, 9; 7:8, 12, a letter written between 1 and 2 Corinthians; Col. 4:16, a letter sent to Laodicea). Other circumstances support the conclusion that Paul's letter production was much greater than what is reflected in the canon. As will be argued in the following discussion, the canonical letters of Paul may be dated to the period A.D. 51–61, with even the earliest extant letters displaying a characteristic structure that Paul must have developed in the years between his conversion (A.D. 36) and the writing of the latest preserved letter (c. A.D. 61).

In several canonical letters, friends of his also figure as coauthors so that Paul appears to have been the leader of a literary team (e.g., 1 Thess. 1:1: Paul, Silvanus, and Timothy). Furthermore, his letters indicate that Paul generally used secretaries (*amanuenses*), adding only words of greeting in his own hand (2 Thess. 3:17; Gal. 6:11; 1 Cor. 16:21; Rom. 16:22; Col. 4:18; Philem. 19). For this reason, too, the Pauline correspondence must be assumed to be more extensive than that found in the canon. In addition, the importance of Paul's epistolary endeavors is evidenced by his insistence that the letters be read publicly (1 Thess. 5:27; Col. 4:16). No doubt the literary activity of Paul, who forcefully and enthusiastically spearheaded the church's mission initiatives, went far beyond the selection now ensconced in the New Testament.

This expansion of his production with the aid of collaborators and stenographers implies that questions of authenticity and integrity should not be treated in the individualistic terms that came to characterize the higher criticism of the nineteenth century and continues even today.

Paul himself once emphasized that he was able to adapt his preaching to Jews, Greeks, and other peoples according to conditions that would facilitate their conversion (1 Cor. 9:19–22). It is, therefore, not fair to deny, as is often done, that Paul could have written in a variety of styles. The authenticity of the letters should not be judged merely on the basis of a comparison with the critic's a priori "standards." On the contrary, because Paul must have also produced a considerable number of letters in a variety of situations beyond those represented in the NT canon, he was certainly able to adopt various styles and forms of expression. This ability to diversify is enhanced even more when Paul's preference for collaborators and stenographers is kept in the forefront. These "co-compositionists" may well have contributed a passel of variation, such that each letter does not always represent the same type or subtype, and parts within the same letter do not always fit well together. Beyond even those considerations, the very practice of dictation implies that disconnections, interpolations, and fluctuations may, for psychological reasons, have emerged in the original composition and are not necessarily the result of scribal errors or deliberate changes of a later hand.

Thus, the modern notion of a writer sitting in his or her study and producing a manuscript complete with copyright ought not be applied to questions of authenticity and integrity in the Pauline epistles. It is anachronistic to regard Paul as such a man of letters. But this modern stereotyping is often practiced when scholars are convinced they can separate genuine Pauline epistles from so-called deutero-Pauline or even pseudepigraphic compositions, or even allocate parts of an extant letter to different originals. This practice becomes extremely dubious when research is based primarily on the inherited results of critical studies or upon ingenious suggestions of renowned scholars. At an international meeting of New Testament professors some years ago, one lecture consisted of a careful summation of German contributions to the division of Pauline epistles into authentic and nonauthentic components. It was remarked afterward that if all of the speaker's radical criticism were to be trusted, Paul could not have written letters but only postcards. There is a certain ironic truth to this caricature in that Paul probably inscribed with his own hand only a few words of greeting. Nevertheless, his personal responsibility for the letters remains the fundamental point.

It is true, on the other hand, that disagreement is also found among the numerous scholars who are eager to distinguish between Pauline and pseudepigraphic elements without considering the teamwork to which Paul himself referred. Characteristic examples are the different opinions about the authorship of Colossians or the integrity of Philippians. Regardless of a scholar's stance in such a debate, the argument is based on the general belief that Paul was obliged to follow (critically established!) theological and stylistic principles when he wrote his letters, with the result that variations in the message and transitions in the discourse are stamped as secondhand.

Anachronistic criticism of this type is made questionable by the historical circumstances gleaned from the text itself: (a) that Paul possessed willingness and capacity to adapt his communications to different audiences; (b) that he produced many letters beyond those preserved in the canon; (c) that he worked in collaboration with valued friends who may often have influenced his thoughts and words; (d) that he regularly dictated the letters so that his stenographers may also have contributed to the style, with Paul writing only a short greeting at the end. For these reasons it seems legitimate to suggest a less narrowminded approach to the Pauline correspondence than that generally found in modern discussions on the authenticity and integrity of the letters.

To secure a correct historical picture of the Pauline correspondence, one should also set aside dogmatic interests and traditions. For centuries the attitude of theologians toward Paul's letters had been dominated by a concern for orthodoxy; and when scholars representing higher criticism began to play a leading part, they established a fixed idea of Pauline "orthodoxy" as the criterion for authenticity. Ever since, the scholarly eagerness to discern original and interpolated elements of the Pauline correspondence has been based on these theological or ideological considerations. Another expression of this dogmatic bias is the rather ironic phenomenon that conservative theologians risk being accused of unorthodoxy if they do not believe that every Pauline letter is genuine, whereas liberal theologians fear being accused of unorthodoxy if they do not believe that certain Pauline letters are spurious. Paul's personal testimony concerning his versatility and willingness to be a Jew among Jews and a Greek among Greeks in order to win and keep as many believers as possible speaks against the use of these dogmatic criteria. What is most questionable is that historical references found in Acts and the Pauline correspondence are carelessly suppressed in favor of theological verdicts.

Certainly the author of Acts was not able to describe Paul's activities with complete accuracy, nor did he intend to do so. His purpose was to secure a positive appreciation of the apostle's work for Christ. This intent, however, does not mean that Luke was as ignorant as many modern theologians believe. Although he never quoted the letters of Paul, this fact merely indicates that Paul's messages were not yet spread as holy writ in the church when the Book of Acts was composed. Nevertheless, there are numerous instances where names and dates found in Acts and the letters of Paul correspond. A striking example is Luke's awareness of Paul's earning his living as a tentmaker in Corinth, before the arrival of Silas and Timothy from Macedonia allowed him to devote his full energy to preaching (Acts 18:3, 5). This detail corresponds closely to what Paul tells the Corinthians, reminding them of the support from Macedonia that enabled him to give up his "breadwinning" in Corinth (2 Cor. 11:9). Unintentional concords of this kind between Acts and the letters of Paul are found far more often than many scholars are wont to admit. Instead of judging Luke incognizant or incompetent, critical scholars should rather use the information in Acts as far as possible to understand the history of the Pauline correspondence. Regarding names, dates, and other personal or geographical details found in the Pauline letters—for instance, such passages as, "The greeting is by my own, Paul's hand" (2 Thess. 3:17) or "Go to join me in Nicopolis" (Titus 3:12)—it does not seem plausible that all such items would have been interpolated by postapostolic editors or "producers" to enable readers of the period A.D. 65–100 to believe in Pauline historicity and authorship. Christians living under the Flavian emperors had more serious concerns than reconstructing Pauline nomenclatures and itineraries simply to satisfy antiquarian interests. Their more pressing problems were with the imperial religion and the danger of persecution.

It is common knowledge that pseudepigraphy was indeed practiced in Judaism and Christianity, and the canonical dignity of the Pauline corpus is not alone sufficient proof that all elements were shaped by the apostle. Yet it seems improbable that editors and writers of the postapostolic years A.D. 65–100 who wanted to impose a quasi-Pauline message upon their contemporaries would have bothered matching so many names and dates with what still might have been known about the activity of Paul, Timothy, and other apostolic collaborators. It is more likely that they either would have rendered pious reports of apostolic miracles like the authors of the Abgar letters and other Christian apocrypha or, like John in Revelation and the writer of First Clement, would have commented on the growing problem of martyrdom in the church. Neither trend is supported by the names and dates occurring in the Pauline corpus. Interest in apostolic miracles and concern for problems caused by the Roman authorities do not characterize any of the letters found in the New Testament under Paul's name. On the contrary, each letter is filled with realistic admonitions to congregations and to fellow workers known generally from Paul's other letters and from the story of Paul in Acts. The addressees were obviously living in a society not yet hostile to believers.

The popular practice of classifying some writings euphemistically as "deutero-Pauline epistles" (2 Thessalonians, Colossians, Ephesians), and calling the pastoral epistles "pseudepigrapha" (1–2 Timothy, Titus) implies an aversion to speaking openly of falsifications. Moreover, attempts to attribute these documents to authors living in the postapostolic period and writing under the name of Paul are stained with historical deficiencies. Admittedly, there are particularities in the vocabulary of the letters in question that make it possible to suppose they were not formulated by Paul alone, as was probably the case for Galatians or Romans (Gal. 1:1; Rom. 1:1), but were written in collaboration with an assistant. The relevant letters also reflect a certain degree of development in church life and organization, which nonetheless does not extend beyond what could be expected during Paul's lifetime.

The essential point is that dating the writings dubbed "deutero-Pauline" and the "pastoral epistles" several years after Paul's death fits neither with the concrete names and dates that they contain nor with the problems that occupied the postapostolic generation.

Against modern attempts to question the authenticity of several Pauline epistles because of apparent disjunctions and inconsistencies, it may be observed that little agreement is found among the opposing theories. More seriously, every such partition and vivisection gives rise to even greater difficulties, namely, explaining why and how an integration was later carried through. The structure of the letters is not always consistent, but this is understandable in light of Paul's ardent personality, his use of coeditors and stenographers, his habit of dictating the text, and the rhetorical character of the messages.

Details in the individual letters will be analyzed in the following survey to show that it seems possible—without artificial surgery and division, and in conjunction with the information about Paul given by Luke in Acts—to connect every letter of the Pauline correspondence to the circumstances and particulars of the remaining twelve letters. Because the biblical revelation possesses a dignity of its own, independent of chronological judgments, this investigation is undertaken not to meet apologetic or ideological interests, but to approach historical probability to the extent that one person's critical sifting of this evidence may allow.

# 3. Overview of the Chronology

According to Luke in Acts, shortly after contributing to the martyrdom of Stephen in Jerusalem and on his way to persecute Christians in Damascus, the young Pharisee and Roman citizen, Saul of Tarsus, was converted and became Paul the Christian missionary (Acts 7:58; 8:3; 9:4, 15; 22:3, 15; 26:16). Paul mentions his own conversion from Jewish zealotry to Christian service in his letter to the Galatians (Gal. 1:13–17). The historical circumstances allow dating his conversion to A.D. 36, as will be demonstrated. Remarkably enough, the high priest was able to instigate the killing of Stephen without seeking permission from the Roman procurator in Caesarea, who normally had to concur with any executions (John 18:31). This exception was possible during an interregnum in the year 36, when there was no imperial procurator in Palestine and the Roman governor of Syria appointed a powerful new high priest named Jonathan and permitted him to reign independently over the Holy Land (Josephus, *Antiquities* 18:90, 95). Equipped with such power during the interregnum in 36, Jonathan was able to sanction the stoning of Stephen in Jerusalem and permit Paul to persecute Christians as far as Damascus (Acts 9:2). Only one year later, the authoritative Jonathan was replaced by another high priest who had to obey a new imperial procurator (*Antiquities* 18:123, 237). Consequently, the martyrdom of Stephen and Paul's subsequent conversion took place in A.D. 36. Following his baptism in Damascus, Paul stayed for some time in what he called Arabia, the Syrian desert outside Damascus inhabited by Nabateans, before returning to Damascus to preach (Acts 9:22; Gal. l:17). Because of a Jewish plot, he fled through a window in the wall and escaped to Jerusalem (Acts 9:23–29; 2 Cor. 11:32–33). According to Paul, this contact with the church in Jerusalem took place "three years" after his conversion (Gal. 1:18); but because according to the conventional rhetoric of chronology it was customary to count both the initial and the concluding years as whole years, he actually meant "two years later," or A.D. 38. This date corresponds to the last year of the Nabatean King Aretas IV (9 B.C.–A.D. 38), whom Paul mentioned in connection with his escape from Damascus (2 Cor. 11:32). To avoid difficulties raised by the Jewish Hellenists in Jerusalem who had recently attacked Stephen, Paul was sent after two weeks to Tarsus (Acts

9:30; Gal. 1:18–24), from where Barnabas called him a few years later to assist him in Antioch (Acts 11:25–26). During a famine that struck the Holy Land around A.D. 46 (Josephus, *Antiquities* 3:320–21, 20:51–53, 111), the church of Antioch supported the Christians in Jerusalem with the aid of Barnabas and Paul (Acts 11:30). Subsequently, the church of Antioch sent Barnabas and Paul to preach in Cyprus and Asia Minor (Acts 13:1–14:28), dating Paul's first journey, led by Barnabas, to the years 47 and 48. The admission of uncircumcised Gentiles to the church was then discussed at the apostolic council in Jerusalem (Acts 15:1–31; Gal. 2:1–10). Paul himself said that he came to Jerusalem for this reason "after fourteen years" (Gal. 2:1). Adjusting this expression to mean "after thirteen years," with the starting point of Paul's conversion as A.D. 36, the apostolic council took place in the year 49.

Paul led his second journey himself, assisted by Silvanus of Jerusalem and Timothy of Derbe (Acts 15:36–18:22), who also figure as coeditors of the two letters connected with this journey, 1 and 2 Thessalonians. After preaching again in Asia Minor, Paul continued on to Europe, visiting Philippi and Thessalonica in Macedonia, and Athens and Corinth in Greece. This journey may be dated to the years 50–54 for the following reasons. Presuming Paul started from Antioch some time after the apostolic council of A.D. 49, his activity in Asia Minor may have included parts of the years 50–51, after which he may have spent the latter part of the year 51 and the first half of 52 in Macedonia. In any case, Paul is explicitly said to have worked afterward in Corinth for eighteen months (Acts 18:11), being confronted there with the Roman proconsul Gallio (18:12). An inscription placed by Gallio at Delphi states that he was the proconsul of Greece during the year A.D. 52, making it possible to date the activity of Paul in Corinth to the latter part of 52, the whole year 53, and the first months of the year 54. Thus his return from Corinth to Antioch (18:18–22) may have occurred in the spring and summer of 54.

Paul's third journey began soon afterward (Acts 18:23–21:15), and it may be dated to the years A.D. 54–58. It took the apostle through Galatia and Phrygia to Ephesus, from there to Macedonia and over some part of Illyricum (Rom. 15:19), down to Corinth again, then back to Macedonia, and by ship along the coast of Asia to Caesarea and Jerusalem. During this journey Paul is described as spending considerable time in Ephesus, preaching for three months among the Jews and then for two years among the Gentiles (Acts 19:8, 10). In order to collect money for the church in Jerusalem (2 Cor. 8:4), he also stayed for an extended period in Macedonia and is reported afterward to have been in Greece for only three months (Acts 20:3). If the apostle began his third journey in A.D. 54, he would have preached in Ephesus during the years 55 and 56, visited Macedonia in A.D. 57, and stayed in Corinth during three winter months of 57–58. From there he returned to Macedonia, leaving Philippi for Asia Minor and Palestine shortly before Easter (Acts 20:6), so that he must have reached Jerusalem in the summer of A.D. 58.

This third journey provided the framework for the apostle's most important letters; the subsequent analysis of details shows that among them were Galatians, 1 Corinthians, 1 Timothy, 2 Corinthians, Romans, and Titus. It may be further observed that although the first and second great journeys of Paul were undertaken during the reign of Claudius (A.D. 41–54), his third journey took place during Nero's first years as emperor (A.D. 54–68). Under both emperors the political situation facilitated the spread of the gospel in the Greek world, even under Nero, who had not yet developed his despotic tendencies. Among the Jews, however, Nero's well-known enthusiasm for Hellenism sparked new waves of zealotism, fanning unprecedented terror and murder (Josephus, *Antiquities* 20:160, 164).

Paul was confronted with this zealotism when he arrived in Jerusalem in A.D. 58. The leader of the Jerusalem church, James, is reported to have declared that there were thousands of Jewish Christians eagerly defending the law (Acts 21:20). Moreover, when Paul went into the environs of the Temple, he was attacked by a Jewish mob that accused him of breaking the law, and Paul would have been stoned if the Roman tribune had not put him in prison (Acts 21:27–36). To avoid further Jewish zealot attacks on Paul, the officer then sent the apostle to Felix, the Roman procurator in Caesarea.

Although Felix made no decision at Paul's trial, he kept the apostle in custody at his residence (Acts 23:23–26:32). This, in fact, was Paul's first extended imprisonment, previous incarcerations lasting only a night or so (Acts 16:23; 2 Cor. 6:5). Felix had been installed by Claudius in A.D. 52; but after A.D. 54 Felix found little support from the new emperor, Nero, though he was allowed to retain his post until A.D. 60. This latter date is corroborated by Josephus (*Antiquities* 20:179, 182—Eusebius' [*Chronicle* 2:155] suggestion of A.D. 56 is much too early). Well-known political developments also speak in favor of the year 60 as concluding the procuratorship of Felix. In A.D. 59, Nero killed his mother and was able to "expunge" certain officials whom she and her powerful friend Pallas, Felix's brother, had protected. Hence it becomes clear that it was Felix's less than certain position under Nero that prevented him from delivering any decision in the Jewish-zealot accusations against Paul while the apostle lingered on in prison from the fall of A.D. 58 to the spring of 60. This pivotal period of erupting tensions among Romans, Jewish zealots, and Jewish and Gentile Christians matches the circumstances of Paul's captivity in Caesarea as well as the decisive responses reflected in the letters of Philemon, Colossians, Ephesians, and 2 Timothy (as will be shown in more detail below).

A short time after Felix had been replaced in Caesarea by Festus—an effective politician who had much better relations with Nero—Paul risked an appeal to the emperor Nero (Acts 25:1, 11) and was promptly sent to Rome (27:1). This so-called fourth journey of the apostle began in the fall (27:9), was interrupted by a shipwreck at Malta (28:1), and only after three months (28:11) proceeded on to Rome (28:14), where Paul was allowed to stay in a private room guarded by a soldier (28:16). At the end of Acts, Luke states that Paul remained in this rented lodging for two years (28:30). Because he most likely traveled from Malta to Rome in the spring of 61 (according to 28:11 he sailed from Malta in a ship that had just wintered there), the stay in Rome of Acts 28 covered the rest of the year 61, the whole of 62, and perhaps the beginning of 63.

In the treatment below, Philippians will be linked to the Roman captivity. There are no indications that any other letters were written by Paul in Rome, either during the two years mentioned in Acts or at some later point.

What happened to Paul after his years in Roman custody (A.D. 61–62) is not known from any historical reports. However, it seems probable that he was liberated in A.D. 63, for Acts ends optimistically with Paul able to continue his preaching (Acts 28:23, 30–31). Likewise, it can be assumed that Paul was able to fulfill his desire to go from Rome to Spain (Rom. 15:24, 28). In 1 Clement, a valuable postbiblical document written in the name of the Roman church in A.D. 95, Paul is said to have come to the "utmost west" (1 Clem. 6:7), which, from the Roman perspective, refers to Spain. No other journeys of Paul, possibly undertaken after the Roman trial was over, are indicated by any literary sources. Numerous imaginative reconstructions based on the pastoral epistles have been attempted; but the details contained in the Pastorals connect them with the activity of Paul during the years known from Acts and his other epistles, as will be demonstrated below. The only further occurrence that can be established is Paul's martyrdom in Rome along with Peter's during the Neronian persecution of A.D. 64 or early 65, as evidenced in the Roman 1 Clem. 5:2–7 and supported by early references to Peter's martyrdom (John 21:19; Ascension of Isaiah 4:3).

The thirteen letters comprising the Pauline corpus will be dated below between A.D. 51 and 61 within the larger period of the church's development as sketched above; namely, between A.D. 36, the year of Stephen's martyrdom in Jerusalem, and A.D. 62, the last date historically available before Paul's martyrdom in Rome in A.D. 65.

# THE CHRONOLOGY OF THE THIRTEEN CANONICAL LETTERS

If allowance is made for the circumstances pointed out above (see "Questions of Method and Procedure"—the apostle's adaptability, his preference for oral dictation, the rhetorical character of his messages, and the considerable influence of his coeditors and shorthand-writers), it is feasible to date the Pauline letters of the New Testament between the years A.D. 51–61, a period in which Paul undertook the second, third, and fourth journeys described by Luke in Acts. This time frame is suggested without claiming that Paul necessarily wrote every line himself; on the other hand, the only correct and honest procedure a priori is to treat the names and dates in the extant texts seriously rather than degrading them from the outset as merely various types of camouflage.

Taking these points into account, the letters of the Pauline corpus will be treated below in a chronological sequence, the order of which is argued from case to case. Writings especially debated in critical scholarship will be more thoroughly discussed than the others.

## Early Palestinian Jewish–Jewish Christian Tension

### 1. 2 Thessalonians (A.D. 52, summer)

The earliest Pauline letters found in the canon are generally thought to be 1 and 2 Thessalonians. Although a number of scholars consider 2 Thessalonians deutero-Pauline, written in imitation of Paul in 1 Thessalonians, the arguments used against Paul's authorship are both contestable and contradictory.

First of all, 2 Thessalonians, like 1 Thessalonians, contains no highly developed ideas on "justification" as is characteristic of Galatians and other later Pauline letters. The two letters to the Thessalonians speak only of holiness and sanctification (1 Thess. 3:13; 4:3, 6, 7; 5:23; 2 Thess. 2:13), but not of righteousness and justification. If, as the literary critics in question suggest, a postapostolic writer wanted to bless readers living in the period A.D. 70–100 with a letter imitating Paul's style and concepts, he or she would not have omitted the well-known Pauline emphasis upon justification. Therefore it seems likely that both 1 Thessalonians and 2 Thessalonians were written before Galatians.

Another obstacle in dating 2 Thessalonians to the years 70–100 is the exhortation to pray for Paul and his companions, wishing them success in preaching the gospel and escape from evil aggressors (2 Thess. 3:1–2). No such reconstruction of Paul's concerns during his early missionary activity would have impressed readers living in the postapostolic period, when the gospel was already widely spread in the Greek world. It would also have been particularly silly to ask those later readers to pray for Paul and his collaborators when everyone knew the apostle had been dead for years.

The usual objections to the Pauline background of 2 Thessalonians are willful inversions of positive evidence found in the text itself. Because the styles of 1 and 2 Thessalonians are consistently the same, it is more natural to ascribe a common authorship rather than declare 2 Thessalonians a skilled imitation. It is even more crass to regard the final greeting (2 Thess. 3:17) as a mark of falsification simply because it contains a remark, extraneous to the main discourse, that Paul wrote this greeting with his own hand. The purpose of this graphic annotation was not to authenticate 2 Thessalonians, which the bearers of the letter would be able to do in any case, but rather to help the readers distinguish Pauline epistles in general from other circulars that were being erroneously aligned with Paul (2:2). Further, when 2 Thess. 2:15 is taken into consideration with its injunction to "hold to the traditions you have already been taught, whether by mouth or through our letters," then Paul's added "signature" for his readers makes perfectly good sense (2 Thess. 3:17).

What has especially led critical scholarship to deny the authenticity of 2 Thessalonians is the character of the eschatological teachings in the second chapter (2 Thess. 2:1–12). To counter this unwarranted skepticism, it must be observed that apocalyptic foretokens of the parousia, corresponding to those mentioned in 2 Thessalonians and including the "abomination of desolation" referred to in the Book of Daniel, were already in the Jesus traditions as recounted eventually by the Synoptic Gospel writers (Matt. 24:4–41 with par.). It is not correct to date this speech after the fall of Jerusalem in A.D. 70, for the destruction of the city took quite other forms than what Jesus is reported to have said about the abomination of desolation. The first half of the eschatological scenery developed in 2 Thessalonians (2:1–12) is parallel to the apocalyptic speech of Jesus. Here all the details are based on utterances of Daniel about the coming abomination that makes desolate and about related phenomena (2 Thess. 2:3–4—apostasy caused and adoration claimed by the powers of destruction, as in Dan. 11:31, 36; 2 Thess.

2:7—the mystery of lawlessness presently active, as in Dan. 2:18–47; cf. Matt. 24:12).

The second half of the apocalyptic passage in 2 Thessalonians (2:9–12) is built on a polarity between truth and falsehood that is especially characteristic of Qumran texts. In 2 Thessalonians, the idea of "truth" occurs twice in 2:10, 12 and again in 2:13, each time in opposition to a "lie," "deceit," and "lawlessness" (2:7–12 passim), and such dualism is often found in the Qumran texts (e.g., in 1QS 3:19; cf. "sons of the light" in 1 Thess. 5:5 and 1QM). Also to be considered is that Qumran believers were much occupied with apocalyptic traditions, including those found in Daniel. Paul's Pharisee background certainly enabled him to produce a similar eschatological teaching when he worked in Thessalonica, so that he could ask the readers there: "Do you not remember that I said this when I was still among you?" (2 Thess. 2:5).

The purpose of recalling and elaborating this apocalyptic tradition in 2 Thessalonians was to warn the readers not to be disturbed and upset (2 Thess. 2:2a, *me saleuthenai mede throeisthai*) by misconceptions about the Day of the Lord. Their believing that the time had already arrived (2:2b) had caused the readers to give up normal work in society (3:6, 10). The apocalyptic chapters of the Synoptic Gospels contain similar warnings of Jesus against premature anticipation of the future parousia and consummation (Matt. 24:6//Mark 13:7 *me throeisthe*//Luke 21:9 *me ptoethete*, followed by a number of corresponding warnings against untimely expectations). The evangelists quoted these words of Jesus because a corresponding fervor of eschatological rapture had evidently overcome people in the Jerusalem church. Social factors contributed to a similar enthusiasm in the Hellenistic diaspora, with the newly converted proletarian expecting to receive material welfare in the new kingdom, leading poorer members of the house-churches in Thessalonica to anarchy, strike, and parasitism (2 Thess. 3:6–12).

The picture that 2 Thessalonians provides of eschatological impatience and social unrest in the congregation corresponds to what Acts and 1 Thessalonians relate about Paul's initial experiences in Thessalonica.

First there is the remarkable fact that 1 Thessalonians, which can be dated to Paul's stay in Corinth (see below), reflects several circumstances that correspond to information in 2 Thessalonians. One passage of 1 Thessalonians mentions that Paul had consented to work alone in Athens, having sent Timothy to Thessalonica to strengthen the believers and exhort them not to be shaken (*sainesthai*) in the present troubles (1 Thess. 3:2–3). In very similar words, 2 Thessalonians deals with the endurance of the readers amid various troubles (2 Thess. 1:4) and warns them not to be disturbed (*salleuthenai*) or upset (2:2). The latter passage finds a further counterpart in

Acts, where the Jews of Thessalonica go to the nearby city Beroea to disturb (*saleuein*) and stir up the believers there (Acts 17:13). Another instructive connection between the two letters is the passage where Paul felt relieved when Timothy returned from the Thessalonians with good news about their steadfastness (1 Thess. 3:8, *stekete*), and the corresponding exhortation to that steadfastness (2 Thess. 2:15, *stekete*). Here the exhortation to steadfastness in 2 Thessalonians must be understood to precede the passage in 1 Thessalonians about steadfastness having been observed in Thessalonica. Furthermore, both letters contain similar warnings against refusal to work and "parasitism" upon others (1 Thess. 4:1–12; 2 Thess. 3:6–12), supported by references to Paul's working night and day for his living (1 Thess. 2:9; 2 Thess. 3:8), and both culminate in general exhortations to work for daily bread (1 Thess. 4:11; 2 Thess. 3:10–12). In the same context, 2 Thessalonians reports that Paul had just heard of the strike in question (2 Thess. 3:11), whereas the corresponding passage in 1 Thessalonians contains no less than four clauses indicating that Paul had told the Thessalonians earlier to refrain from such parasitism and to work honestly with their hands (1 Thess. 4:1, 2, 6, 11). Thus there is reason to date 2 Thessalonians before 1 Thessalonians, a numerical inversion of little consequence, since only the length of the letters determined their canonical order.

With the aid of Acts, the historical situation of the two letters can be illustrated more exactly. On his second journey, Paul, accompanied by Silas and Timothy, came from Philippi to Thessalonica (Acts 17:1), probably in the fall of 51 (see "Overview of the Chronology"). Because of a riot instigated by Jewish merchants, Paul and Silas proceeded westward to Beroea, where the Jews of Thessalonica are said to have caused new troubles (17:13, *saleuontes*). To avoid complications, newly converted Christians of Beroea brought Paul by ship to Athens, while Silas and Timothy stayed behind in Macedonia, but were asked to join Paul in Athens as soon as possible (17:14–16a). As mentioned above, 1 Thessalonians shows that Timothy then visited Paul in Athens but was sent back to Thessalonica soon afterward in order to strengthen and comfort the believers and to find out whether they had maintained their faith (1 Thess. 3:1–5). Paul's anxiety is reflected in 2 Thessalonians, where he first praises his readers for their previous endurance (2 Thess. 1:10) and then warns against being distressed or upset and yielding to the fervor of eschatological rapture (2:2) of which he had just heard, implying that those who refused to work were being fed by rich brethren (3:10–11). It is probable that Timothy took 2 Thessalonians along with him when he was sent from Athens back to Macedonia (as mentioned then later in 1 Thessalonians). Together with Silas (or Silvanus), Timothy also figures as coauthor of the letter (2 Thess. 1:1), though Silvanus seems to have been sent back to some other place in Macedonia (see below). At any rate, the above-mentioned sending of Timothy to Macedonia shows that 2 Thessalonians was composed in Athens. This is further confirmed by Paul's complaint about being threatened by perverted and evil-minded people and not finding much belief (2 Thess. 3:2), which sounds like the difficulties with the philosophers and the limited success Paul had in Athens, according to Luke (Acts 17:32–34). Paul subsequently traveled from Athens to Corinth, where he was led before Gallio (Acts 18:1–17). According to his inscription, Gallio was governor of Greece in A.D. 52. This extrabiblical evidence dates the activity of the apostle in Athens, including the writing of 2 Thessalonians, most likely to the summer of 52.

Built on a simple logical structure, 2 Thessalonians begins with advice on "doctrinal" questions (1:1–2:12) and follows with ethical admonitions (2:11–3:18).

## 2. 1 Thessalonians (A.D. 52/53)

The historical situation of First Thessalonians can be reconstructed from notices found in Acts, 2 Thessalonians, and 1 Thessalonians itself.

According to Luke in Acts, the apostle Paul left Athens for Corinth, center of the Roman province of Greece (Acts 18:1), where Gallio was governor in the year 52. For some time, Paul earned his living in the service of his Jewish Christian colleagues Aquila and Priscilla (18:3); but when Silvanus and Timothy arrived from Macedonia, he was able to devote his full attention to the gospel (18:5). This new commitment was possible because the two collaborators came to Corinth with support for Paul from the churches in Macedonia (2 Cor. 11:9). According to the opening sentence of 2 Thessalonians, Silvanus and Timothy had previously joined Paul in Athens (2 Thess. 1:1), but in 1 Thessalonians the apostle writes that he quickly agreed to be left alone in Athens in order to let Timothy obtain further news from Macedonia (1 Thess. 3:1–2). In fact, both assistants were sent back to Macedonia, not only Timothy, who is singled out in the text. This dual sending is made clear by the passage in Acts about Silas (Silvanus) and Timothy coming from Macedonia to Paul in Corinth (Acts 18:5), although it appears that Silas was sent to some other city of Macedonia. At a later point Paul will include in a letter to the Corinthians a retrospective of Paul's initial preaching in Corinth that confirms that both Silvanus and Timothy assisted him there (2 Cor. 1:19).

In 1 Thessalonians the apostle looks back to his days in Athens (1 Thess. 3:1), which indicates that he was in Corinth at the time of his writing of 1 Thessalonians. After referring to Timothy's expedition from Athens to Thessalonica (1 Thess. 3:2), he mentions that his delegate had just returned to him with good news from Thessalonica (3:6). This return corresponds to the arrival of Silas and Timothy in Corinth, with support from Macedonia referred to in Acts 18:5. Timothy's news about Thessalonica greatly consoled Paul (1 Thess. 3:7). To hear now that his earlier admonitions (2 Thess. 2:15, *stekete*) had indeed led the readers to be steadfast in the Lord (1 Thess. 3:8, *stekete*) filled him with joy and gratitude (3:9). On the whole, 1 Thessalonians is more optimistic than 2 Thessalonians. For instance, Paul calls the "faith," "love," and "hope" of the Christians in Thessalonica (1 Thess. 1:3) a model for all believers in Macedonia, Greece, and everywhere else (1:8). He writes that the word preached by him had enabled them to be patient in various sufferings, caused now by Gentiles, and he draws a parallel to the concurrent troubles of Palestinian Christians brought about by nonbelieving Jews (2:13–14). It is in this context that Paul blames the Jews for previously persecuting him (2:15) and for continuing to impede his efforts to preach to the Gentiles (2:16). Both complaints were undoubtedly connected with Paul's recent experiences known from Acts; that is, his earlier expulsion by Jews from Thessalonica and Beroea (Acts 17:5, 13) as well as his later troubles with Jews in Corinth (18:6, 12).

All these details confirm that 1 Thessalonians was produced in Corinth during the eighteen months of Paul's activity there (Acts 18:11). Paul possibly reached Corinth in the fall of 52, when Gallio served as governor and had decided not to support the Jewish attack on Paul (Acts 18:15). Because this Jewish provocation most likely influenced Paul's complaint about hostile Jews (1 Thess. 2:16), the letter must have been written some time after the trial, dating 1 Thessalonians to the end of A.D. 52 or the beginning of 53.

As in 2 Thessalonians, Silvanus and Timothy are mentioned as coauthors of the epistle (1 Thess. 1:1). Perhaps they were sent with 1 Thessalonians to Macedonia—as was the case with 2 Thessalonians—but no evidence is available to prove this suggested parallel. Silvanus is known later to have gone to Rome (1 Pet. 5:12), and the next reference to Timothy implies that he was sent from Ephesus to Corinth during Paul's third journey (Acts 19:22; 1 Cor. 4:17).

In 1 Thessalonians, the behavior distinctive of the recipients' Christian faith is described in more positive terms than in 2 Thessalonians. The improvement that had taken place in the intervening period was evidently connected with a moderation of the eschatological tension. In 2 Thessalonians the apostle had to combat an anarchy in Thessalonica that had been provoked by the false notion that the "Day of the Lord" had already arrived (2 Thess. 2:2). A correct understanding of eschatological foretokens had to be impressed upon Paul's readers (2:3–12). But according to 1 Thessalonians, Paul had received comforting information from Timothy. To be sure,

Paul repeats his admonitions regarding a life together that must be "pleasing to God" (1 Thess. 4:1–12), but he then restricts the eschatological lesson to explanations concerning the resurrection of the dead (1 Thess. 4:13–18) and exhortations to be prepared for the end, whenever it does come (5:1–11). The priority of 2 Thessalonians is thus confirmed by the progression of faith and love on the part of the Thessalonian congregation, made especially clear when Paul, in the midst of great adversity, says he was relieved and "now could really live" when Timothy came to him in Corinth with good news about the strength and steadfastness of their faith (1 Thess. 3:6–8).

Concerning the structure, 1 Thessalonians, like 2 Thessalonians, can be divided into two sections: one dealing with personal circumstances (1 Thess. 1:1–3:13), and the other with admonitions (4:1–5:28).

## Rising Zealotism

### 3. Galatians (A.D. 55)

Chronologically, the letters to the Thessalonians are followed by the letter to the Galatians.

The date of this letter is controversial because of two well-known competing theories: (1) the north-Galatian and (2) the south-Galatian theories. The crucial point is the extent of the area indicated by "Galatia" (Gal. 1:2), for a more precise determination of the geographical territory intended by Paul becomes decisive in adjudicating the competing chronologies of each theory.

1. According to the north-Galatian theory, the letter was addressed to inhabitants of the geographical region Galatia, which surrounded Ancyra in north-central Asia Minor, a town corresponding to modern Turkey's capital Ankara. This region received its name from the Galatians, three Celtic tribes that had settled there during the third century B.C. Paul was not thinking of his readers as Celts but called them "Galatians" (3:1) as inhabitants of Galatia, whether he used this expression in a stricter or wider sense; for him the readers included both Jews and Greeks (3:28).

2. According to the south-Galatian theory, Paul was referring to the Roman province founded by Augustus in the year 25 B.C. One half of this province comprised the region Galatia in the north, the other half Pisidia, Lycaonia, and various districts in the south, including the cities of Iconium, Lystra, and Derbe, which Paul had visited on his first journey (Acts 13:51–14:24).

Part of the uncertainty in choosing between these two options is that Paul mentions his initial visit to the Galatians with the following words

(Gal. 4:13): "You know that it was in a state of weakness that I preached the gospel to you the first time (*to proteron*)." Here the expression "the first time" shows that Paul had preached more than once in Galatia before writing the letter; that is, he must have been there at least twice. The date of Galatians depends on which of the journeys described in Acts was connected with Paul's visit to the Galatians. If the apostle spoke of Galatia in the sense of the Roman province—the south-Galatian theory—then his earlier visit took place during the first journey, which brings Paul to Pisidia and Lycaonia within the southern half of the Roman province in question (Acts 13:51–14:24). Consequently, the second visit would have been part of the second journey, when, according to Acts, Paul "passed through Phrygia and the Galatian country" (16:6). Because this visit to Galatia may be dated to A.D. 50 or 51, shortly after the apostolic council in A.D. 49, Galatians could have been written as early as 51. If this is the case, however, it is difficult to locate a suitable place of composition, considering that Paul hurried on from Galatia to Macedonia (Acts 16:7–10).

Supposing that Paul instead used the expression "Galatia" only for the region in the northern part of the Roman province—maintained by those who prefer the north-Galatian theory—then his first visit did not occur until his second missionary journey, in which context the Galatian region is mentioned explicitly for the first time (Acts 16:6, as quoted above). Accordingly, Paul's second visit to the readers would have taken place during his third missionary journey, which Luke describes similarly: "[Paul] went through the Galatian country and Phrygia" (18:23). From this perspective the date of Galatians would be A.D. 55, some time after Paul had returned from his second journey, implying a stay in Corinth from the fall of the year 52 to the spring of the year 54 (see "Overview of the Chronology"). According to Luke, the apostle began his third journey shortly after returning from the second. Paul started from Antioch and traveled through Galatia and Phrygia (Acts 18:23) in order to reach Ephesus (19:1), where he preached to the Jews for three months (19:8) and then to the Gentiles for two years (19:10). Later he refers to a three-year stay in Ephesus (20:31); but considering the custom of including the initial and concluding years, this reference can be understood to correspond to the previously mentioned "three months plus two years." In light of the chronology suggested for Paul's third journey, A.D. 54–48 ("Overview of the Chronology") his three months among the Jews in Ephesus may be dated approximately to the last part of A.D. 54, and his two years among the Gentiles to A.D. 55 and 56.

Assuming the north-Galatian theory, Paul would probably have written Galatians in the year 55, during the first half of his long stay at Ephesus. Such a localization fits well with the assumption that Paul composed his severe letter to the Galatians shortly after his second, evidently disappointing, contact with the readers.

This last point favorable to the north-Galatian theory is supported by Luke's use of geographical names in reporting Paul's journeys through Asia Minor. In the context of the first journey, he refers to Lycaonia and Pisidia without indicating their political connection with Galatia (Acts 14:6, 11, 24), and the name "Galatia" actually never occurs in Acts, although names of Roman provinces like "Asia" are common. It is only the above-mentioned expression, "the Galatian country" (*choran*), that is used in the relevant passages of Acts, and together with Phrygia, this phrase refers to regions visited by the apostle during his second and third journeys (16:6; 18:23). Most likely, Luke meant the region in the north around Ancyra when he mentioned the "Galatian country."

Furthermore, in the days of Paul there is no evidence that official proclamations and inscriptions ever used the name of Galatia for the whole of the Roman province with Ancyra its capital; rather, such references followed the pattern found in Acts, listing the geographical districts in the province: "Galatia, Pisidia, Lycaonia," and so forth. It is only in later works of geographers and historians that "Galatia" is used alone to designate the Roman province, apparently for the sake of brevity.

The superiority of the north-Galatian theory is also supported by the probable date of Paul's confrontation with Peter in Antioch (Gal. 2:11–21). Just before this event is mentioned, Paul refers to the agreement reached with James, Peter, and John at the apostolic council in Jerusalem, when the equality of Jewish and Gentile believers was acknowledged (2:1–10). Later, under pressure of Jewish zealotic trends, Peter withdrew from table communion with uncircumcised Christians in Antioch (2:12). With the apostolic council held in A.D. 49 (see "Overview of the Chronology"), it does not seem possible that Peter had already changed his mind by the year 50, as must be asserted on the basis of the south-Galatian theory, which dates Galatians to A.D. 51. The north-Galatian theory, which dates Galatians to A.D. 55, grants Peter a longer time to reverse his practice, and the judaizing movement behind this "about face" is conveniently explained by the sudden intensification of zealotism and the rise of sicarian terror after the enthronement of Nero in A.D. 54 (Josephus, *Antiquities* 20:158–67a).

For these various reasons it seems probable that Paul wrote Galatians in Ephesus during the year 55, and that his readers lived in the region Galatia, of which Ancyra was the capital. After returning from his second journey in A.D. 54 and finding Peter under the influence of increasing Jewish nationalism in Antioch, Paul soon departed on his third journey.

Before he journeyed through Phrygia to Ephesus (Acts 18:23; 19:1), Paul passed through Galatia and to his disappointment also found the Christians there impressed by a legalistic Judaism (Gal. 1:6; 3:1–5). In great agitation Paul wrote to the Galatian believers—this time, however, without mentioning any coauthor (1:1).

The letter to the Galatians is stamped by Paul's attacks on a justification secured by works of the law (2:4, etc.) and by proofs for the exclusive value of belief in the redemptive work of Christ (2:16, etc.). The structure of the entire letter is determined by these two concerns. Of the six chapters in Galatians, two contain biographical material illustrating the absolute importance of grace and faith, and two contain ethical admonitions to secure the freedom of the believers:

| | |
|---|---|
| Introduction | 1:1–5 |
| Biographical material | 1:6–2:21 |
| Dogmatic arguments | 3:1–4:31 |
| Ethics (admonitions) | 5:1–6:18 |

The special value of Galatians has always been its clear exposition of justification by grace and faith alone.

## 4. 1 Corinthians (A.D. 56, spring)

Chronologically, the next letter to be considered is 1 Corinthians, and in this case the place and date are easy to determine with the aid of Paul's own indications and Luke's corresponding reports.

It can be inferred from the text that Paul wrote the letter in Ephesus (1 Cor. 16:8, 19) after his fight with antagonists there, whom he compared to wild beasts (15:32, *kata anthropon etheriomachesa*, "humanly speaking, I fought with beasts"). This metaphor certainly alludes to the riot of the silversmiths described with dramatic verve by Luke (Acts 19:23–40). More exactly, Paul states that he composed the letter during the Easter season (1 Cor. 5:7–8; cf. 16:6, 8) and before the Pentecost festival of the relevant year (16:8) while planning to go from Ephesus through Macedonia to Corinth (16:5).

These specifications correspond to what Luke writes in Acts about Paul's experiences in Ephesus during the three months and two years he spent there (Acts 19:8, 10), and, as stated above in the discussion of Galatians, one can date Paul's stay in Ephesus to A.D. 55 and 56. Paul is depicted in Acts as very successful for a time in Ephesus and Asia (19:10, 20), and for this reason, he was attacked by the silversmiths (19:23–40). Accordingly, the riot occurred during the second half of his stay in Ephesus, that is, in A.D. 56.

Because the apostle indicates that he composed 1 Corinthians before Pentecost, the epistle can thus be dated to the spring of 56.

Between the founding of the Corinthian church in A.D. 52 and the composition of 1 Corinthians in A.D. 56, Paul had written an earlier letter to the Corinthians (1 Cor. 5:9) and had received a letter from them (7:1) discussing concrete problems of the Christian life.

As coauthor of 1 Corinthians, the apostle mentions a Christian brother by the name of Sosthenes (1 Cor. 1:1). Because several parts of the letter betray knowledge of the present situation in Corinth, it seems likely that this Sosthenes was identical with the synagogue leader in Corinth whom the Jews are alleged to have punished because of his adherence to Paul (Acts 18:17). Besides what Paul may have learned from Sosthenes, the apostle had also received news of a schism from members of a Christian house-church led by a woman named Chloe (1 Cor. 1:11).

Just before the account of the silversmith's hostility (Acts 19:23), Paul is said to have planned a visit to Macedonia and Greece (19:21). Although he did not leave until later, Paul sent Timothy and Erastus to Macedonia while he remained for a considerable time in Asia (19:22). In fact, Paul probably sent his delegates not only to Macedonia but also to Greece, for apparently their expedition was intended to replace his own postponed visit to both countries (19:21). Erastus was most likely from Corinth, for he can be identified with a treasurer of this city from whom the Roman church had received a greeting (Rom. 16:23). The condensed report of Luke further shows that Timothy and Erastus left as the silversmiths had already begun to assail Paul, for the text actually reads (Acts 19:23): "At that time a not very modest tumult dealing with the Way [i.e., the Christian gospel] took place (*egeneto*)." Paul thus sent Timothy and Erastus to Macedonia and Greece while he was exposed to the riot in Ephesus, and it was only after the end of the uproar that he himself was able to leave for Macedonia and Greece (20:1–2).

Luke's statement that Timothy was sent to Macedonia and probably also to Greece, as observed above, finds an exact parallel in 1 Corinthians, where Paul writes in response to the deplorable schism in the church of Corinth: "For this reason I have sent Timothy to you . . . who is going to remind you of my ways/principles in Christ, as I teach about them everywhere in every church" (1 Cor. 4:17). Here the most natural assumption is that Timothy was sent with this same letter to readers in Corinth. In the last chapter Paul asks the Corinthians to receive Timothy in friendship and without contempt (16:10–11a), a concern possibly related to Timothy's young age (cf. 1 Tim. 4:12). The readers were also requested to equip Timothy for a safe return to Paul in Ephesus, which the apostle emphasizes by saying: "I wait for him together with the brethren" (1 Cor. 16:11b).

Evidently, Paul wrote 1 Corinthians in the spring of 56 and sent the letter to Corinth with Timothy while he remained behind in Ephesus. Paul may have expected Timothy's return in the summer or fall of the same year (A.D. 56) before he himself would proceed to Macedonia and Greece once the riot in Ephesus had subsided, as stated by Luke in a brief summary (Acts 20:1).

Paul's reasons for writing 1 Corinthians were twofold: (1) He was shocked by the news of a schism in the congregation that caused people to cling to individual authorities like Paul, Apollos, and Peter, and thus letting it appear that Christ was divided (1:10–13a). (2) Preceding correspondence and recent information had shown that several practical and fundamental questions had to be treated, such as marriage (5:1), knowledge (8:1), the eucharist (11:17), spiritual gifts (12:1), and the resurrection (15:4).

The structure of 1 Corinthians is triptych-like. In each of four major sections Paul first deals with a problem A, then discusses a topic B, and thereafter returns to a topic connected with A, as illustrated by the following summary:

|       |                                       |           |
|-------|---------------------------------------|-----------|
|       | Introduction                          | 1:1–9     |
| (I)   | A. Schismatic tendencies              | 1:10–17   |
|       | B. Wisdom and knowledge               | 1:18–2:16 |
|       | A. Individual authorities             | 3:1–4:21  |
| (II)  | A. Incest                             | 5:1—13    |
|       | B. Lawsuits                           | 6:1–11    |
|       | A. Fornication, chastity, matrimony   | 6:12–7:40 |
| (III) | A. Prejudices against meat            | 8:1–13    |
|       | B. Freedom                            | 9:1–27    |
|       | A. Self-control                       | 10:1–11:1 |
| (IV)  | A. Men and women in worship           | 11:2–16   |
|       | Lord's supper                         | 11:17–34  |
|       | Spiritual gifts                       | 12:1–31   |
|       | B. Fraternal love                     | 13:1–13   |
|       | A. Spiritual gifts                    | 14:1–40   |
| (V)   | Resurrection and consummation         | 15:1–58   |
| (VI)  | Practical instructions                | 16:1–24   |

The singular and enduring importance of 1 Corinthians lies in Paul's tactful and sensitive treatment of practical questions that had arisen in Corinth, and that may arise in every church. A golden thread is found in his emphasis upon the cross as nullifying any intellectual pretension (1:18–19) and in his identification of Christian knowledge (*gnosis*) with humble love (8:1; 13:2).

## 5. 1 Timothy (A.D. 56, summer/fall)

Using the available textual evidence without theological prejudice, 1 Timothy can be connected with references to the end of Paul's stay in Ephesus and to Timothy's return from Corinth as treated above in the discussion of 1 Corinthians and Acts.

As observed, Paul himself writes that Timothy had been sent by the apostle from Ephesus to Corinth (1 Cor. 4:17), probably in the spring of 56. Paul had wanted to visit Corinth himself (16:5), but provisionally he stayed in Ephesus and waited there for Timothy's return (16:11), expected possibly in the summer or fall of the same year. In addition, Luke provides the following relevant information (Acts 20:1): (1) when the conflict with the silversmiths was over, Paul gathered the disciples in Ephesus; (2) after encouraging and advising them at length (*parakalesas*), he bid farewell to the Ephesian church and (3) departed for Macedonia. In 2 Corinthians there is further material about his departure. After recounting the struggle in Asia (2 Cor. 1:8), Paul states that he preached in Troas and then in Macedonia (2:12–13), where he later, together with Timothy, wrote 2 Corinthians (1:1).

The picture offered by these documents is absolutely in harmony with the situation described in the ingress of 1 Timothy (1 Tim. 1:1–3): "Paul ... to Timothy, my genuine child in the faith: ... Just as I asked you to stay in Ephesus, while I went on my way to visit Macedonia, so the purpose remains that you admonish certain people not to spread wrong ideas." The passage shows that Paul and Timothy had been together in Ephesus and that Paul had requested that Timothy remain there and preach against heresy, while the apostle himself prepared to leave for Macedonia. As is evident from the information gathered above from 1 Corinthians, Acts, and 2 Corinthians, this is precisely what happened in the year 56: Having sent Timothy from Ephesus to Corinth, Paul eagerly waited his return (1 Cor. 16:11). Paul then left for Troas and Macedonia, where he stayed for a considerable time occupied with a gift for Christians in Judea, so that his visit to Corinth was delayed (2 Cor. 1:15, 23; 2:12–17; 8:1). Because none of the texts say that Timothy immediately followed Paul, he may well have remained behind in Ephesus, just as 1 Timothy indicates. It is true that 2 Corinthians mentions Paul and Timothy as coauthors of the letter (2 Cor. 1:1). But because this document contains apologies for Paul's delays in Troas and Macedonia, 2 Corinthians could not have been written until a year or so after Paul left Ephesus. Timothy could very well have stayed for a while in Ephesus before joining Paul in Macedonia. What the opening verses of 1 Timothy reveal about Paul and Timothy in Ephesus agrees with the information furnished by 1 Corinthians, Acts, and 2 Corinthians about Paul's last days in Ephesus before he went to Macedonia in the year 56.

No other circumstances in the life of Paul can be made to fit here. Regardless of whether 1 Timothy is Pauline or pseudepigraphic, attempts to place Paul again back in Ephesus sometime after his captivity in Rome are based on pure speculation.

## Excursus

At this juncture, an excursus on the authorship of the Pastorals, together with the group known as the "captivity epistles," is appropriate:

Three of the letters that belong to the Pauline corpus—1 Timothy, 2 Timothy, and Titus—are called "pastoral epistles" because they deal with pastoral duties and problems. In scholarly discussions of their authorship, their authenticity is often called into question, along with the "captivity epistles" Colossians and Ephesians, so-called because they allegedly were written during an imprisonment of Paul. [Second] Timothy especially is linked to the captivity epistles, because this letter too apparently stems from an imprisonment (2 Tim. 1:8). As is well known, the authenticity of all these epistles has sometimes been accepted, sometimes rejected, and the various theories fall mainly into three categories: (1) The pastoral and captivity epistles derive from Paul or at least from a disciple who represented his ideas. (2) The epistles contain biographical fragments that go back to Paul and his circle, but were later combined with theological arguments inserted by church leaders propagating the so-called early Catholicism of the postapostolic period. (3) The pastoral epistles are pseudepigraphy, and the two captivity epistles are deutero-Pauline, the latter term being a euphemism expressing no vital connection to the activity and letter writing of the apostle while he was alive, so that in fact the epistles are erroneously attributed to Paul.

To be sure, 1 Timothy and Titus, as well as Colossians and Ephesians, represent anomalies within the Pauline corpus. But although they differ in part from other Pauline epistles in their diction and program, they do share common characteristics when they are compared with each other. What has especially led critical scholarship to doubt the Pauline authorship of these epistles is their emphasis on the "church" as the subject of Paul's main concern. On the other hand, the names and dates contained in these epistles coordinate with material in Acts and in noncontroversial Pauline epistles. These seemingly contradictory elements complicate the scholarly discussion.

From a historical point of view, independent of theology, one should ask whether the peculiarity of these epistles was not due to the intended readers, residents of Asia Minor, where a heavy baroque style called Asianism was the rhetorical ideal. It is possible that Paul, who could be a Jew among Jews and a Greek among Greeks (1 Cor. 9:20), was able to adapt himself to his Hellenistic colleagues Timothy and Titus as well as to the Hellenistic believers in Colossae and Ephesus. From this perspective, perhaps also in collaboration with an assistant, he may well have been responsible for the special style and ecclesiastical agenda articulated in these particular epistles. The other alternative does not seem very reasonable, because it implies that anonymous representatives of a later orthodoxy and hierarchy must have unearthed or fabricated Pauline names and dates in order to promote the so-called early Catholicism, without using the older Pauline letters in a consistent way as models for their vocabulary and message. Independent of learned traditions stemming from renowned scholars (which Francis Bacon called *"idola theatri"*), every student of the pastoral and captivity epistles ought to consider which solution to the question of authorship offers fewer difficulties in clarifying their provenance. Given the alternatives, it would seem more promising to explain the background of the pastoral and captivity epistles if Paul was their author or at least the person who authorized the letters.

The descriptions of historical events and persons in the Pastorals and deutero-Paulines do indeed harmonize, in large measure, with the overarching picture of Paul's activity as detailed in other Pauline letters and the Book of Acts—a fact that becomes inexplicable if the letters are the product of later ecclesiastic writers. Proponents of pseudepigraphy suggest that unknown authors some twenty, fifty, or ninety years after Paul's death took pains to mention names and dates from Acts or the letters of Paul in order to delight their contemporaries with new Pauline letters. This they would have done, on the one hand, without rendering convincing imitations of Pauline expression or concepts and, on the other hand, without including discussions of problems essential for the postapostolic church, such as martyrdom and the attitude of the state toward Christianity.

This negation of Pauline responsibility is in fact nothing but an indelicate anachronism. To be sure, detailed information on personal affairs belonged to antiquity's convention for the writing of letters, whether the correspondence be actual letters or literary epistles. As has been demonstrated by H. Koskenniemi, a Finnish classics scholar, in antiquity a dynamic exchange between the customs and rules for actual letters and those for literary epistles occurred. The influence of such an interchange can be seen in letters written by ordinary people as well as qualified authors, among the latter of which the apostle Paul must be counted. Manuals circulating in the Roman world, especially two that carry the names of Demetrius and Proclus, offered advice on letter composition. They recommended that writers of letters or epistles include explicit references to the friendship and intimacy of the correspondents or to other personal data, references commonly found both in private letters written on papyrus and in public communications composed at a literary level.

Thus, from a stylistic point of view, the personal messages in the pastoral and captivity epistles have analogies in actual letters as well as in literary epistles of antiquity. This factor, however, does not have the slightest bearing on the question of authenticity; for here, as always, overlapping of literary genres is no proof for determining a fictitious work. It is only when the extant references to personal details contradict a historical framework otherwise known, that evidence for a work's artificial character may be granted.

Moreover, the formal distinctions between private letters and general epistles posited by Adolf Deissmann and later authorities never did exist. Sometimes a personal letter was garnished with rhetorical features; sometimes a rhetorical epistle was oriented to personal affairs. This interweaving of private and literary elements appears in the whole of the Pauline correspondence, including the pastoral and captivity epistles.

Even the earlier Pauline letters contain personal messages to be extended to all readers, as shown by the following examples: "I adjure you by the Lord to let the epistle be read to all the brothers and sisters" (1 Thess. 5:27); "Paul... and all the brothers and sisters with me to the churches in Galatia" (Gal. 1:1-2); "Paul... to the church of God represented in Corinth... along with all who invoke the name of our Lord Jesus Christ in every place, theirs and ours" (1 Cor. 1:1-2).

This open, public nature of the letters enhances the rhetorical flavor of the entire Pauline correspondence, and the letters in question are to be understood as literary substitutes for public addresses where even the personal notes serve oratorical and homiletical purposes. Examples of this convention occur in some of Paul's earliest correspondence: "However, now when Timothy has come to us and brought us good news about your faith and your love, and reported that you always have a pleasant memory of us, longing to see us just as we long to see you—for this reason, brothers and sisters, we felt comforted about you in spite of all your trouble and distress, that is, on account of your faith, because now we come to life if you continue to stand firm in the Lord" (1 Thess. 3:6-8).

Such organic combinations of personal and rhetorical elements are found in the entire Pauline corpus, indicating that Paul was acquainted with the norms of ancient epistolary style. Classical examples of this personal-rhetorical strategy, though published with higher literary pretensions, are the famous epistles of Cicero and Seneca that were addressed to individual relatives or acquaintances but were intended for particular reading circles or for general consumption. The personal notices found in such compositions may be regarded as more or less spontaneous and at the same time as more or less stereotyped; but their literary function does not as such offer any criterion with which to judge the amount of truth behind them. The same is true of the Pauline letters. Because Hellenistic literary conventions both for private letters and public epistles appear already in Paul's earliest correspondence, the apostle and his coauthors would certainly have been able to apply these conventions to later writings such as the pastoral and captivity epistles. The rhetorical style and ecclesiastical contents of these epistles do not provide any evidence against the factuality of the personal notices in the letters.

After all, the historical credibility of the personal details in the pastoral and captivity epistles must be decided on the basis of their content—not their literary style. If the biographical and geographical data in these epistles stood in blatant contradiction to facts otherwise known, as is the case with apocryphal legends about the apostles, it would then be appropriate to question their authenticity. No such contradiction, however, can be found here. Just the opposite is true, for the biographical and topographical indications in 1 Timothy, 2 Timothy, Titus, Colossians, and Ephesians can be tallied with a whole array of incidents that are known from other letters of Paul and the Book of Acts. An unbiased, close inspection yields a congruous picture, consisting in part of inconspicuous details, such that suggestions of later and deliberate textual adjustments are out of the question.

Whereas the oratorical peculiarity of the three pastoral and the two captivity epistles cannot be denied, their distinctive character can best be explained as a concession to the original hearers or readers; namely, residents of Asia Minor, where the aforementioned baroque style of Asianic rhetoric was cultivated and where the apostle Paul of Tarsus was at home. On the other hand, this rhetorical particularity is relativized by the fact that earlier Pauline epistles already display oratorical devices. Furthermore, the apparently special position of the letters under discussion is offset by the fact that nearly all the names and dates agree with items found in Acts and other epistles of Paul, and this essential agreement cannot possibly be ascribed to deliberate fabrication.

The topics treated in the pastoral and captivity epistles appear to display an alleged "progression" of thought when compared with older Pauline letters. But here again this difference has to do with accommodation to Paul's hearers and readers. 1 Timothy, 2 Timothy, and Titus were meant to instruct collaborators of Paul on such matters as leadership and instruction in the community (1 Tim. 1:3; 2:1; etc.). For these practical reasons the admo-

nitions possess a more ecclesiastical orientation than the letters addressed
to the community of believers as a whole. With respect to Colossians and
Ephesians, it should also be remembered that the envisaged audiences or
reading circles were residents of Phrygia and Asia who were already familiar with several of the distinctive ideas in these epistles, such as "mystery"
(Eph. 1:9) and "fullness" (Col. 2:9; Eph. 1:10). Neither can the ecclesiastical
duties mentioned in the three pastoral epistles be used for a precise dating of
these writings, for no timetable can be established for the "progression" of
such ideas. Whenever this development is attempted in modern scholarship,
the basis inevitably includes some aprioristic scheme that ultimately begs the
question.

These general observations, especially with regard to specific names and
dates, are discussed below for each individual letter.

## 5. 1 Timothy (continued)

Attention must now be paid to the circumstances surrounding Paul's advice
to his younger colleague. While the apostle was setting out for Macedonia, he directed his "spiritual child" Timothy to remain in Ephesus (1 Tim.
1:3). As sketched above (See "Overview of the Chronology"), this direc-
tive corresponds to information in Acts and the Corinthian letters about
events that took place in A.D. 56. Paul had sent Timothy from Ephesus to
Macedonia and Corinth (Acts 19:22a; 1 Cor. 4:17) while he himself remained in Ephesus (Acts 19:22a), eagerly awaiting the young man's return
(1 Cor. 16:11) before setting out for Troas and Macedonia (Acts 20:1; 2 Cor.
2:12–13).

When the epistle mentions Timothy remaining in Ephesus while the
apostle himself was leaving for Macedonia, the text does not say that Paul
had already left, but that he was about to depart (1 Tim. 1:3, *poreuomenos*
[pres. part.]). First Timothy was therefore written while both Paul and Timothy were still in Ephesus, and the epistle can be understood to correspond
to the public farewell speech that Luke alludes to in connection with Paul's
departure for Macedonia (Acts 20:1, *parakaleusas*, "having admonished
them," that is, the disciples in Ephesus). Another concrete example of a
farewell sermon replete with admonitions is recorded by Luke in his account
of Paul's later speech in Miletus before the Ephesian elders (Acts 20:17–35).
It is easy to see that all the instructions and exhortations found in 1 Timothy, though nominally addressed to Paul's assistant Timothy, were actually
formulated with a broader audience in mind, so that 1 Timothy is actually
a written speech.

Throughout 1 Timothy it is clear that the whole congregation in Ephesus
and even outsiders were intended to hear the message, whereas much of the

content would appear quite trivial and superfluous if Timothy were the only hearer or reader. The repeated warnings against false teachers (1 Tim. 1:6–11; 4:1–5; 6:3–10) were certainly not reserved for the ears of Timothy alone. Paul was not compelled to remind Timothy of his own conversion and call to the apostolic ministry (1:12). But this reference to his past experience is most reasonable when a broader audience is kept in mind. By directing Timothy to organize common prayer and parish leadership (2:1–3:13), as well as social life in the community (5:1–22), Paul is instructing Timothy in front of the whole congregation. All of these messages were undoubtedly intended to teach the community and to communicate important information to this wider circle.

In full accord with this public character of the presentation is the pronounced rhetorical style. The apostle declares twice in a dignified manner: "The saying is sure and worthy of every affirmation" (1:15; 4:9). Other emotive phrases of this kind are the following: "This charge I entrust to you, my child Timothy" (1:18); "In the presence of God and Christ Jesus and the elect angels, I adjure you to heed this without prejudice" (5:21); "But as for you, man of God, shun this and pursue righteousness, piety, faith, love, endurance, humility" (6:11). Paul is seen throughout as a speaker who, standing before Timothy and the assembled community, prepares for his imminent departure by exhorting the members of the congregation through the instruction of his youthful substitute.

This community address as backdrop for 1 Timothy corresponds exactly to the setting indicated in Acts concerning Paul's departure from Ephesus. "Having called together the disciples and exhorting them, he bid them farewell, left them and went to Macedonia" (Acts 20:1). Moreover, as reported by Luke, Paul's farewell message at Miletus in front of the Ephesian elders (Acts 20:17–35) is a homily performed in a similar public situation. Although the speech was formulated by Luke, its ecclesiastical context and rhetorically shaped contents offer interesting analogies to those admonitions that constitute 1 Timothy.

Consequently, 1 Timothy can be classified as a public address delivered in Ephesus after Timothy had taken 1 Corinthians to Greece and returned to Ephesus in the summer or fall of the year 56. In part, 1 Timothy was intended as a letter of introduction for "the young man" who was to serve as leader of the Ephesian church in Paul's absence. This setting implies then that Timothy must have remained in Ephesus for a while, and in fact his activity there probably lasted most of a year, for Timothy next appears in the documents as coauthor of 2 Corinthians (1:1), a letter sent by Paul from Macedonia in the summer of A.D. 57 (2 Cor. 8:10; 9:2, "since last year," referring back to the collection mentioned in 1 Cor. 16:1).

During the year in question, Paul worked in Troas and Macedonia (2 Cor. 2:12–13). Timothy probably joined him in the latter country due to difficulties in Ephesus, as suggested by a passage in 2 Corinthians referring in the "we-form" to serious afflictions suffered in Asia (1:8–11). In 1 Timothy, as well as in 2 Timothy, which also mentions Ephesus, there are corresponding references to pugnacious opponents about to cause or already causing troubles in the city (1 Tim. 1:4, 7, 20; 6:4, 20; 2 Tim. 1:15; 2:16, 18, 23; 4:14). Luke also reports that Paul, accompanied by Hellenist disciples, including Timothy (Acts 20:4), avoided Ephesus on his return from Greece to Asia (20:16) and in Miletus spoke to the presbyters of Ephesus about the devastating activity of "seducers" (20:29–30). All these passages support the assumption that Timothy replaced Paul in Ephesus, as indicated in 1 Timothy, and that he later, under pressure from agitators, joined Paul in Macedonia, as intimated in 2 Corinthians.

Thus there is good reason to date the public recitation of 1 Timothy in Ephesus and Paul's subsequent departure for Troas and Macedonia to the summer of A.D. 56. After this Timothy probably worked in Ephesus in accord with Paul's instructions for around a year before joining Paul in Macedonia when tensions in Ephesus began to accelerate. The preceding discussion was intended to make this provenance credible, the point being that 1 Timothy agrees with circumstances in the life of Paul known from various documents, so that the epistle cannot be called a forgery post mortem. Paul was at least the initiator of the message, although its oratorical style does not exclude contributions of a colleague like Luke, whose report on Paul's oration in Miletus (Acts 20:17–36) provides a most illuminating analogy to the rhetorical thrust of 1 Timothy.

The purpose of the speech presented in 1 Timothy was (A) to warn Timothy and the Ephesians against heretical tendencies, and (B) to give instructions on church discipline.

(A) Evidently the heresy was a sort of Judaism, known partially from Galatians, but here reinforced by special claims that were based on genealogies (1:4). This Jewish pretentiousness (cf. 2 Cor. 11:22) led to legalism (1:7; cf. Titus 3:9), asceticism (4:3; cf. Col. 2:21), and materialism (6:5; cf. Phil. 3:19). The concluding rejection of a "falsely so-called knowledge" (6:20) corresponds with Paul's words against the Corinthian overemphasis on wisdom and knowledge (1 Cor. 1:18–2:16). This "knowledge" was only a preliminary stage of the later philosophy referred to as gnosticism.

(B) These warnings alternate with instructions on church discipline and social order, prayer (2:1), bishops and deacons (3:1, 8), elders (5:1), and other social groups. Because these instructions are intended for a church leader, they are more detailed than those in such community addresses as

1 Thessalonians or 1 Corinthians. But this greater specification does not prove that 1 Timothy was composed at a time later than any other Pauline correspondence.

The structure of 1 Timothy consists of repeated alternation between the two motifs A and B:

| | | |
|---|---|---|
| Introduction | | 1:1–2 |
| (I) | A. Judaistic legalism rejected | 1:3–20 |
| | B. Church discipline | 2:1–3:16 |
| (II) | A. Asceticism rejected | 4:1–10 |
| | B. Social order | 4:11–6:2 |
| (III) | A. Materialism rejected | 6:3–21 |

Modern churches and their members are not confronted with the same problems as those encountered by Timothy in Ephesus. Nevertheless, 1 Timothy challenges clergy and laity alike through its warnings against a self-righteous religious propaganda that has continued on and occurs today in many forms. First Timothy emphasizes sound faith and true love in the church.

## 6. 2 Corinthians (A.D. 57, summer)

Paul's experiences in Ephesus and Asia during his third journey form the background of the next letter to be considered, 2 Corinthians. It presupposes that Paul had recently encountered great distress in Ephesus (2 Cor. 1:8) and had left Asia for Troas and Macedonia (2:12–13; 7:5; 8:1).

The date of 2 Corinthians was probably the summer of A.D. 57, for Paul writes here about the collection, which he (according to 1 Cor. 16:1) had planned for Jerusalem. He mentions that the Greek congregations had been preparing a contribution "since last year" (2 Cor. 8:10; 9:2), with which he was familiar because Timothy had returned to Ephesus from Corinth in the summer of the year 56 (see "Overview of the Chronology"). While writing 2 Corinthians, Paul was occupied with the same collection in Macedonia (8:1–4; 9:2). Timothy had recently joined the apostle there (see "Overview of the Chronology"), so that he was able to coauthor 2 Corinthians with Paul (1:1). In fact, Timothy's literary collaboration must have been particularly substantial in 2 Corinthians, because the word "we" is used here twice as often as in the longest Pauline letters ("we": 108 times in 2 Corinthians; cf. 59 times in Romans and 54 times in 1 Corinthians).

Whereas the first visit encompasses Paul's stay in Corinth from the fall of A.D. 51 to the spring of A.D. 53, there must have been a second visit before the one announced in 2 Corinthians, for Paul alludes to his presence among them as causing sorrow (2:1) when the congregation had received his sharp reprimands (13:2). Some time later, in order to explain his attitude, Paul wrote a letter to Corinth "with many tears" (2:3–4; 7:8, 12), and the context shows that he sent it with Titus, a Greek believer who had assisted Paul at the apostolic council (Gal. 2:1–3). Titus probably went to Corinth from Troas, for Paul said he expected to see him there again (2 Cor. 2:13a), and it was because Titus did not appear in Troas that Paul left for Macedonia earlier than planned (2:13b). When Titus finally met with Paul in Macedonia, the apostle was relieved to hear of the positive effects of his critical, "tearful" letter (7:6–16).

On this occasion, Titus even asked the apostle to let him continue the collection initiated in Corinth (8:5, 16), and for this purpose was sent back to Corinth, supported by delegates of the Macedonian churches (8:18–24; 9:3–5; 12:18). Like the preceding critical letter, 2 Corinthians was probably sent with Titus to Corinth (8:17, 23; 12:18), while Paul remained in Macedonia somewhat longer before leaving for Greece (12:14, 20; 13:1–2, 10). On the way, the apostle passed through western Macedonia, reaching the border of Illyricum (Rom. 15:19), a Roman province northwest of Macedonia, whose region along the west coast was called Dalmatia (2 Tim. 4:10).

In 2 Corinthians there are thus several references to circumstances that kept Paul from coming to Corinth as soon as previously promised (1 Cor. 16:5–7). On the one hand, Paul did not want to cut short his fruitful activity in Troas and Macedonia (2 Cor. 2:12–17); on the other, the ill feeling palpably expressed in Corinth after his second visit also made him postpone his third visit (1:23–2:2). Instead, on two occasions he sent Titus to Corinth, once from Troas with the letter "written in tears" (2:3; 7:7–8) and once from Macedonia with 2 Corinthians accompanied by faithful collaborators to prepare Paul's own arrival there (8:18; 9:5; 12:1, 18; 13:1).

Naturally, the long delay of Paul's expected visit provoked disappointment and criticism in Corinth, and he found it necessary to defend himself. Paul had indeed promised to go directly from Ephesus to Corinth (1 Cor. 16:5; 2 Cor. 1:16). But he had changed his itinerary in order to fulfill the promises of God (2 Cor. 1:20) and to spare the Corinthians painful discussions (1:23), working longer in Troas and Macedonia (2:12–13). In connection with this disappointment and irritation, Paul encountered a graver difficulty, raised in Corinth by people who questioned his apostolic legitimacy. They said Paul had not presented a letter of recommendation like some other preachers in Corinth (2 Cor. 3:1; 5:12; 10:12; 12:11, cf. Apollos' letter of recommendation brought from Ephesus to Corinth, Acts 18:27). Paul defended his apostolic dignity by referring to the Corinthian church that he himself had founded (2 Cor. 3:2) as well as to his ministry of the new covenant (3:4–5:10). Furthermore, he mentions personal qualifications and spiritual achievements that his competitors were proud of, but which he possessed to an even greater degree (10:7–12:13): Paul does not say who his adversaries were, but their pretensions were evidently based on claims of Jewish lineage (11:22; cf. 1 Tim. 1:4, "genealogies") and of visionary experiences (2 Cor. 12:1; cf. Col. 2:16–18, against judaistic observances and boasting of visions). The popular veneration of these so-called superapostles in Corinth (2 Cor. 11:5) led Paul to repeat and intensify his warnings in the last part of the letter (10:1–13:13).

As a combination of apologetic explanations and polemical admonitions, 2 Corinthians has a particularly eruptive style. Paul himself felt that his anxiety had thrown him off balance (11:1, 16–21). Nevertheless, the letter is a homogeneous composition, for all its parts describe the same historical situation during the apostle's third journey. Each section exhibits Paul's endeavors to make the readers understand this situation as well as the importance of the genuine apostolic ministry and their own responsibility in response to his unalloyed apostolic message.

Attempts to divide 2 Corinthians into different writings destroy the logical coherence, which is evident in spite of the passionate prose. The last four chapters (10–13) in particular have been lopped off by scholars in order to recover the letter "written in tears" that Paul earlier had sent to Corinth (2:4). The following objections to this truncation must be raised, however: (1) Whereas the letter written in tears is said to have grieved a member of the congregation, whom the assembly had rebuked but then forgiven (2:2, 5–11), the last four chapters of 2 Corinthians make no mention of this. In addition, it is impossible to explain how these four chapters would have been removed from the usual epistolary framework in order to be glued directly to 2 Corinthians. (2) To be sure, Paul displays his offensive and defensive weapons (6:7) more aggressively in the last four chapters than before. Yet this can be explained on a personal level, for chapters 10–13 are no longer dominated by the we-forms characteristic of the preceding chapters that indicate Timothy's coauthorship. From the very beginning of this section Paul speaks emphatically in the singular: "I myself, Paul, am now admonishing you" (10:1). To enable his Christian "armament" to come to the fore effectively (10:4), he deploys rigorous and rhetorically charged argumentation (11:1–2, 16–17). Paul also had external reasons to intensify the polemics, given the fact that the congregation had come under the influence of popular speakers who claimed to possess powerful qualities (10:7, 13; 12:11, etc.) backed up by authoritative written recommendations (10:12, 18). These new circumstances offer sufficient explanation for the severe tone in chapters 10–13, whereas their separation from the epistle causes insurmountable difficulties.

In spite of the impulsive leap, 2 Corinthians is a coherent unit in which apologetic discourse alternates with polemical warning. Like 1 Corinthians, the epistle called 2 Corinthians is partly based on the logical pattern A B A as follows:

|        |                                               |            |
|--------|-----------------------------------------------|------------|
| Introduction |                                         | 1:1–2      |
| (I)    | Apology for delay of third visit              | 1:3–2:27   |
| (II)   | A. Legitimation required                      | 3:1–3      |
|        | B. Paul and the apostolic ministry            | 3:4–5:10   |
|        | A. Legitimation delivered                     | 5:11–6:10  |
| (III)  | A. Preparation for the visit                  | 6:11–7:4   |
|        | B. Events in Macedonia                        | 7:5–16     |
|        | A. Collection before and during the visit     | 8:1–9:15   |
| (IV)   | A. Warnings in view of the visit              | 10:1–6     |
|        | B. Paul and the apostolic pretenders          | 10:7–12:13 |
|        | A. Desires in view of the visit               | 12:14–13:13 |

The importance of 2 Corinthians for modern readers is not to be sought in the historical identification of the apostolic pretenders whom Paul combated, although their eventual connection with gnosticism or some other movement occupies most scholars today. One has only to observe that different kinds of pretentious prophets and preachers, coming from outside, have always raised and still raise difficulties in Christian communities. A substantial and positive value of 2 Corinthians, however, is found in the practical suggestions it offers regarding a pastor's care for his or her parish and the meaning of his or her ministry.

## 7. Romans (A.D. 58, early)

The continuation of Paul's third journey as described in Acts together with the relevant letters of Paul implicates Romans as the canonical letter that follows 2 Corinthians.

According to Luke in Acts, Paul's stay in Macedonia during his third journey was followed by a three-month visit to Greece, before the apostle decided to return through Macedonia to Syria (Acts 20:2–3). No doubt, this stay in Greece brought Paul mainly to Corinth, a realization of his intention to visit the Corinthians a third time (2 Cor. 12:14; 13:1).

Paul wrote the epistle to the Romans during this stay in Corinth, which according to Acts was as short as three months. The localization is confirmed by mention of his approaching return to Jerusalem with the money collected in Macedonia and Greece (Rom. 15:25–26) and by the reference to Phoebe in Cenchreae, the eastern harbor of Corinth (16:1–2), where she was hostess of a house-church and the protectress (Gk., *prostatis*, Lat., *patrona*) of foreign believers, including Paul. When the apostle sent her to Rome with warm commendations, he evidently was indicating that she was to take the letter with her. Further evidence of the Corinthian provenance is the notice that Gaius was currently Paul's host (16:23), for this man had been baptized by Paul in Corinth (1 Cor. 1:14).

There is no reason to doubt that Luke was essentially correct in his statement that Paul, after rather extensive activity in Macedonia, spent only three months in Greece (Acts 20:2-3). Paul also indicates in Romans that he passed through some part of Illyricum near the west coast of the Balkans after his stay in Macedonia (Rom. 15:19), so that his third visit to Corinth was further delayed. It thus seems probable that Paul was able to stay there for only approximately three months, as reported by Luke. In Romans, the apostle explicitly states he was going to leave for Jerusalem with the money collected in Macedonia and Greece (15:15-16), so that the epistle was most likely composed toward the end of Paul's three months in Corinth. Taking into consideration the apostle's extensive activity in Macedonia during A.D. 57, before he arrived in Corinth via Illyricum, his letter to the Romans may be dated to the beginning of A.D. 58. A confirmation of this estimate is found in Luke's account of Paul's return after his three months in Corinth and his passage through Macedonia accompanied by numerous collaborators (Acts 20:3-5). Here begins a we-report of the apostle and his company leaving Macedonia for Troas before Easter, and of Luke himself and some friends traveling from Philippi to Troas after this feast (20:6-7). It is most likely, then, that Paul wrote Romans in Corinth just before leaving for Macedonia so that the epistle has good reason to be dated to the beginning of the year 58.

In this case, Paul wrote to a church he had not yet visited, and in the ingress he gives a solemn declaration, with no mention of a collaborator, of his appointment to preach the gospel (Rom. 1:1-7). He then indicates the purpose of the letter—to prepare his coming to Rome after preaching in many different countries (1:10-15).

Luke knew that Paul had expressed this intention when he was in Ephesus (Acts 19:21), and Paul himself spoke of having had such a desire for several years (Rom. 15:23). The original impulse came from Paul's contacts with Aquila and Priscilla in Corinth (Acts 18:2), for these Jewish Christians were from Rome and therefore able to inform Paul about the incipient church there. Although they had moved to Greece around A.D. 50 because Claudius had ordered the Jews to leave Rome (Suetonius, *Claudius* 25:4), they, like other Jews, were allowed to return after a certain time, and in the letter to the Romans they receive the apostle's very first greeting (Rom. 16:3-5a).

The appearance of the Christian believers Aquila and Priscilla in Corinth shows that a Christian congregation existed in Rome before A.D. 50, making it the oldest European church known from available documents. Because there is no evidence of a personal founder, one has to assume that Christians moving to Rome, possibly as merchants like Aquila and Priscilla, had begun to assemble in private houses and had thus given rise to the Roman church. Many were probably Jews, for in his letter Paul often mentions the people of Israel and the Jewish believers (Rom. 1:16; 2:9–10, 17, 29; 3:1, 29; 9:1–11:36; 14:1; 15:1, 8). Because many Jewish inhabitants of Rome lived in Trastevere near what is now the Vatican, the first Roman house-churches may have developed there.

Paul was known among Jews and Christians as the leading representative of a mission to the Gentiles. When preparing his visit to Rome by letter, he had to explain what the gospel meant to him as it related to both Jews and Gentiles. He introduces this exposition with this proclamation: "I am not ashamed of the gospel, for it means the power of God leading to salvation for every believer, first the Jew and then the Greek" (Rom. 1:16). This divine power remained the apostle's topic, and he endeavored to prove that it results in justification and salvation on the basis of belief in what God, in Christ, does for sinful human beings (3:23–25), whether Jews or Gentiles (3:29). Awareness of Jewish elements in the Roman congregation led Paul to further statements on justification and salvation (4:1–8:39), on the present callousness and final salvation of Israel (9:1–11:36), and on the mutual solidarity of believers who fulfill different functions in the parish or take different attitudes toward Jewish observances and Christian liberty (12:1–15:14).

Writing again of his desire to visit Rome (15:15–33), Paul remarks that his preaching had reached the regions between Jerusalem and Illyricum (15:19) and that he hoped, after bringing the collected money from Corinth to Jerusalem (15:25), to be helped by the Roman congregation in reaching Spain in his missionary activity (15:24, 28). Though he felt there could be difficulties in Jerusalem (15:31), Paul did not know at the time that he would be arrested there and sent to Rome as a prisoner. Nevertheless, as discussed above (see "Overview of the Chronology"), there is some evidence that, after two years in Roman custody, Paul was possibly able to reach "the utmost west," that is, Spain.

It is the section with greetings to numerous persons (16:3–16) that has caused doubts that chapter 16 could have been written to Rome and members of a congregation whom Paul had never visited. In order to find another possible destination for chapter 16, some expositors have pointed out that Aquila and Priscilla were in Ephesus two years earlier (1 Cor. 16:19) and that older manuscripts call the next person greeted, Epaenetus, a firstfruit of *Asia* (instead of *Greece* as in the majority of texts). For these reasons it has been suggested that chapter 16 of Romans is connected with Ephesus, where Paul had spent considerable time (Acts 19:8, 10). Against this hypothesis it must be noted that chapter 16 cannot have existed as a separate letter, and the supposition that it may have been added to a copy of Romans sent to Ephesus implies a contradiction in the text, for the other chapters explicitly refer to Rome. It must also be acknowledged that Priscilla and Aquila as well as Epaenetus and other persons listed may have moved to Rome recently from places where Paul had first met them. Priscilla and Aquila may, on earlier occasions, have also mentioned the names of individual Christians in the Roman church to Paul.

In this context there is special reason to highlight Phoebe, whom the apostle obviously commissioned to deliver the letter. In the recommendation of her to the readers, she is portrayed as the "deaconess" of the church in Cenchreae, the eastern harbor of Corinth (16:1). This designation implies she had the financial means to be hostess of the house-church there. Moreover, when she is characterized as the "protectress" (Gk., *prostatis*, Lat., *patrona*) of many believers including Paul himself (16:2b), it is clear she was a person of social standing and influence who could take political responsibility for strangers who did not enjoy the civil rights of the Roman colony of Corinth. Paul had most likely asked her to deliver the letter, because her financial resources, social position, and travel experience allowed her to undertake the voyage and find her way to the addressees. This social position makes Phoebe comparable to other important women in contact with Paul, such as Lydia in Philippi and Priscilla in Rome, Corinth, and Ephesus, whose business activity took them around the Mediterranean world. It is therefore reasonable to presume that Phoebe, on some of her journeys, had met several of the persons mentioned in chapter 16 and that she could have helped Paul assemble an impressive list of persons to greet. This assumption is confirmed by the fact that no less than seven of the persons greeted are women, five of them praised for their charitable work like that of the deaconess Phoebe. By following the well-known French advice, "Cherchez la femme," one is able to explain how Paul knew of so many Christian women in Rome and their merits. A further circumstance, which speaks in favor of Rome as the destination of chapter 16, is the occurrence of several Latin names in the list of greetings: Junias (Junianus), Ampliatus, Urbanus, Rufus, Julia. In addition, some of the persons greeted are identified as Paul's "countrymen," namely, Andronicus and Junias (16:7) and Herodion (16:11). This demarcation appears understandable only in light of Paul's desire to be accepted by Jewish believers in Rome; such allusions to his own Jewish descent would by no means have reduced his difficulties in Ephesus.

The fourth section of Romans 16, which lists persons sending greetings to the readers (16:21–23), also suggests Rome and not Ephesus as the destination of chapter 16. Timothy is introduced here as Paul's collaborator (16:21a), a detail of obvious interest to readers not yet acquainted with him, but an awkward truism for readers in Ephesus who knew Timothy quite well. Remarkably enough, Titus does not appear among those who send greetings, although Paul had warmly praised his preparation for the collection in Corinth (2 Cor. 8:6, etc.). As will be argued below, for the letter bearing his name, this apparent lacuna is explained by Titus' absence from Corinth when Paul wrote to the Romans. Concerning the next three persons mentioned—Lucius, Jason, and Sosipatros (16:21b)—emphasis upon their Jewish origin points again to Roman readers as was true for Andronicus and the others mentioned in the second section (16:3–16). The final greetings of the fourth section are from Gaius and Erastus (16:23). Gaius is portrayed as the host of Paul and the whole church, indicating that he was a resourceful and important citizen in Corinth, probably even more important than Phoebe of the suburb Cenchreae.

In an earlier letter Paul also mentions Gaius as one of the first persons baptized in Corinth (1 Cor. 1:14). Erastus is described as the city treasurer, implying high social status. In both cases Paul wanted to show that persons of rank in Corinth supported his letter, which would of course facilitate his visit to Rome. Those who believe that Ephesus was the destination of Romans 16 are compelled to deny that this Erastus was probably the same Erastus mentioned by Luke as sent with Timothy to Corinth while Paul remained in Ephesus (Acts 19:22). The notation in Romans about his high office at Corinth would be senseless for Christians in Ephesus who already knew him as the Erastus who had been sent to Corinth from their city.

A decisive proof for the original connection of Romans 16 with the preceding chapters is the greeting inserted by Tertius, the shorthand-writer used by Paul for this epistle (16:22). Here is the only instance in which the name of Paul's stenographer is disclosed, the reason no doubt being that Tertius was happy to have completed a demanding work. It would have been strange to slip in this exceptional announcement if Tertius had written only chapter 16, whether as a separate or an additional unit.

Consequently, there are no historical reasons to separate Romans 16 from chapters 1–15. It must be admitted, however, that the fifth section of this chapter, containing a liturgical prayer generally called a doxology (Rom. 16:25–27), raises questions about its original position due to variations in the manuscript sources. Most older manuscripts include the doxology at the end of chapter 16, but in the papyrus $p^{46}$ it occurs after chapter 15 and in codices Alexandrinus and Porfirianus (A and P) after chapters 14 and 16, whereas codex Boernerianus (G) leaves an empty space after chapter 14. The confusion may have been caused in the second century by Marcion's edition of the Pauline epistles, which omitted the last chapters of Romans. In any case, the doxology seems to have been a liturgical formula that could be used in different contexts.

As observed above, it is possible to place Romans in a concrete historical situation and show that Paul formulated the letter in view of his intended visit to the Roman church (Rom. 1:8–15). However, this special setting for the epistle led the apostle to present his missionary program in more general terms in order to avoid eventual misunderstandings. Paul's main concern here was to show that both Jews and Greeks, two fundamental categories of humankind, are saved from sin and death if they accept in faith what God by grace has done for them in Christ (1:16). Pious works do not save, for both Jews and Greeks are sinners (1:18–3:20), and God prefers in his majesty to practice his own righteousness in which he justifies sinners and leads them to salvation by faith in Christ (3:21–31). Paul then illustrates this justification by faith with the example of Abraham (4:1–25) and discusses the liberation of human beings from negative principles of existence (5:1–8:39), and also expatiates on Israel's future salvation (9:1–11:36). Knowing that Christians in Rome are of both Jewish and Gentile background, Paul emphasizes the unity of all believers in his annexed exhortations (12:1–15:14), before he concludes with personal matters (15:15–16:27).

The structure of Romans may be illustrated in more detail by this scheme, where the logical pattern A, B, A is found once again in the discussion on Israel and in the subsequent exhortations:

| | | |
|---|---|---|
| Introduction | | 1:1–7 |
| (I) | Desire to visit Rome | 1:8–15 |
| (II) | The gospel, a power issuing in righteousness for Jews and Greeks by faith | 1:16–17 |
| (III) | All are sinners, both Jews and Gentiles | 1:18–3:31 |
| (IV) | Justification by faith: | |
| | (a) was prefigured in Abraham | 4:1–25 |
| | (b) liberates the believer from | |
| | the wrath of heaven | (5:9) 5:1–21 |
| | " the destructive power of sin | (6:1) 6:1–23 |
| | " the elenctic function of the Law | (7:1) 7:1–25 |
| | " the corruption of death and flesh | (8:2–3) 8:1–39 |
| (V) | The people of Israel | |
| | A. originally elected | 9:1–29 |
| | B. though presently emphasizing works according to the Law | 9:30–10:21 |
| | A. will come to faith when all Gentiles are converted | 11:1–36 |

The church has always recognized the exceptional importance of Romans, but particularly during the Reformation the impact of the letter's emphasis on grace and faith became especially obvious. Luther called Romans a light that illuminates the entire scripture, and Melanchthon described it as a compendium of Christian doctrine.

## 8. Titus (A.D. 58)

The circumstances surrounding the letter to Titus can be seen as following upon the historical situation in which Romans was written.

First, it may be recalled that Paul's valuable assistant Titus had been sent to prepare the collection in Corinth for the benefit of the church in Jerusalem (2 Cor. 8:6, 17).

Remarkably enough, however, in Romans Titus is not included among those eight friends of Paul who, like Timothy, send greetings from Corinth to the imperial capital (Rom. 16:21–23). This can only mean that he was absent from Corinth when Paul writes Romans. Because the letter sent to Titus states that Paul had asked his Greek assistant to stay on the island of Crete and install presbyters there (Titus 1:5), the absence of Titus in the greeting list of Romans can be explained quite naturally by concluding that he was in Crete when Paul greeted the Romans from Corinth.

As stated above (see Romans) Paul wrote Romans toward the end of his stay in Corinth. According to Luke in Acts, the apostle had spent three months there and then concluded his third journey with a triumphal return through Macedonia and along the coast of Asia Minor to Caesarea and Jerusalem (Acts 20:9–21:17). Sailing along the coast of Asia Minor brought Paul to places where a letter could be sent to Crete by a ship on a normal route.

A suitable explanation for the provenance of the letter to Titus is that Paul sent the letter to his friend in Crete while he passed the west coast of Asia on his way to Jerusalem; that is, in the spring or early summer of A.D. 58 (see "Overview of the Chronology"). Details supporting this assumption will be studied below.

Apart from the hint offered by the omission of Titus' name in Romans, there is no situation in the life of Paul, as far as it is known from his letters or from Acts, that helps date the activity of Titus in Crete. On the journey to Rome, the short time that the ship anchored off the south coast of Crete at Fair Havens in the vicinity of Lasea (Acts 27:8) did not allow the prisoner Paul to undertake any mission on the island, and there is no mention of Titus as his fellow traveler. Furthermore, the letter addressed to Titus does not give the slightest clue that the apostle is a prisoner. Consequently, either this letter must date from before Paul's imprisonment in Jerusalem, Caesarea, and Rome during the years 58–62 (Acts 21:33–28:31) or after this period. The first alternative opens up possibilities of aligning several details of the letter with circumstances known from Romans and Acts. The second alternative provides nothing more than an insubstantial freehand sketch. Under these circumstances the first alternative is clearly preferable.

Assuming the first alternative, it is true that Luke does not describe the conditions under which Paul may have instructed Titus to leave Corinth and work in Crete. However, Luke was not informed of the details concerning the activity of Paul and Titus during the third journey, and the course of the relevant narration in Acts discloses that Luke remained in Macedonia while Paul visited Corinth. He could only summarily tell of Paul's three months in Corinth before Paul's return to Macedonia (Acts 20:3). Here the scanty account stands in sharp contrast to the rich information that Luke subsequently presents in we-form depicting Paul's return to Macedonia, together with numerous Hellenistic friends, and the journey of the whole company from Philippi to Miletus (20:4–15). No doubt Luke had stayed in Macedonia and Philippi while Paul was in Corinth, which easily explains why the author of Acts does not mention Titus' activity in Corinth during Paul's third journey. Thus Luke's absence from Corinth would also explain why Titus' mission from Corinth to Crete is never mentioned in Acts, even though a hint of this omission can be found in the lacuna of Romans 16.

Regarding the greetings from Paul's collaborators in the last chapter of Romans, the curious absence of Titus after the reference to Timothy (Rom. 16:21) represents a specific historical situation. In this context Paul cannot possibly have ignored or forgotten Titus. Failure to mention his appreciated collaborator can only be due to the fact that Titus was no longer in Corinth when Paul dictated Romans.

Indeed, Titus' absence from Corinth corresponds exactly to his activity in Crete as reflected by Paul in the following words: "For this reason I let you stay in Crete, in order that you should arrange the rest of the matters and install presbyters in each city, as I told you" (Titus 1:5). It may be assumed that Paul, after coming to Corinth in the fall of the year 57, had sent Titus from there to Crete and let him stay on the island in order to organize parish life among people won for the gospel, either by others or converted through him. The expression "I let you stay in Crete" does not imply that Paul had been with Titus on the island, but that he had his collaborator remain there when he himself left Corinth for Macedonia (Acts 20:3; Rom. 15:25). Paul's eagerness to let Titus include Crete in the countries already reached by the gospel was only a natural consequence of the apostle's ambitious impulse to bring the gospel to each of the Greek countries before going on to Italy and Spain (Rom. 1:4; 15:19, 24, 25, 29; cf. Nicopolis in Titus 3:12).

In the letter to Titus there is material not only to illustrate what the apostle expected his collaborator to accomplish in Crete (Titus 1:5–3:11), but also to indicate what Titus was to do after receiving the letter (3:12–14). The latter reference sheds light on the situation in which the letter may have been written. Paul indicates here that he planned to send either Artemas or Tychicus to replace Titus in Crete, and that he wanted Titus to meet him in Nicopolis where he intended to spend the winter (3:12).

Artemas is not mentioned in other texts, whereas Tychicus is known from Acts as one of the Hellenistic collaborators who accompanied Paul on his return from Corinth through Macedonia and along the coast of Asia Minor to Jerusalem (Acts 20:4). It is also possible to identify Nicopolis, for even if there were several towns with this name, it must have been clear to Titus, without further directives, which one was meant. This holds true for antiquity's most famous Nicopolis, a harbor in Epirus south of Dalmatia and Illyricum, which Paul had certainly mentioned to Titus. After extending his activity as far as the border of Illyricum (Rom. 15:19), Paul must have passed Epirus on his way to Corinth, where Titus was still occupied with the collection (2 Cor. 8:17). It was in this Nicopolis that Paul said he intended to spend the winter (Titus 3:12b), and he obviously expected to sail from this important navigational center to Italy and from there to Rome and Spain (Rom. 15:22–24). Paul had preached earlier on the border of Illyricum, and his request that Titus join him in Nicopolis probably indicates that he wanted both to review and to expand the missionary activity in the neighboring countries during the winter until a ship would be available for a passage to Italy.

When writing the letter, Paul did not know whether he would send Artemas or Tychicus to replace Titus in Crete (Titus 3:12). But because Tychicus is later mentioned in connection with other responsibilities (Col. 4:7; Eph. 6:21), it seems likely that Paul sent Artemas. In any case, it is probable that Titus was replaced and that he left Crete for Nicopolis without knowing that Paul would be arrested in Jerusalem; for in a captivity letter Paul later states that Titus had gone to Dalmatia (2 Tim. 4:10), thus expanding the missionary work intimated by his departure for Nicopolis.

These observations help settle the chronological and geographical framework of the letter to Titus. After the introduction, Paul states that Titus had been asked to stay in Crete, although the apostle himself was leaving Corinth (Titus 1:5, "I left you behind"). Consequently, the message to Titus was produced some time during Paul's subsequent journey through Macedonia and along the coast of Asia Minor to Caesarea and Jerusalem. At the end of the letter, Paul greets Titus in the name of all the friends present with him at that time (Titus 3:15)—in this instance not a local congregation but a traveling company. In a we-report, Luke describes the journey and states that Paul and his entourage spent a week in Troas shortly after Easter—that is, A.D. 58 (Acts 20:4–6)—then sailed from Assos along the islands of Mitylene, Chios, Samos, and, deliberately avoiding Ephesus, came to Miletus (20:13–15).

As will be shown below, the letter to Titus is in the style of a public speech, reminiscent of the address during the apostle's stay in Miletus as reported by Luke (Acts 20:17–38). It is possible that Paul's communication to Titus was conceived as a public oration in Miletus. It may have been in this situation that the apostle took up the plan to send Artemas or Tychicus from Cnidus or Rhodes along the usual maritime route to Crete (cf. Acts 21:1; 27:7).

Like 1 Timothy, the message to Titus is more a public address than a private letter. It deals with ecclesiastical projects and problems prevalent in the churches of Asia Minor, such as the organization of community life through the help of presbyters (Titus 1:5–9), social order in the church (2:1–10), and the difficulties caused by judaistic tendencies (1:10–16; 3:9–11). Nominally, the letter was written for Titus and Crete, but it mentions several points about which Titus did not have to be instructed and contains little information specifically relating to Crete, where Paul had stayed only briefly, if at all. Actually, the text strikingly fits conditions in Asia Minor, where Paul had firsthand experiences. What the apostle presented as instructions to his representative in Crete was evidently to be made known first to the Asian communities through a public reading in Miletus. Later, the letter was probably circulated in the surrounding areas.

The letter to Titus, like 1 Timothy, is marked by pronounced rhetorical diction. One example of this is the following passage (Titus 2:11–14): "For the grace of God has been revealed as being salvific for all human beings, educating us, so that we might avoid godlessness and secular cupidities, living diligently, rightly, and piously in the present aeon, and looking forward to the blessed hope that we have in the glorious epiphany of our great God and Savior Christ Jesus, who sacrificed himself for us in order to deliver us from all lawlessness and purify for himself a people of his favor who are zealous for good works." Such a solemn proclamation was certainly not meant for Titus alone but rather for a Christian and Gentile audience whom the apostle desired to enlighten directly.

The original connection of the letter with Miletus is confirmed by Paul's ironic quotation of the ancient philosopher Epimenides, "Cretans are always liars . . ." (Titus 1:12). Citing this well-known antinomy, penned by a known Cretan, in no place would have been more fitting than in Miletus, where early Greek philosophy was developed.

Luke also records a similar oration given in Miletus by Paul (Acts 20:17–35). Here the audience consists of presbyters who were asked to come from Ephesus to Miletus (20:17). Parts of this homily deal with Paul's earlier problems in Ephesus, but there are several positive recommendations and negative judgments that resemble those in the letter to Titus. In both cases the important ecclesiastical functionaries are called "presbyters" (Acts 20:17; Titus 1:5) and even "bishops," though only in the sense of pastors (Acts 20:28; Titus 1:7). The congregation for which they are responsible is characterized in similar Old Testament terms, being on the one hand a people of holy inheritance (Acts 20:30; cf. Titus 3:7) and on the other, a people of divine favor (Titus 2:14). In both cases Paul complains about the activity of Jewish disturbers (Acts 20:19; Titus 1:10; 3:9–11) and rapacious deceivers who are compared to savage beasts (Acts 20:29—wolves; Titus 1:12—evil animals) who snatch away many disciples through their perverted teaching (Acts 20:30; Titus 1:11). These similarities do not imply that one text influenced the other, for important differences in the orientation and in the vocabulary are apparent. Luke can have remembered and summarized a speech given by Paul to the Ephesian presbyters, whereas the letter was composed by Paul in the form of a speech addressed to Titus, but with the intention that it should be heard by a similar assembly. The *tertium comparationis* lies in the connection of both speeches with Miletus and their concentration on problems that occupied Paul in Roman Asia. Luke knew that Paul had given a speech in Miletus and, in his usual fashion, has reconstructed characteristic elements of it. This evidence from Acts, together with topical similarities found in the letter to Titus, suggests that the latter document is a rhetorical composition first meant to be heard in Miletus.

With respect to the ecclesiastical subjects treated, the letter to Titus is somewhat reminiscent of 1 Timothy, but it is shorter and has a less complicated structure:

| | | |
|---|---|---|
| Introduction | | 1:1–4 |
| (I) | Presbyters installed, disturbers rejected | 1:5–16 |
| (II) | Social order | 2:1–10 |
| (III) | Universality of grace, loyalty toward society | 2:11–3:11 |
| (IV) | Personal notices | 3:12–15 |

The letter to Titus is especially attractive in section III, which contains an impressive meditation on the universality of God's grace (2:11–3:8). A consequence of this universality is loyalty toward society (3:1–2). The believers should remember that they were erring like the Gentiles until they were cleansed in the bath of regeneration (3:3–7).

# Paul's Captivity

## 9. *Philemon* (A.D. *59*)

The final group of Pauline letters is the captivity epistles. On the basis of their own indications of historical circumstances, they will be analyzed in the following order: Philemon, Colossians, Ephesians, Second Timothy, and Philippians.

In spite of its brevity, the letter to Philemon contains two elements of fundamental importance for establishing the chronology of the captivity epistles. These are especially significant because the authenticity of Philemon is generally accepted in critical scholarship.

First it should be observed that Paul describes his captivity as a new situation in his life (Philem. 9b): "Still being the old man Paul, but now also a prisoner of Christ Jesus, I appeal to you. . . . " He wanted Philemon to forgive his slave Onesimus for running away and to receive him gently because, on Paul's initiative, he was now being sent back (vv. 10–12). In order to soften the anticipated anger of Philemon, Paul appealed to his reader's compassion. Not only could Paul emphasize his confidence in Christ and love toward Philemon (vv. 8–9a); he could also now claim to have become a prisoner for the sake of Christ (v. 9b). The point was that Paul had become more intimately bound up with the Lord than ever, for in his old age he was now also suffering as a captive for Christ. When speaking in this context of being "but now (*nuni de*) also a prisoner," Paul explicitly presents his captivity as a new experience in life.

This information is decisive for the question concerning which captivity is being referred to in the letter. Paul had occasionally been in jail for a night or so (Acts 16:23; 2 Cor. 6:5; 11:23; Rom. 16:7), but that was very different from an extended captivity as a prisoner in chains (Philem. 13). His reference to a "fight with animals" in Ephesus (1 Cor. 15:32) has been used to suggest an imprisonment; but the phrase is a metaphor, as proved by the specification "figuratively (humanly) speaking" (*kata anthropon*), by which Paul indicated his difficulties with the silversmiths. On the whole, the popular assumption of a captivity in Ephesus is not based on any evidence, but on pure speculation. It is directly refuted by Luke. According to Acts, the tumult unleashed by the silversmiths was truncated by the chancellor (mayor) of Ephesus, who then helped Paul to escape (Acts 19:40)—the opposite of putting him in the state prison that was under his jurisdiction. The captivity mentioned in Philemon must therefore be sought elsewhere. No extended imprisonment implying a new situation in the life of Paul can be discovered until the apostle was arrested in Jerusalem at the end of A.D. 58 and brought to Caesarea (Acts 23:31–33), where he was imprisoned for two years, 59–60 (24:27). The beginning of this captivity was no doubt the background of Paul's appeal to Philemon's compassion (9b): "Now also a prisoner of Christ Jesus." The letter probably dates from early 59.

The striking analogies existing between the nomenclature of Philemon and Colossians must also be considered:

|             | *Philem.* | *Col.*      |                                          |
|-------------|-----------|-------------|------------------------------------------|
| Archippus   | 2         | 4:17        | (identified as at home in Colossae)      |
| Onesimus    | 10        | 4:9         | (identified as at home in Colossae)      |
| Epaphras    | 23        | 1:7; 4:12   | (identified as at home in Colossae)      |
| Mark        | 24        | 4:10        | (presented as the nephew of Barnabas)    |
| Aristarchus | 24        | 4:10        | (according to Acts 27:2 with Paul in Caesarea) |
| Demas       | 24        | 4:14        |                                          |
| Luke        | 24        | 4:14        |                                          |

In the letter to the Colossians, the three first persons mentioned in this list of common names are described as inhabitants of Colossae. Therefore it is generally acknowledged that the recipient of the letter to Philemon must have been a friend of Paul living in the same city.

An indirect connection between the two letters is found in the person of Tychicus. Although he is not mentioned in Philemon, he was commissioned by Paul to deliver the letter to the Colossians and was to be accompanied by Onesimus, the slave mentioned in Philemon (Col. 4:7–9). The delivery of Ephesians to its readers was also to have been Tychicus' responsibility (Eph. 6:21, 22).

In short, Paul wrote the letter to Philemon, a resident of Colossae, at the beginning of his imprisonment in Caesarea in early 59. The reason for the letter was the escape of Onesimus from his master and Paul's decision to send him back.

This charming billet, which came to be known simply as "To Philemon," reflects Paul's personality more than many of his other canonical letters. Apparently under the influence of Paul's compelling character, Onesimus had left his master in Colossae and sought the apostle's company in Caesarea. Because Onesimus is called a "child" (v. 10), he may have been an enthusiastic teenager. However, unlike many charismatic leaders, the apostle, in this delicate affair, did not want to misuse his appeal. Instead, he sent the young man back, and he even promised to reimburse Philemon for any money this servant may have carried off in funding his own escape (vv. 18–19a).

## 10. Colossians (A.D. 59)

The remarkable correspondence in personal names between Philemon and Colossians supports the conclusion that Colossians was also written during Paul's two-year imprisonment (A.D. 59–60) in Caesarea (Acts 24:27). It is highly improbable that a so-called deutero-Paulinist would have taken the names from a private note to Philemon and used them to secure historical credibility for a later composition that was meant to impress Christians in Phrygia. The only reasonable explanation for the correspondence of the names is the assumption that Philemon and Colossians were produced at the same time, and this concurrence is strongly supported by the fact that both letters mention the sending back of Onesimus to Colossae (Philem. 12, 17; Col. 4:9).

Like the letter to Philemon, the epistle to the Colossians contains a clause that, as the text explicitly states, Paul added in "my own hand" (Philem. 19; Col. 4:18), implying that a secretary had written out the main text. Paul apparently dictated Colossians together with two collaborators: Timothy figures as coauthor in the ingress (Col. 1:1), and in the subsequent text a Colossian preacher and teacher by the name of Epaphras is described as one who had arrived with recent information about the Christians in Colossae and the neighboring cities of Laodicea and Hierapolis in the Lycus valley (1:7; 4:12–13). As residents of Asia Minor, these persons most likely would have contributed to the Asiatic eloquence—characteristic of Colossians— that has led a number of expositors to doubt Paul's personal responsibility for the letter.

The church of Colossae in Phrygia, although not founded by Paul alone, was at least connected with his first journey, which brought him and Barnabas to Antioch near the border of Pisidia and Phrygia in the year A.D. 47 (Acts 13:14). Luke reports on their great success among Jewish proselytes and Gentiles in Antioch (13:43, 48), which caused the gospel to spread "in the whole country" (13:49). The gospel may then have reached Colossae two hundred kilometers farther west along the important Roman road crossing the country there. Paul's reference to Barnabas (Col. 4:10) also indicates familiarity of the readers with the leader of the evangelization in Antioch and the surrounding areas.

Further indications found in Acts show that Paul may have actually visited Colossae and other cities in the Lycus valley during his third journey, around A.D. 55. Journeying through Galatia and Phrygia (Acts 18:23), he is portrayed as passing through "the upper parts" of the country before arriving in Ephesus (19:1). From the Ephesian perspective, these upper parts were the valley of the river Maeander and its southern tributary, Lycus, where Colossae was situated. Luke's references to these regions were certainly meant to show that Paul visited congregations already existing there, like the church of Colossae. In his letters to Philemon and the Colossians, Paul also mentions several acquaintances in Colossae by name, such as Philemon, Onesimus, Archippus, and Epaphras. The last-mentioned friend had told Paul of the Colossian believers' affection for him (Col. 1:8). Paul clearly had had contact with several believers in Colossae before he dictated the letter in question.

Paul also extended his admonitions to people in Colossae who had never seen his face (2:1). This utterance, however, refers to neophytes who had been converted and instructed by Epaphras (1:7) in the four years after Paul's visit to Colossae, and in itself does not support any theory of post-Pauline authorship.

All attempts to make Colossians a deutero-Pauline composition of the period A.D. 70–100 are rendered null and void by documents that demonstrate that Colossae lost its cultural importance through an earthquake in 61. Situated on the southern bank of the river Lycus in Phrygia, Colossae was only seventeen kilometers distant from the big and rich city of Laodicea to the west, also on the Lycus river. In fact, in Colossians Paul mentions Laodicea as the recipient of another letter sent at the same time (but now lost) (Col. 4:16). According to Tacitus, Laodicea was destroyed in A.D. 61 by an earthquake (Tacitus, *Annals* 14:27:1), and because the whole region was known as a center of repeated catastrophes (Strabo, *Geography* 12:8:16), it can be inferred that Colossae was destroyed on the same occasion. Tacitus does not mention Colossae, for what interested him was only the fact that Laodicea was soon rebuilt by its inhabitants. However, precisely because he does not refer to Colossae, one can assume that it was not rebuilt in any noteworthy way. This conclusion is confirmed by the total silence about Colossae characteristic of documents after A.D. 61; earlier texts refer to it as an important city, known for its wool industry. No mention of Colossae is found in passages about Laodicea formulated during the last half of the first Christian century (Pliny, *History* 5:105; Rev. 1:11; 3:14; *Sibylline Oracles* 3:471; 4:106 e.p.). Particularly striking is the witness of Revelation from around A.D. 95, where the seven churches of Asia include Laodicea but not Colossae (see passages quoted above). This lacuna proves without doubt that for the author no Colossian congregation of importance existed. Furthermore, a later historian complements the information of Tacitus without depending upon it; namely Eusebius, who states that Laodicea, Hierapolis, and Colossae were destroyed by an earthquake in the year 62 (Eusebius, *Chronicle*

1.21.22, ed. R. Helm, p. 183). All of this literary evidence speaks against scholarly inclinations to date Colossians between A.D. 70 and 100. No forger would have been interested in producing a quasi-Pauline letter to Colossae in a period when no city or at least no church of importance existed there. It is true that Colossae has not yet been excavated, and the archaeological evidence will perhaps change the picture. But provisionally, the literary witnesses are plain enough to invalidate any degradation of Colossians to a deutero-Pauline creation.

Returning to the remarkable correspondence of the names cited in Philemon and Colossians, it may be emphasized once again that both letters refer to Onesimus' being sent back to Colossae (Philem. 12, 17; Col. 4:9). Moreover, Colossians mentions Tychicus as the bearer of the letter and guide for the young man (4:7–9). Thus Philemon and Colossians were undoubtedly composed and delivered at the same time during the first part of Paul's captivity in Caesarea from A.D. 59–60, dates supported by the extrabiblical sources cited above.

Also interesting is the request to welcome Mark when he comes to Colossae (4:10). He is identified as the nephew of Barnabas, indicating that he was not yet known to the readers. Barnabas, however, had been in the region during Paul's first journey through Pisidian Antioch, as mentioned above. The itinerary of 2 Timothy, to be analyzed below, shows that Paul at a later point did send Mark from Caesarea through Lycaonia and Phrygia to meet Timothy in Troas (2 Tim. 4:11). Paul already had Mark in mind to visit Colossae when he requested that Mark be welcomed.

The purpose of Colossians was to admonish neophytes, to whom "the word of truth" had recently been preached and who needed to be rooted more firmly in what they had been taught (2:7). As he expressly admitted, Paul had not personally met them (2:1); but from their preacher and teacher, Epaphras, he had heard of their belief and love (1:4, 7–8). That neophytes were the primary audience is also confirmed subsequently by characteristic topics rhetorically crafted. In the apostle's liturgical hymn on Christ (1:14–21), who is the head of the church (1:18), the closing introduces the recent conversion and reconciliation of the readers through the gospel they have heard (1:21–23). The rejection of speculations and traditions not based on Christ (2:8–15) includes a declaration that the baptism, which the readers had received, was founded upon a circumcision not made with hands, but one that led to the forgiveness of sins through their death and vivification with Christ (2:11–13). Such baptismal imagery also appears later in an ethical section (3:1–17): "You have died" (3:3); "Now put away (like old clothes)..." (3:8); "Take off the old self... and put on the new one" (3:9–10).

The apostle's earlier experiences in Phrygia and the information recently provided by Epaphras led Paul to include certain religious terms and to reject outright various heretical tendencies that the Phrygian neophytes would have encountered. Thus he let his admonitions be colored by expressions not so typical of earlier letters, such as "fullness," "insight," and "mystery" (1:9, 10, 19, 26, etc.), concepts that may have been common in Phrygia because of its religious rites, including "mysteries." Furthermore, the apostle inserts an extensive warning against what he termed a "philosophy" (2:8a), a new expression referring to an old topic in other of his correspondence. This religious speculation is connected with judaistic asceticism, including a dependence on legalistic and materialistic "elements" (2:8, 20). The apostle had already encountered a similar judaistic heresy in the neighboring country of Galatia (Gal. 4:3, 9). Hence such conceptualizations and warnings, more or less peculiar to Colossians, can be understood as Paul's attempt to face head-on the issues at hand by adapting local terminology and vernacular, stimulated in part by the presence of Epaphras.

Regarding the structure, the four chapters of Colossians may conveniently be divided into two parts, the first dealing with dogmatics and the second devoted to ethical questions:

| | | |
|---|---|---|
| Ingress | | 1:1–2 |
| (I) | Dogmatics | 1:3–2:23 |
| | Instruction through Epaphras | 1:3–8 |
| | Participation in Christ | 1:9–2:23 |
| | Rejection of Judaistic doctrine and practice | 2:4–23 |
| (II) | Ethics | 3:1–4:6 |
| | Seeking heavenly values | 3:1–4 |
| | Laying off the old nature | 3:5–9 |
| | Putting on the new self | 3:10–17 |
| | Duties of household members | 3:18–4:1 |
| | Prayer and wisdom | 4:2–6 |
| (III) | Personal notices | 4:7–18 |

Modern readers of Colossians will do right if they concentrate their interest on the challenging and refreshing admonitions contained here.

## 11. Ephesians (A.D. 59)

In its vocabulary, diction, and concepts, Ephesians closely resembles Colossians, although it is about a third longer. The striking analogies may be understood as proof of a common or at least similar origin. But these parallels have also led to the opposite hypothesis, that Ephesians was produced by a deutero-Paulinist who imitated Colossians.

Several times it has been emphasized in the preceding arguments that dogmatic judgments—which classify units of the Pauline corpus as deutero-Pauline or pseudepigraphic—by regularly overlooking names and dates, including pertinent information in Acts, neglect precisely the kind of evidence that would divulge a literary-historical coherence between one Pauline letter and the rest of his corpus. As seen above, the *onomastica* of Philemon and Colossians offer just such an example of authorial coherence. Moreover, the fact that this convergence of names does not at the same time include exactly the same sequence of names in each of the letters argues more for a common setting of author and circumstance than for the claim of redactional imitation.

Admittedly, this appeal to common names and dates is not applicable to Ephesians, because the only personal names occurring here are those of Paul, Jesus (Eph. 1:1), and Tychicus (6:21). Nevertheless, if Ephesians had been copied from Colossians, why would the author have omitted Timothy's name when he is mentioned in the latter as Paul's coauthor (Col. 1:1)? And why are all the other names in Colossians missing in Ephesians except that of Tychicus, who is described similarly in both letters as Paul's delegate to the recipients (Col. 4:7–8; Eph. 6:21–22)? No theory of imitation offers a suitable explanation of this inconcinnity. The only adequate explanation for the composition of Ephesians will require an examination of the letter itself in order to profile its distinctive epistolary qualities and historical referents and thus establish its relation to other Pauline letters and their historical settings.

The textual evidence shows that Ephesians was probably not meant to be read in Ephesus alone. Although a majority of manuscripts contain the full text of the first clause—"Paul, apostle of Christ Jesus by the will of God, to the holy ones who live in Ephesus and are faithful in Christ Jesus" (Eph. 1:1)—the words "in Ephesus" do not appear in Papyrus 46 or the original text of Codices Vaticanus and Sinaiticus. In the letter to the Romans, also written in the name of Paul without reference to a coauthor, a similar phrase was used (Rom. 1:7): "To all who live in Rome as the beloved of God, as called and holy." Unlike the letter to the Ephesians, the place name (Rome) appears in all of the sources. Due to the lacuna found in notable manuscripts of Ephesians, however, it seems doubtful that "in Ephesus" belonged to the original text. Instead, a blank space may have been left for different names. Because the name "Ephesus" never occurs again in the letter, it is possible that Ephesians was meant to be heard or read in different churches, as Colossians was also intended to be read in Laodicea (Col. 4:16). It should also be recalled that Tychicus was to provide various hearers and readers with additional oral information about Paul's present situation (Eph. 6:21–

22). Because this native of Asia Minor (Acts 20:4) was sent to Colossae for the same purpose (Col. 4:7–8), it seems probable that he was also expected to forward Ephesians to readers living along the road beyond Colossae, particularly in Laodicea and other cities of Phrygia and Asia.

Thus Ephesus may have been the final destination of the letter, which is indirectly reflected in the majority of manuscripts (Eph. 1:1). Subsidiary evidence is offered by 2 Timothy, which contains the corresponding notice: "I have sent Tychicus to Ephesus" (2 Tim. 4:12). Provided that the names and dates in 2 Timothy are taken seriously, as suggested below, this declaration about Tychicus supports the assumption that Ephesians was carried by him along the Maeander valley to Ephesus.

By referring to 2 Timothy it is possible to explain why Timothy is not mentioned in Ephesians as coauthor, although Colossians in its own context ascribes this function to him (Col. 1:1). According to 2 Timothy, Paul at some earlier point had sent Timothy to work in Troas (2 Tim. 4:13), and it is quite possible that Ephesians was composed somewhat later than Colossians, when Timothy was no longer with Paul in Caesarea. In any case, Tychicus seems to have departed with both letters in his charge when Timothy was not present (Col. 4:7–8; Eph. 6:21–22).

The historical context in which Ephesians was produced can thus be at least preliminarily reconstructed: Paul wrote the letter in Caesarea shortly after the composition of Colossians, when Timothy was no longer present, and both messages were probably sent with Tychicus sometime during the year 59. Further details depicting the literary genre and historical setting of Ephesians support these suggestions.

Ephesians was not written for any particular congregation, and the author does not allude to any personal acquaintances, not even in Ephesus where the apostle had worked for a long time. This silence is due to the fact that Paul's hearers and readers are regarded as neophytes, as also in Colossians, whom the apostle had not personally met: "Now having heard of your belief in the Lord Jesus" (Eph. 1:15); "You must no longer live as the Gentiles with their vain mind" (4:17); "You have not learned about Christ in this way, insofar as you have heard of him and been taught in him" (4:20–21). References to baptism in Ephesians as well as Colossians are particularly appropriate for new Christians: "You have been sealed by the Spirit" (Eph. 1:13b); "Preserve the unity of the Spirit in the bond of love. There is one body and one Spirit...one Lord, one belief, one baptism" (4:3–5); "Put off...the old character...put on the new one" (4:22–24). It is evident that Ephesians was shaped rhetorically for neophytes as the apostle's address to a number of churches.

Because the author was not familiar with any special conditions in the communities of his intended audience, he gave the exposition a general Christian orientation. At the same time, he drew inspiration from his own situation in the place where he composed the oration, similar to what was observed above concerning the problems of Asia that are addressed in the letter to Titus. The author in Ephesians not only refers to his present captivity (3:1; 4:1), but also presents a picture of Christianity largely influenced by experiences in his current surroundings.

From this perspective, a passage in Ephesians dealing with the reconciliation of Jews and Gentiles in Christ helps place the composition of the homily in Caesarea: "You were at that time without Christ, excluded from the state of Israel and strangers in relation to the covenants of promise, having no hope and being without God in the world. But in Christ Jesus you, though once being far off, have now been drawn near in the blood of Christ. For he is our peace, he who has made both parts into one and dissolved the wall between them that produces exclusion, that is to say, hatred. In his flesh he has abolished the law of commandments according to its precepts, in order, by establishing peace, to create in him the two into one new organism. And (this he did) in order to reconcile both partners to God in one body through the cross, in his communion (with death) extinguishing the hatred" (Eph. 2:12–16).

The wall envisioned here to symbolize the separation and hostility between Jews and Gentiles must be understood in its historical context. This wall was not some spiritual obstacle between the soul and heaven. Rather, this barrier refers explicitly to an instrument for the separation of Jews and Gentiles here on earth, namely, the famous wall in the Herodian Temple of Jerusalem that divided the outer court of the Gentiles from the inner courts reserved solely for Jews. Josephus describes a wall between two main parts of Solomon's Temple using an expression similar to that found in Ephesians 2:14—*to mesotoichon* (Josephus, *Antiquities* 8, 71, *ho mesos toichos*). In his description of the Herodian Temple, Josephus speaks of a high wall separating the court of the Gentiles from the inner courts, and here again similar words are used (Eph. 2:14, *mesotoichon tou phragmou;* Josephus, *Jewish War* 5, 195–96, *teichos and peripephragmenon*). In front of the wall there was a fence on which Herod had placed tablets of stone threatening every heathen intruder with death (Josephus, *War* 5, 193–94, *Antiquities* 15, 417), of which Greek and Latin fragments have been found. In the days of Paul this wall between the outer court of the Temple and the inner parts, called the sanctuary, aptly symbolized the religious separation of Jews and Gentiles.

Important also is the fact that Paul himself had been confronted with this wall of partition in a most violent way. Jews from Roman Asia accused him in Jerusalem of previously bringing a Gentile into the inner courts of the sanctuary—in spite of the prohibition. Within the Temple precincts the volcanic reaction of the multitude to these charges was to lead ultimately to Paul's incarceration in Caesarea (Acts 21:27; 26:32). This disastrous experience offers an excellent explanation for the metaphor of the "wall" used in Ephesians to illustrate that Christ had extinguished this former separation between Jews and Gentiles. It is very likely that this metaphor should be ascribed to Paul and his personal recollections during the days of his ensuing imprisonment in Caesarea.

In addition, "hatred," mentioned twice in the text as epitomizing the attitude of Jews and Gentiles to each other (Eph. 2:14, 16), was particularly evident between Jews and Greeks in Caesarea when Paul was a prisoner there, A.D. 59–60.

From the days of Antiochus Epiphanes there had been religious and political tension between Jews and Greeks in the Holy Land as well as in various Hellenistic cities. Shortly before Paul was brought to Caesarea, the Jews of that city had begun to claim that they, and not the Greeks, were the rightful citizens, because it had been Herod who had founded the city. This assertion led to furious street battles during Paul's imprisonment, culminating in a process in Rome, along with the outbreak in Caesarea in A.D. 66 of the Jewish war against Rome as an outcome of this hatred (Josephus, *Antiquities* 20, 173–84).

In response to such outrages it was only natural for the author of Ephesians to encourage Gentile hearers or readers to understand that as Christians they are no longer "strangers" or "settlers" (Eph. 2:19a). Instead, they are called "fellow-citizens" together with "the holy ones" and inhabitants of God's house (2:19b). "Holy ones" was an honorary title often used by Paul to describe the Christians in Jerusalem (cf. 1 Cor. 16:1; 2 Cor. 8:4; 9:1, 12; Rom. 15:25, 31). The collection he arranged for them proves that he regarded the Jerusalem congregation as the earthly center of the church. Gentile believers receiving the message of Ephesians should thus realize that, although they do not belong to the state of Israel and do not stand under the covenants of the Jewish people (Eph. 2:12), they are no longer aliens but citizens of a holy commonwealth of which the Jewish believers in Jerusalem form the center (2:19). Accordingly, they can regard themselves as inhabitants of God's house, built on Christ as the cornerstone, who had established the apostles and prophets as the foundation (2:20). Historically, in Paul's eyes, these apostles and prophets were the first ministers of the church (1 Cor. 12:28; Eph. 4:11), a claim through which Paul again draws attention to Jerusalem. On the whole, the graphic illustrations of Christian citizenship point to the Jewish church in Jerusalem where the gospel had originated. During the bloody fights over citizenship between non-Christian Jews and Gentiles in Caesarea, the Gentile neophytes are portrayed by Paul as possessing a citizenship of higher value, indeed, one characterized by this communion with the holy ones in Jerusalem and God's house built with the cornerstone of Christ and the one foundation of apostles and prophets.

These sublime declarations of citizenship attest historically that Ephesians echoes the exigencies of the time of Paul's captivity in Caesarea (59–60). Through his imagery of the "wall and hatred" between Jews and Gentiles, the apostle was recalling a dramatic and recent experience of his own (Eph. 2:14). By underscoring "Christian" citizenship, he was in fact responding to the hotly debated and socially contested religio-political issue that, above all, had stamped the Caesarea of Paul's experience of imprisonment there (2:12, 19–22).

Consequently, it seems impossible not to regard Paul as the authority behind Ephesians and his captivity in Caesarea as the backdrop of the letter. Stylistic peculiarities may indicate the assistance of a collaborator; but there is no reference to any such person in the text, and it does not seem impossible that Paul was able to address neophytes in Asia Minor with the solemn rhetorical diction found in Ephesians. Chronologically, Ephesians may have been written somewhat later than Philemon and Colossians since Timothy is not mentioned. But A.D. 59 must still be the year of composition, because Tychicus was expected to take all three letters with him, delivering the letters to Philemon and to the Colossians in Colossae, before continuing on with Ephesians (cf. Col. 4:7—Tychicus with Philemon's servant Onesimus in 4:9, who was returned to Colossae—and Eph. 6:21, where Tychicus is still mentioned but not Onesimus).

The letter known as Ephesians is thus based on an image of the church influenced by two factors: (1) Paul's appreciation of the Jewish believers in Jerusalem as the root from which the Gentile believers received their holiness (cf. Rom. 11:16; 15:27); (2) his recent dramatic experiences of the hatred between Jews and Gentiles in Jerusalem and Caesarea. Paul, however, expands this perspective beyond Jerusalem and Caesarea by addressing new believers in churches of Asia Minor who should be aware that, in spite of the notorious tension between Jews and Greeks throughout the world, there is a fundamental unity of Jewish and Gentile believers in Christ.

For his audience of Phrygian and Asian neophytes, the apostle endeavors in the first two chapters of Ephesians to make this unity clear. He repeatedly uses "we" for himself and Jewish believers in general, and "you" for the Gentile neophytes:

> In order that we, who have earlier come to hope in Christ, should con-
> stitute a praise of his glory; in whom you also who have come to belief,
> after hearing the word of truth—the gospel of your salvation—have

been sealed by the promised Holy Spirit" (Eph. 1:12–13). "Although
you were dead because of your transgressions (2:1)...and we, too,
once lived in the lusts of our flesh (2:3a)...you are saved by grace"
(2:5c). "Therefore remember that you once, you Gentiles in the flesh
who are called uncircumcised..., that you at that time were separate
from Christ and excluded from the state of Israel" (2:11–12a). "But
in Christ Jesus you, who once were far off, have now come near in
the blood of Christ" (2:13). "You are no longer strangers and settlers, but you are fellow-citizens with the holy ones and inhabitants
of God's house built on the fundament of the apostles and prophets
where Christ is the cornerstone" (2:19–20).

All these changes between "we" and "you" illustrate the incorporation of
the Gentile neophytes into a commonwealth whose center was still being
conceived as the Jewish believers and apostles in Jerusalem.

Ephesians 3, containing a prayer, and chapters 4–6, filled with admonitions to the neophytes and their families, present no such we-forms. Instead,
from the very beginning of chapter 3, they are dominated by an interplay
of "I" and "you." "For this reason I, Paul, the prisoner of Christ Jesus for
your sake..." (3:1).

With respect to the exhortations of Ephesians 4–6, it should be observed
that Paul's first concern was the neophytes' unity in the Holy Spirit (4:3).
This unity is authentic because there is only one body, one Spirit, one hope
based on the same calling, one Lord, one belief, and one baptism (4:4). Here
the calling, the hope, and the belief of the neophytes are cited as prerequisites
for baptism, and the following exhortations deal generally with conduct
worthy of Christian baptism, as, for instance, the admonition to "take off
the old nature and put on the new" (4:22–24).

Similar to Colossians, several expressions in the Ephesian paraenesis are
reminiscent of dualistic terms found in Qumran texts. There is, for example,
a moral controversy between fraud and truth (4:14c-15a), and even an ex-
istential difference between darkness and light (5:8, 11, 13, 14)—concepts
well known from the Qumran movement (cf. remarks above on Colossians).
Such expressions could easily have been chosen in a Palestinian environment,
as is the case if Paul dictated Ephesians in Caesarea.

The purpose of Ephesians was to admonish Gentile neophytes in Asia
Minor. The "doctrinal" chapters 1–3 can be regarded as an introduction
to the paraenetic sequel; and the ethical admonitions in chapters 4–6, pre-
ceded by the prayer in chapter 3, form the substantial part of the apostle's
message. Like Colossians, the structure of Ephesians consists of two parts,
one dogmatic and one ethical.

| Introduction |  | 1:1–2 |
|---|---|---|
| (I) | Dogmatics | 1:3–3:21 |
|  | Christ the eternal initiator of election and salvation | 1:3–23 |
|  | Equality of Jewish and Gentile believers in Christ | 2:1–22 |
|  | Prayer, concerning the universality of the gospel | 3:1–21 |
| (II) | Ethics | 4:1–6:20 |
|  | Unity in the spirit | 4:1–16 |
|  | Laying off heathen vices | 4:17–5:20 |
|  | Duties of household members | 5:21–6:9 |
|  | Putting on the armor of God | 6:10–20 |
| (III) | Personal notice, wish of peace | 6:21–24 |

In spite of their heavy rhetorical style, the dogmatic chapters 1–3 provide fundamental instruction on the nature of the church; and from the ecumenical perspective that these chapters provide, the primary importance of Jewish Christians is highlighted for all non-Jewish Christians of any period. The ethical chapters 4–6 are especially apt to impress readers of this fascinating letter. The apostle's declarations on love within a Christian marriage (5:25–33) and his admonitions to put on the armor of God (6:10–18), for instance, are particularly compelling.

## 12. 2 Timothy (A.D. 60)

The onomasticon and reconstructible itinerary of 2 Timothy provide reasons to connect it geographically to Philemon, Colossians, and Ephesians. In particular, the names of Paul's colleagues in 2 Timothy are remarkably comparable to those of Philemon and Colossians (summarized above for Philemon) and are supported as well by a passage in Titus:

| 2 Timothy | Other letters |
|---|---|
| Timothy 1:2 (addressee, currently in Mysia) | Col. 1:1 (coauthor) |
| Demas 4:9 (currently in Thessalonica) | Philem. 24; Col. 4:14 (sends a greeting) |
| Crescens 4:10 (currently in Galatia) |  |
| Titus 4:10 (currently in Dalmatia) | Titus 3:12 (sent to the Nicopolis south of Dalmatia) |
| Luke 4:11 (still with Paul) | Philem. 24; Col. 4:14 (sends a greeting) |
| Mark 4:11 (sent to Timothy in Mysia) | Col. 4:10 (expected to pass through Colossae) |
| Tychicus 4:12 (sent to Ephesus) | Col. 4:7 (sent to Colossae); Eph. 6:21 (sent with the letter to the Ephesians) |

It is unreasonable to ascribe these intricate correspondences to deliberate redactional manipulation. Culling personal names from the other letters and presenting them in a new order with additional geographical information would have been senseless for a later author of 2 Timothy and his readers. Rather, the personal details in 2 Timothy are unmistakably based on the desire to provide updated information about the circumstances of each of the collaborators mentioned. Compared with the other letters and their nomenclature, 2 Timothy reflects a somewhat later stage of Paul's captivity.

Thus precisely through, rather than despite, these personal details, 2 Timothy reveals that it was intended for a wider audience. For example, Timothy hardly needed to be reminded of the faith that Paul had received from his ancestors and that Timothy himself had received from his mother and grandmother (2 Tim. 1:3, 5). But such personal allusions were valuable as homiletic appeals to the hearers and readers of the letter wherever it was to be recited. Such references as Paul's captivity for the benefit of the elect (2:9–10), the recalling of his trials in Antioch, Iconium, and Lystra (3:11), or the depiction of his abandonment in prison (4:10–11) were all obviously made to serve didactic rather than biographical purposes.

This desire then to instruct a wider circle of disciples is expressed programmatically by Paul in this exhortation (2 Tim. 2:2): "What you have learned from me, entrust to faithful people who will be able to instruct others as well." Indeed, the entire structure of the letter underscores this orientation to a wider audience. In the first and third sections, the text alternates between "you" and "I" (1:3 "you," 1:11 "I"; 2:1 "you," 2:8 "I"; 3:10 "you," 4:6 "I"), so that a reciprocal model for disciple and master becomes apparent. An earnest, if not ceremonious, paraenetic tone pervades these passages (e.g., 3:10–11: "But you have followed me in my teaching, conduct, program, belief, patience, love, steadfastness, persecution, suffering... "). The author of this epistle obviously did not write his intimate collaborator Timothy to inform him of basic biographical details or to impress him with his literary grandiloquence. Rather, he wanted to inform the leaders and members of the communities who would come in contact with the letter about Paul's conduct and posture and the tasks outlined for his collaborator. All of this exhortation is intended to fortify their faith and loyalty while at the same time offer practical guidelines for their life together.

The open homiletic character of 2 Timothy, then, in no way implies that the personal details are to be reduced to literary flourish or even to the imaginative collage of a later forger. Only if a historically impossible picture were to emerge would such judgment be warranted. Here, however, all the personal and geographical items form a strikingly coherent image that not only fits with other documents, but also mirrors well-known events in the life of Paul.

Even the itinerary or the travel route of the epistle can be traced through its distinctive messages that were to be delivered by the bearer of the letter at each point along the way. According to 2 Timothy, Mark was instructed to take the letter to Mysia and link up with Timothy (4:11b). From there both of them were to pass through Troas on their way back to Paul (4:13). Mark and three other companions of the apostle mentioned in 2 Timothy—Demas, Luke, and Tychicus (4:10–12)—are also referred to in the other captivity epistles (Philem. 24; Col. 4:7, 10, 14). As is evident from the chart above, these letters were written when these colleagues were all together with Paul, that is, in Caesarea (Philem. 9—"And now also a prisoner"). Moreover, the details surrounding these fellow workers in 2 Timothy imply that Timothy had been a member of the same circle in Caesarea (Col. 1:1) and would now be brought up to date about his colleagues' current activities. But such news would also have been of interest to Christians along the letter's path who had the opportunity of hearing or reading the message.

Consequently, the provenance of 2 Timothy must be Caesarea, and Mark was to bring the letter by way of the Cilician gates through Asia Minor to Timothy in Mysia. In every respect, the remaining allusions to cities and districts laced throughout 2 Timothy attest this itinerary. Chronologically, the letter's origin must therefore be placed during the two-year captivity of Paul in Caesarea, but somewhat later than Philemon, Colossians, and Ephesians, that is, A.D. 60.

The short notice concerning Onesiphorus, who lived in Ephesus (1:16, 4:19), and his presence in Rome (1:16–18a) should not be misunderstood. It does not imply that Paul wrote 2 Timothy while a prisoner in Rome. Concerning Onesiphorus, this passage states the following (1:16–18a): "He was not ashamed of my chains, but (a) though being in Rome, (b) he searched eagerly for me, and (c) found me. (d) May the Lord let him find mercy in the presence of the Lord on that Day."

As the order of the events described proves, Onesiphorus did not (a) sail from Ephesus to Rome to visit Paul in jail, but simply happened to be in Rome at the time (*genomenos en,* like *genesthaiekei* in Acts 19:21). He then became anxious concerning Paul's whereabouts when he did not find him in Rome as expected (see below). It is for this reason that his earnest searching (b) and his visit to the prisoner (c) are presented (d) as marvelous deeds to be rewarded specially by the Lord at the day of judgment.

Had Paul been imprisoned in Rome, no rigorous search would have been necessary, because any Christian could have shown Onesiphorus the way to the prisoner. A visit with the apostle would then have been a matter of

course, hardly an extraordinary act of love. With Caesarea as the place of
custody, however, this extant geographical detail in 2 Timothy provides a
far less trivial perspective: Not knowing of Paul's confinement, Onesiphorus
had expected to meet up with him when he himself was in Rome, because
Paul, when he was earlier in Ephesus (the home of Onesiphorus) had spoken
of his intention to visit Rome (Acts 19:21, cf. Rom. 15:22–24). Not finding
Paul in Rome, Onesiphorus began a fervent search for him and eventually
found him in Caesarea. In this light, his act of compassion appears worthy
of Paul's effusive praise.

To be sure, this explanation requires that Onesiphorus traveled exceptionally far to visit Paul, but such an undertaking would not have been
unthinkable for him. He had certainly already demonstrated his zeal through
his particularly effective support of the communities in Ephesus (2 Tim.
1:18b); and like the home of Aquila and Priscilla (1 Cor. 16:19), the house
of Onesiphorus constituted a center for the Christians of Ephesus (2 Tim.
4:19). For this reason and because he is mentioned immediately after Aquila
(ibid.), Onesiphorus too may well have been an entrepreneur in Ephesus. Because Aquila and Priscilla were able to pursue business alternately in Rome,
Corinth, and Ephesus (Acts 18:2, 18–19, 26; 1 Cor. 16:19; Rom. 16:3;
2 Tim. 4:19), similar business travels are not inconceivable for Onesiphorus.

To summarize, Onesiphorus did not journey to Rome to visit Paul. The
apostle had mentioned his plans to visit Rome during his last stay in Ephesus
during the winter of 56/57 (Acts 19:21). Therefore, when Onesiphorus, in
Rome for other business, did not meet up with Paul as expected, he eagerly
sought him out, eventually finding him as a prisoner in Caesarea. It is only
from such a scenario that Paul's intense praise of Onesiphorus in 2 Timothy
becomes explicable.

When the travel route of the letter is studied in this light, additional evidence is illumined. The letter's path can be reconstructed on the basis of
its rhetorically targeted messages, reinforced by the fact that Mark was to
present these messages orally in each of the towns of his itinerary through
Asia Minor in tandem with his reading of the letter to gathered believers
(2 Tim. 4:11: "receive Mark" [that is, when he comes to Mysia where Timothy was located]). Paul had already urged that his messages be spread in
the congregations of Colossae and Laodicea in a similar fashion (Col. 4:16).
This policy of writing letters as circulars lends practical significance to seemingly unnecessary comments in 2 Timothy. Even the praise of Onesiphorus,
discussed above, was evidently included for such purpose.

The reference to Paul's religious heritage (2 Tim. 1:3) makes sense immediately if it is kept in mind that from Caesarea Mark was to go to Tarsus
first. Here in Paul's hometown, the open letter to Timothy would bolster the

faith of the Christians. Moreover, recalling the traditions of his own family would have been useful in view of the judaizing current in Asia Minor represented by Hymenaeus and Alexander (1 Tim. 1:20; 2 Tim. 2:17; 4:14). The same holds for the rather solemn and sermonic appeal to the faith of Lois and Eunice, the grandmother and mother of Timothy. Because these Jewish women lived in Derbe, Timothy's home (Acts 16:1), the reference to their genuine Christian faith was meant to make an impact on the believers there. After the visit to Derbe, Mark was to press on to the Christians in Lystra, Iconium, and the Pisidian Antioch, where he was to encourage the hearts of these believers as Paul harks back to his endurance of persecution in these towns during his first missionary journey (2 Tim. 3:11). From the epistle to the Colossians, written in Caesarea a few months earlier, it is clear that Paul had planned on Mark making a subsequent visit to Colossae: "When he comes to you, receive him with hospitality" (Col. 4:10). In this context, Mark is described as the cousin of Barnabas (ibid.), a person well known in Colossae from the days when Barnabas had conducted the evangelization in Pisidian Antioch (Acts 13:14) and the surrounding areas (13:49). The mystery of elective grace, prevenient and now revealed, as well as the suffering of Paul for the sake of the elect are themes characteristic of Colossians and, interestingly enough, they are also found in 2 Timothy (Col. 1:26–27; 2 Tim. 1:9–10; 2:10). Second Timothy intimates Ephesus as the next stop for Mark, where the family of Onesiphorus should learn of the apostle's gratitude for his loyalty, and where the community would be made aware of Paul's concerns about false teaching and especially for those who had fallen away (1:15; 2:16–18; 4:14). Mark finally was supposed to reach Timothy in Mysia and return with him to Paul after picking up the apostle's coat and some of his books in Troas (4:11, 13, 21a). Because the apostle had actually visited Troas in the spring of 58 (Acts 20:6), his request to fetch these objects appears reasonable. If written many years later, such obscure details in 2 Timothy could only appear trite and nonsensical.

Paul further mentions that he had sent Tychicus to Ephesus (2 Tim. 4:12). As the other captivity epistles imply, Tychicus had first presented Colossians and Philemon to the Colossian congregation (Col. 4:7–9) before going on through various communities to Ephesus with the Ephesian circular (Eph. 1:1; 6:21). It was here in Ephesus that Timothy was to make contact with Tychicus. At the same time, Paul warns Timothy about the coppersmith in Ephesus by the name of Alexander (2 Tim. 4:14), who seems to be identical with the Jewish silversmith mentioned by Luke at the uproar in Ephesus (Acts 19:33) and with one of the judaizing apostates there (1 Tim. 1:20). On the other hand, Paul sends greetings to good friends in Ephesus, namely Priscilla, Aquila, and the family of Onesiphorus, whereas Erastus

(Acts 19:22) is noted as remaining in Corinth (2 Tim. 4:19–20a). After their stay in Ephesus, Timothy and Mark were supposed to visit Trophimus in Miletus, where he had been left behind because of illness (4:20b). From here they should proceed by ship, for it was evidently with an eye to sea connections that Paul urged Timothy to come with Mark before winter (4:21a). Paul needed Timothy's as well as Mark's help because, of all the friends belonging to the apostle's group, only Luke was now at his side (4:11). According to Philemon and Colossians, several Jewish and Greek Christians had been with the apostle at Caesarea in A.D. 59: Timothy, Tychicus, Epaphras, Aristarchus, Jesus Justus, Mark, Luke, and Demas (Philem. 23–24; Col. 1:1; 4:7, 10, 14). Two of these men, Aristarchus and Epaphras, were fellow prisoners and would not have been able to be of much service (Philem. 4; Col. 4:10; Acts 27:2). The Jewish friend Jesus Justus (Col. 4:11) probably did not belong to the inner circle of associates; in any case, he is not mentioned again. Concerning Timothy, Tychicus, Mark, Demas, and the otherwise unknown Crescens, it is implicitly and explicitly clear from 2 Timothy that they had departed for various countries a few months earlier (2 Tim. 4:10–12). Remarkably, these personal details coincide exactly with the descriptions of Paul's collaborators in Philemon and Colossians, with the exception of Jesus Justus who is not mentioned in 2 Timothy.

Is it conceivable therefore that the list of names in 2 Timothy is the result of literary imitation based on earlier captivity epistles? The predominating interests of the apostolic and postapostolic generation speak against this supposition. For them a rapid spreading of the word and stabilization of the church were of the utmost importance and not biographical artifacts. Certainly, legends gradually arose around the apostles and their disciples, but these attached themselves to miraculous episodes. None of this appears in the sober descriptions of 2 Timothy. What is more, in the first and second centuries, when the church was fervently engaged in missionary activity, what would motivate anyone to such great lengths to take names from Colossians and even from the brief letter to Philemon and use them in a totally different sequence and context to give an impression of historical reality? That any postapostolic writer would have done this in order to satisfy historical interests for contemporary readers—without resorting to miracles—seems itself completely miraculous.

On the contrary, the personal statements in Philemon, Colossians, and 2 Timothy develop quite spontaneously into a completely integrated picture of the interruption and delay in Paul's career, A.D. 59–60, when Luke alone was left at his side (2 Tim. 4:11a). It is not conceivable that any member of the ancient church or any representative of the so-called early Catholicism would have adopted historico-critical points of view and endeavored to extract such a coherent portrait from the onomasticon of Philemon and Colossians. Even less imaginable would be a redactional construction of the itinerary by a pseudonymous author. Many passages of 2 Timothy point tacitly or expressly to communities and individuals whom Mark was to encounter along the way. In addition, Timothy's and Mark's return journey is traceable in several instances.

A subsequent reworking and interpolation from such partially concealed elements presupposes a refinement for which there is no precedent and which would not have had the slightest meaning for believers or nonbelievers in the subapostolic period. By holding the itinerary to be original, however, a reasonable picture emerges in agreement with facts known from other sources, implying that 2 Timothy was dictated in Caesarea some months after Philemon, Colossians, and Ephesians; that is, at some point in the year 60.

### 13. Philippians (A.D. 61/62): Paul's Relations with Philippi and His Exhortations to Peace*

The Acts of the Apostles, 1 Thessalonians, and 2 Corinthians, as well as Paul's letter to the Philippians, all shed light on Paul's relationship with the congregation in Philippi. The internal affairs of the Philippian congregation are of course most fully evidenced in Paul's correspondence to them, and it is in the context of his description of their mutual relationship that his exhortation for peace (Phil. 4:7) takes on special significance.

*Paul's Activity in Philippi*

It can be gathered from the sources mentioned above that Paul visited Philippi on three occasions. In his letter to the congregation he expresses his hope for a visit, and opinion is divided whether this wish coincides with one of the three known visits. It will be postulated below that this passage refers to a fourth visit of Philippi, the fulfillment of which cannot be proved.

1. *The First Visit.* During his second missionary journey, Paul made his initial visit to Philippi and founded a Christian congregation there (Acts 16:12-40). Assuming the widely accepted date of A.D. 49 for the apostolic council, which is mentioned just prior to this passage (Acts 15:1-29), and reckoning that the year and a half that Paul spent in Corinth after his time in Philippi (Acts 18:10) occurred between the fall of 51 and the spring of

---

*Lecture at a conference of the Pauline Society for Historical Studies in Kavala, Greece (*Pauleios Etaireia istorikon Meleton*), June 25-29, 1986. The topic of the conference was "Peace." The German text of the lecture was translated by Rebecca Reese, Basel, and was revised by the editors.

53—as supported by the Gallio inscription—the first visit to Macedonia and Philippi may be dated to the first part of A.D. 51.

According to the vivid account in Acts, Paul had come to Troas with Timothy and Silas. While they were there, Paul saw in a vision a Macedonian man who said: "Come over to Macedonia and help us" (Acts 16:8–9). Immediately following this plea, the passage begins a first-person-plural narration, the first of the book's "we-passages" (Acts: 16:10–17; 20:5–15; 21:l–19; 27:1–28:16). The writer's introductory remark reads as follows: "Immediately we sought to go on into Macedonia, concluding that God had called us to preach the gospel to them" (Acts 16:10b). By using the we-form, the author apparently wanted to show that he also experienced the events in Macedonia and was explicitly included in the work of spreading the gospel. Moreover, it is striking that the very next we-passage is Paul's and his companions' final departure from Philippi, and that both occurrences, though separated by considerable distance in time and events, are recorded with such meticulous detail (Acts 16:10–17; Acts 20:5–6 ["God had called us to preach the gospel...." "But we set sail after the days of unleavened bread," 16:10 and 20:6]). The precise descriptions in these two passages as well as their association with Philippi imply that the author was active in Macedonia, at least in part, during the time that Paul worked in Athens, Corinth, and Ephesus. Thus this coincidence between the first and second we-passages might well be because of the author's special association with Philippi and the Pauline Macedonian mission.

Although the question of the authorship of Acts lies outside the primary scope of this article, the following points deserve mention: (a) The obvious stylistic similarities between the we-passages and the text of Acts as a whole imply a common origin. (b) The author responsible for the text was apparently someone who accompanied Paul on his journeys. That the author did not deal with Paul's teaching on justification by faith in as much detail as some theologians would wish was due to his preoccupation with the description of the mission itself, instead of Paul's theology. (c) According to tradition, this companion of Paul is the Luke mentioned in the captivity epistles (Philem. 24; Col. 4:14; 2 Tim. 4:11). This attribution is not arbitrary; since the second century the Gospel of Luke has been associated with this nonapostle (*euaggelion kata Loukan* in papyrus Bodmer (papyrus $p^{75}$, written before A.D. 200). A better solution to the question of authorship has not come to light.[1] Paul's companion, Luke, can in fact be regarded as the author of the third Gospel and the Book of Acts. The "we" suggests that Luke was active as a preacher in Philippi and Macedonia, although he wanted to remain anonymous in the company of Paul, Timothy, and Silas.

After the reference to Paul's dream, Luke relates in his first we-report that Paul and his colleagues traveled as quickly as possible from Troas to Samothrace and, on the following day, to Neapolis, the seaport of Philippi, now known as Kavala (Acts 16:11). From there they travelled the ten miles to Philippi by way of the *Via Egnatia,* the Roman road connecting Byzantium with Epirus. Philippi, described by the author as "a leading city of the district of Macedonia and a Roman colony," was in fact, like the Roman colony Corinth in Greece, an important city. The capital city of Roman Macedonia was Thessalonica, however, and the main city of the Eastern district was Amphipolis. As a result, exegetes often claim that this ascription is simply incorrect. But this conclusion appears quite unfounded if one were to understand Luke's own missionary activity as concentrated in the environs of Philippi. It would only be natural for him to regard the city named after Philip II as a leading city in eastern Macedonia.

Originally, Philippi was a Greek and Thracian settlement known as Krenides (Strabo 7, 331 fr.41). Because of the gold mines in the vicinity, Philip II, the father of Alexander the Great, expanded and renamed the settlement. In the first century B.C. the city became less important as the mining activity decreased. After the famous battle on the plains around Philippi in 42 B.C., Antony, victor over Caesar's murderers Brutus and Cassius, developed the city and surrounding areas as a Roman colony for his retired soldiers. Each former soldier received a house with land as well as slaves to work the property. When Octavian defeated Antony near Actium in 41 B.C., he confiscated the Italian property of other of Antony's soldiers and moved them to Philippi, thus further augmenting the colony (Cassius Dio 51,4,6).

At this time the colony was allowed to call itself *Colonia Julia* after Julius Caesar. In 27 B.C., Philippi received the further distinction of being named *Colonia Augusta Julia,* after Octavian had taken the honorific title "Augustus." Inscriptions on coins discovered in Philippi reflect the increasing honor accorded the colony: after 42 B.C.—*Colonia Victrix Philippensium;* after 31 B.C.—*Colonia Julia Philippensium;* after 27 B.C.—*Colonia Augusta Julia Philippensium.*

As was common in the Roman empire, veterans in such colonies received Italian and occasionally even Roman citizenship; the former was the case for the residents of Philippi. Luke relates in his first mention of the city that Paul's opponents emphasized their status as Roman citizens to the officials in Philippi (Acts 16:21, "not lawful for us Romans ... "). Discovering their prisoner's Roman citizenship was a nasty surprise for the officials who had arrested and mistreated Paul (Acts 16:37–39). The strong civic awareness in Philippi is also the reason that Paul exhorted the Christians there to an appropriate conduct in society (Phil. 1:27, *politeuesthe*) and stressed the priority of their citizenship in a heavenly commonwealth (4:20, *politeuma*).

Analogous to Rome, such colonies were governed by senators and magistrates headed by the so-called *duumviri* (two-men), counterparts to the two consuls who served as supreme judges in the colonies. At their disposal were the court servants, two *lictors* with bundles of rods *(fasces)*. According to Luke, the magistrates, *duumviri* and *lictors,* were all involved in Paul's arrest (Acts 16:19, 20, 35: *archontes, strategoi, rabdouchoi*).

Both French and Greek excavations have shed light on the archaeology and topography of the area.[2] The actual city of Philippi was rectangular in shape like a Roman army camp, oriented lengthwise roughly east-west with the east and west gates connected by the *Via Egnatia*. South of the middle section of the main street was the forum, measuring 100 x 50 meters with a podium, or *bema,* adjacent to the street. The sections north of the *Via Egnatia* were on an incline, stretched out over a part of Mount Orbelos, and included the theater. About a kilometer west of Philippi was a stately arch marking the entrance to the area controlled by the city. It is uncertain whether the Jews' place of prayer "outside the gate" (Acts 16:13) was on the plain outside this arch (Collart) or just outside the west gate of the city (Lemerle). At any rate, Paul apparently did not encounter any synagogue inside the city; presumably Roman civic pride (Acts 16:21) prevented the Jews from building a place of worship within the walls.

Paul and his colleagues visited this place of prayer on the next Sabbath and spoke there with some women, among them Lydia of Thyatira, who converted immediately and was baptized with her household (Acts 16:13–15). Lydia, with whom Paul and his group subsequently stayed, was a seller of purple goods, a manager of a textile industry. This textile business is tantamount to the "tentmaking" trade of a Priscilla and Aquila who in Corinth at some later point would employ Paul, also a tentmaker (Acts 18:3). It is certainly understandable that persons of the same trade would be more receptive to offering visitors hospitality as Lydia did for Paul.

The subsequent arrest of Paul and Silas (Acts 16:16–40) was due to the greedy owners of a fortune-telling slave girl who declared that Paul and his companions were "servants of the most-high God." Paul's exorcism of the girl (vv. 16–18) brought an end to her power and to her owners' lucrative source of income, provoking the latter to haul Paul and Silas to the *duumviri* at the forum and accuse them of advocating Jewish customs unfitting for Romans (vv. 19–21). The colonists' Italian citizenship was brought into play, and the plaintiff counted on the skeptical reaction of the government official toward foreign, unaccepted forms of worship in the Roman empire.

Although the Jews had enjoyed religious freedom for the most part since the time of Julius Caesar, Claudius banished the Jews from Rome in A.D. 49 (Acts 18:2). It was only in A.D. 52 that the emperor once again ruled in favor of the Jews in a Jewish-Greek conflict.[3] This turn of events gave Jews in various places such as Thessalonica (Acts 17:5), Corinth (Acts 18:2), and Judaea (1 Thess. 2:14) a renewed sense of self-confidence.

Paul's first visit to Philippi, however, was in A.D. 51, prior to this turn of favor, so that the city official knew only of Claudius' edict of 49. That current state of hostility explains why the Gentile plaintiff stressed above all that Paul and Silas were Jews whose teachings were unworthy of Romans and why the crowd in the forum concurred with these complaints (v. 22a). Under these circumstances the *duumviri* felt justified in flogging Paul and Silas publicly and throwing them into prison (vv. 22b–24). Independent of the subsequent report of a miraculous deliverance from prison by an earthquake and the immediate conversion of the prison guard (16:25–34), Luke relates that Paul and Silas were set free the next day by order of the *duumviri* (16:35–39). After returning to Lydia's house and bidding farewell to the brethren in Philippi, they traveled southwest along the *Via Egnatia* to other Macedonian cities, namely, Amphipolis, Apollonia, Thessalonica, and Beroea (Acts 16:40; 17:1, 10). Paul then continued on to Athens and Corinth, while Silas stayed and worked in Beroea with Timothy, who had accompanied them from Philippi (Acts 17:14).

Paul later recalled the distressing assault in Philippi (1 Thess. 2:2) and thanked the congregation there for the helpful financial support during his time in Thessalonica and afterward (Phil. 4:15–16). To all appearances, Lydia was behind this support, as was Luke, who in his we-report provides witness to his personal engagement in Philippi (above). Later Paul would receive pecuniary support from Macedonia, as Luke subtly hints in his description of the founding of the Corinthian church. According to Luke, after Silas and Timothy had arrived from Macedonia, Paul was able to devote himself solely to preaching without having to work as a tentmaker (Acts 18:5). Paul explicitly confirms this in his second letter to the Corinthians, which he wrote while in Macedonia (2 Cor. 11:9).

2. *The Second Visit.* Paul's second visit to Philippi was connected with his third missionary journey and may be dated to the year A.D. 57 (Acts 19:21; 20:1; 2 Cor. 2:13; 7:5; 8:1; 9:2). Although the relevant texts mention only Macedonia in general and not specifically Philippi, Paul certainly visited the generous congregation, especially because he spent an extended period of time in Macedonia collecting money for the congregation in Jerusalem (2 Cor. 8:1; 9:2; Rom. 15:26).

3. *The Third Visit.* In the year A.D. 58 the apostle again visited Philippi, returning from Corinth after completing the collection for Jerusalem. Accompanied by numerous Hellenists, he proceeded on to Troas (Acts 20:3–6). This second we-report in Acts describes Paul and his companions going

on ahead to Troas while the group connected with the "we" remained in Philippi over Easter and rejoined Paul five days later (20:5–6). This extended visit in Philippi for that holiday shows that the person behind the we-report had strong connections to the congregation and supports the theory of Luke's continual activity in Philippi.

4. *A Possible Fourth Visit.* In his letter to the Philippians, the apostle expresses his hope that he will be released from prison so that he may again visit the congregation (Phil. 1:26–27; 2:24). Whether this desire translates into a fourth visit or was actually fulfilled in the second visit (Acts 20:2) depends, of course, on where the imprisonment took place. Assuming that the plans for a fourth visit were made during Paul's imprisonment in Rome, as will be argued below, the fulfillment of this wish remains doubtful, because the apostle also desired to, and probably did, in fact, visit Spain (Rom. 15:24, 28; 1 Clem. 5:6–7). Between Paul's likely release in A.D. 62 and his martyrdom, which can be confirmed to late 64 or early 65, the time appears too short for both the historically tenable journey to Spain and the realization of his hope to visit Philippi.

## Background and Content of Philippians

Where and when the letter to the Philippians was written depend on whether the imprisonment mentioned in this letter took place in Ephesus, Caesarea, or Rome; the provenance will also affect one's judgment of the letter's content and composition.

a.) In the first chapter of Philippians the apostle speaks of his "chains" (Phil. 1:7, 13, 14, 17), but he does not refer to himself as a "prisoner" (*desmios*) as he does in Philemon and in the related captivity epistles (Philem. 9; Eph. 3:1; 4:1; 2 Tim. 1:8). None of these letters, however, contain any mention of a "prison" (*phulake*), as does Luke's report of the arrest of Paul and Silas in Philippi (Acts 16:23). Paul himself writes that he was on numerous occasions "confined" or "imprisoned" (*en phulakais*) (2 Cor. 6:5; 11:23). But within Paul's argument of listing the many types or quality of persecutions he has endured, the confinements in these two passages refer only to short-term stays in prison like the one in Philippi. An extended imprisonment did not occur until after his arrest in Jerusalem (Acts 21:33–26:32) when he was incarcerated in Caesarea from A.D. 58–60 and then in Rome from 61–62 (Acts 27:1–28:31). Although many commentators assume that the apostle was imprisoned in Ephesus after the silversmiths' riot, there is not the slightest hint of confinement in Luke's description of the episode or in any of the captivity epistles.[4]

This elimination of Ephesus leaves Rome or Caesarea as possible locations of the imprisonment described in Philippians as "chains." Here Paul views his situation more optimistically than in the other captivity epistles. Not only does Paul *not* describe himself as a prisoner; there is also no mention of any fellow prisoners (in contrast to Philem. 22 and Col. 4:10). Rather, the apostle appears able both to receive and to send out his co-workers (Phil. 2:19, 25, 28; 4:18). There was also reason for joy (1:4, 18, 25; 2:2, 17, 18, 28, 29; 3:1; 4:1, 4, 10), because his preaching of the gospel in his current surroundings was finding great success (1:7, 12–14, 18–20; 3:13–14). Moreover, Paul's offer to visit Philippi again (1:26, 27; 2:24) makes clear that he expected to be released soon.

The circumstances detailed in the other captivity epistles are markedly different (see also each letter above). The phrase in the letter to Philemon "now also a prisoner for Christ Jesus" (Philem. 9) indicates that Paul's imprisonment had only recently begun, a development compatible only with his imprisonment in the governor's palace in Caesarea, which began in A.D. 58 (Acts 23:35). Names and details of Paul's colleagues connect Philemon with Colossians, Ephesians, and Second Timothy, and demonstrate that Paul's situation is the same in all four letters. The setting is similar, independent of each letter's authorship, which is subject to dispute in all but the letter to Philemon. The point here is simply that Paul's circumstances are strikingly similar in all four of these letters. Philemon 9 and the analogous details concerning Paul's colleagues connect all four letters to the year 58, the beginning of the imprisonment in Caesarea, which Paul described as a *recent* change in his life (see the arguments above for each letter that Colossians, Ephesians, and 2 Timothy are not later forgeries).

In contrast, in Philippians the apostle is not sitting in prison, and although he wears "chains," these do not hinder his activity. In fact, Paul does not present his "chains" as a new affliction but rather rejoices over the progress of the gospel and reckons with the possibility of a speedy release. These circumstances are compatible only with his situation in Rome during the years A.D. 61–62 when, according to Luke, Paul lived in a rented room guarded by only one soldier, where he was able to preach the gospel unhindered (Acts 28:16–31).

Two special references in Philippians confirm the letter's Roman backdrop:

1. When Paul writes contentedly of the gospel's progress, he emphasizes: "it has become known throughout the whole praetorian guard and to all the rest that my imprisonment is for Christ" (i.e., not because of a crime, Phil. 1:12–13). The addition of "all the rest" to "praetorian guard" reveals that the word *praitorion* refers here to a human collective and not to a ruler's residence (as in Acts 23:35). Epigraphic and literary evidence confirm that "praetorium" when referring to humans was used to denote the imperial

bodyguard who served only in Rome.[5] A corner angle in the northeast section of the old city wall in Rome divulges the site of the barracks of the
praetorian guard; it was in these barracks that the soldier who guarded
Paul was lodged (Acts 28:16, written in we-form). The praetorian guard in
Rome was entrusted with such police duties, and one of the two prefects
was specifically responsible for the prisoners on trial.[6] Because the duty of
guarding Paul was filled in shifts by a number of soldiers who would no
doubt inform their unusually shrewd prefect, Burrus, about the prisoner,
Paul's confident assertion that he was known to the whole praetorian guard
and to everyone else is perfectly plausible.

2. Among the people sending greetings to the Christians in Philippi
through Paul's letter were "especially those of Caesar's household" (Phil.
4:22). Although members of the royal household could certainly be found
in other cities, they were lodged mainly in Rome. Analogous to these
Christian believers, there also existed in Rome a Jewish synagogue of the
"Augustenses."[7] If these "royal" believers were not in Rome, then the point
of the greeting is destroyed. It was an extraordinary triumph for Paul that
he could tell the Christians in the Roman colony Philippi of his success at
the imperial court.

b.) The primary focus of the letter is to thank the Philippian congregation
for the support that Paul had received through Epaphroditus (Phil. 2:25–30;
4:10–20).[8] Epaphroditus had become seriously ill on his way to reach Paul,
and the Philippian congregation had received word of his predicament (Phil.
2:26–27). Once he had recovered, Paul was able to send Epaphroditus back
home (Phil. 2:25, 28).

Rome is often precluded as the letter's place of origin because of its great
distance from Philippi and the lack of sufficient time for the several journeys
between Philippi and Paul's imprisonment that are assumed necessary from
details within the letter. This distance does not prove to be a real problem,
however, because only the time of Epaphroditus' single journey was needed;
namely, the interval between his departure from Philippi and his encounter
with Paul that led to the writing of the letter. If Epaphroditus traveled from
Philippi to Rome, he could have taken advantage of the *Via Egnatia* in
Macedonia and the *Via Appia* in Italy and would have needed only about
six weeks for the journey. Granted, it must have taken somewhat longer,
for he was taken ill along the way. On the other hand, it did not add to his
travel time to send either a letter or message back to his friends in Philippi
to inform them of his illness, which, according to Paul, caused them great
distress (2:26). Epaphroditus' return journey also need not be taken into
account, because he carried the letter with him.

In any case, Paul joyfully expressed his gratitude for the gift that Epaphroditus delivered to him in the name of the Philippian congregation (4:10, 18). As in his first letter to the Thessalonians, Paul also used the opportunity to tell of his experiences and to exhort the congregation, two themes that alternate in both letters.[9] Along with Paul's expression of gratitude, the letter to the Philippians also contains admonition to the congregation and information about Paul's situation. These two themes, information and parenesis, alternate in rhythmic succession:

1. Information (Phil. 1:1–26)
2. Parenesis (1:27–2:16)
3. Information (2:17–30)
4. Parenesis (3:1–4:9)
5. Information (4:10–23)

The letter as a whole is a logical unity. The two pareneses do not interrupt the flow of information but rather complement those sections, and each parenesis is introduced by an admonition that closes the preceding section of information: Philippians 1:26–27: (Inform.) "that ... you may have ample cause to glory in Christ Jesus." (Parenes.) "let your manner of life be worthy." Philippians 2:29–3:2: (Inform.) "Honor such folk." (Parenes.) "Finally, my brethren, rejoice in the Lord ... look out for the dogs."

The compositional structure of the whole displays a logical coherence despite the succession of themes. In view of this unity, modern attempts to make the letter into a composite of several discrete letters of Paul, later pasted together into canonical Philippians, are unfounded. In fact, some of the many, at times rather spectacular, schemes turn out to contradict each other, the result of disparate lines of research. They all tend to inhere with the fatal flaw of failing to explain the rationale or motivation that would ever bring such text fragments together to form the familiar letter to the Philippians. The alternating framework of personal and parenetic sections— a pattern also found in the first letter to the Thessalonians—constitutes instead the very integrity of the letter.

*Purpose and Function of the Exhortation to Peace in Philippians*

The two parenetic sections in Philippians (1:27–2:16; 3:1–4:9) express the apostle's concern for unity in the Christian congregation and thus are theological complements of Paul's personal messages. The following admonitions are particularly notable: "Complete my joy by being of the same mind, having the same love, being in full accord and of one mind" (2:2); "Let those of us who are mature be thus minded" (3:15); "I entreat Euodia and I entreat Syntyche to agree in the Lord" (4:2). In these admonitions the Greek word *phronein,* translated as "to set one's mind" or "to be of one mind" as in the RSV, does not imply an orthodox or dogmatic way of thinking, but rather one of intense interest and engagement. Paul used the verb *phronein* numerous times in this manner: "with minds set on earthly things" (Phil. 3:19); "set their minds on the things of the flesh...set their minds on the things of the Spirit" (Rom. 8:5); *phronein* is used three times in this sense in Rom. 12:16–17; "set your minds on things that are above, not on things that are on earth" (Col. 3:2). With the use of the word *phronein* in Philippians, Paul intended to encourage the readers toward an engaged unity in matters pertaining to God in Christ.

Paul's well-known exhortation to peace (4:7) is the focus of the last part of the letter: "and the peace of God, which passes all understanding, will keep your hearts and your minds in Christ Jesus."

Two remarks concerning the Greek text are necessary: (1) *kai,* which follows the imperative in "have no anxiety about anything" (4:6), indicates consequence and should be translated as "will then." Many parallels to this sense exist in the New Testament: Matthew 7:7; Luke 10:28; Romans 13:3; etc. (2) In verse 7 the main verb (*phrouresei*) appears in the future indicative and not in the present subjunctive, as it is sometimes translated when used liturgically. Paul does not express a wish or convey a blessing here; he instead offers assurance based on the exhortation to prayer that immediately precedes the sentence: "Let all your requests be made known to God. *Then* the peace of God *will* guard..." (4:6–7).

What, however, does Paul actually mean by the word "peace" in Philippians 4:7? Because the apostle speaks here of "the peace of God," he apparently means a state of peace established by God. A similar wish for and blessing of peace appears at the beginning of this letter (Phil. 1:2) and in all other letters of Paul: "Grace to you and peace from God our Father and the Lord Jesus Christ."[10] The form of Paul's greeting or blessing of peace has its roots in the *chairein* of Greek letter style (Acts 15:23) as well as in the *shelam* from Aramaic letters (Ezra 4:17), although Paul transforms both expressions by giving to them a more sublime meaning. He wished the recipients of this letter a "grace" and "peace" that come only from God and his Son. Jesus also spoke of this "higher" peace at the Last Supper with his disciples: "Peace I leave with you, my peace I give to you—not as the world gives do I give to you" (John 14:27).

Paul, however, desired and expected a practical realization of God's peace among human beings. This reality can be seen from Philippians 4:9, where the apostle urges his readers to follow his example: "what you have learned and received and heard and seen in me, do...*then* (*kai...estai*) the God of peace *will* be with you." In a similar way, Paul states in numerous places that the *God of peace* is the source of peace within the church (1 Thess. 5:23; 1 Cor. 14:33; 2 Cor. 13:11; Rom. 15:33; 16:20).

The reference to "the peace of God" in Philippians 4:7 is connected to a series of exhortations to unity in the church. In a more concise form, Paul closes his second letter to the Corinthians with a similar admonition (2 Cor. 13:11): "Mend your ways, heed my appeal, agree with one another, live in peace, and the God of love and peace will be with you." In Philippians the corresponding call for unity appears first in 1:27: "stand firm in one Spirit, with one mind striving side by side for the faith of the gospel." Then with impassioned words, the apostle at the beginning of chapter 2 makes a plea for solidarity among members of the congregation, writing among other things (2:2): "complete my joy by being of the same mind, having the same love, being in full accord and one mind." The hymn to Christ with the motif of *kenosis* as its center (2:5–11) is intended to undergird this exhortation to unity, love, and humility (2:5): "Have this mind among yourselves, which is yours in Christ Jesus, who...." And following the hymn: "Do all things without grumbling or questioning" (2:14). In the last chapter of Philippians the apostle applies this admonition to unity specifically to two women in the congregation (4:2): "I entreat Euodia and I entreat Syntyche to agree in the Lord." Where their differences lay is not mentioned, but the readers of the letter are urged soon thereafter (4:5) to exhibit a "magnanimous spirit to everyone."

The call to peace in 4:7 is introduced by an exhortation to prayer in 4:6: "Have no anxiety about anything, but in everything by prayer and supplication with thanksgiving let your requests be made known to God." Following this exhortation is the assurance in 4:7 that if the believers in Philippi bring all their needs before God with fervent prayer, "the peace of God, which passes all understanding, will guard their hearts and their minds in Christ Jesus."

Similarly, Jesus urged his disciples in the Sermon on the Mount to trust in God's providence and assured them that their prayers would be answered (Matt. 6:25–34; 7:7–11). For Paul, however, the fulfillment of prayer consisted rather in God's bestowing his peace on the congregation so that all hearts and minds would be directed toward Christ Jesus. God's response to prayer implies a peace that exceeds all human understanding (*panta noun*), a gift of heaven in the face of which all intellectual achievement and individual ambition lose their importance.

Of linguistic interest is the chiastic relationship between the phrases "the peace of God" in 4:7 and "the God of peace" in 4:9. In both cases, God is shown as the source of true peace.

Paul lived and worked in an empire that had profited from the *Pax Ro-*

*mana* since the days of Augustus. But Paul's surroundings were marked by constant tension and frequent aggression between Jews and Greeks; though, to be sure, he found this conflict now rendered invalid in Christ (Eph. 2:14–16). With his allusion to God's peace in Philippians 4:7, the apostle did not refer to a political program, but rather to peace within the Christian congregation and in the Christian *oikumene*. This gifted reality is a peace that "passes all understanding," that cannot be conceived or enacted by human endeavor. Nevertheless, at the same time, the importance of this peace of God within the universal church of Christ should not, on the political level, be discounted in its significance for world peace.

## – III –

# Disputed Settings of the Pauline Correspondence

# The Chronology of the
# Pastoral Epistles

In the discussion of the origin of the letters to Timothy and Titus, various hypotheses have repeatedly fallen into three main categories: (a) the Pastorals stem from Paul or possibly were written by one of his co-workers who represented the apostle's own mind; (b) they contain biographical fragments which go back to Paul or one of his acquaintances from the Pauline circle but were later combined with theological arguments of certain "early catholic" church leaders; (c) as pseudepigrapha they possess no direct connection with the life and letters of Paul but rather, *in toto,* are the work of forgers.

A matter of historical honesty and integrity thus emerges as the pivotal issue: Is it feasible to assume that Paul was able to adapt to the immediate environment of his Hellenistic cohorts Timothy and Titus so that as author or authority behind the letters he could assume responsibility for the largely Hellenistic diction, syntax, and way of thinking reflected in the Pastorals (category a)? Or would it be more reasonable to imagine that a representative of the later church orthodoxy and hierarchy could have "mined" or even fabricated Pauline fragments and ideas in order to advance the program of the so-called early catholicism under the name of Paul? According to explanations b) and c) above, the author of the letters must have done all of this without using the nomenclature and phraseology of the well-known letters of Paul as a definitive model in producing the Pastorals. It is precisely at this juncture where one, unbound by *idola theatri,* must choose the explanation that presents the fewest difficulties in clarifying the provenance of these letters.

## 1

From a number of scholarly vantage points, including serious scrutiny of the historical circumstances, the origin of the Pastorals seems considerably

First published as "Chronologie der Pastoralbriefe" in *TLZ* 101 (1976): 82–94. Translation by David P. Moessner.

less difficult to explain when these letters are tied directly to Paul, either as their author or the one who authorized them. Indeed, to assign to a later church leader the detailed scenarios of the Pauline mission creates a much larger problem for historical critical investigation in explaining the fundamental harmonies between the Pastorals and Acts, on the one hand, and between Acts and the remaining Paulines, on the other. To maintain that a person thirty, fifty, or even ninety years after Paul's death took pains to pick out a number of names and dates from Acts and the Paulines in order to delight his contemporaries with private, but spurious, Pauline correspondence—without even bothering to render a persuasive imitation of Pauline expressions and ideas—to assert this is a rather indelicate anachronism, to say the least.

To be sure, detailed information about personal affairs belonged to the ancient style of letter writing not only in private correspondence but also in literary epistolary compositions or "epistles" per se. But this practice led to an exchange of accepted rules between actual letters and literary epistles, conventions which can be detected already in ordinary writers, but especially in such accomplished authors as Paul. Advice for letter writers such as the widely circulated handbooks in the Roman empire of a Demetrius or a Proklos urged explicit references to the friendship and intimacy of the correspondents. This recommended style was put to good use both in private papyrus letters as well as erudite communiqués.[1] So then, if the personal messages in the Pastorals find certain parallels in fictitious letter compositions as well, this characteristic does not have the slightest bearing on the question of their authenticity.

In reality, such formal distinctions between private letters and general epistles as were posited by A. Deissmann in his own day, and later accepted by a great number of exegetes, never did exist. Sometimes an actual private letter was garnished with rhetorical features, a literary epistle oriented to personal affairs.[2] This common practice of interlacing personal and literary elements is displayed throughout the Pauline corpus so that in this respect the Pastorals hardly form an exception.

The earlier Paulines relate personal, more privately oriented messages that at the same time were to be shared among a more open readership: 1 Thess. 5:27: the letter is to "be read before all the brothers and sisters"; Gal. 1:2: Paul and "all the brothers and sisters" with him "to the congregations in Galatia"; 1 Cor. 1:2: "To the church of God in Corinth," "with all those together who in every place call on the name of our Lord" (cf. Col. 4:16: the letter is to be read in Laodicea as well as Colossae). These examples exhibit marked rhetorical phraseology and are to be understood as literary equivalents for public announcements. Moreover, personal messages also served oratorical or homiletical objectives. As typical examples:[3] 1 Thessalonians 3:6–7: "But Timothy has just now come to us from you, and has brought us the good news of your faith and love. He has told us also that you always remember us kindly and long to see us—just as we long to see you. For this reason, brothers and sisters, during all our distress and persecution we have been encouraged about you through your faith." Or 2 Corinthians 8:16: "But thanks be to God who put in the heart of Titus the same eagerness for you that I myself have." On the whole, these letters show that Paul was well acquainted with the norms of ancient epistolary style, including the characteristic interweaving of personal and rhetorical elements (e.g., the formula "remembering/making mention of you" [*mneian poioumenoi*], 1 Thess. 1:2; Rom. 1:9; Philem. 4 et al.).[4]

Similarly, the Pastorals were presented as personal messages and yet styled rhetorically as "open letters." From a literary point of view, the well-known epistles of Cicero and Seneca evince a number of instructive analogies because they were addressed to private individuals and yet intended for the general public. In the personal details of such works, the amount of originality, or conversely, the dependence upon well-defined forms, does not offer any criterion at all with respect to a real or fictional basis for the presentation. If Paul and his colleagues adapted their earlier epistles to the Hellenistic conventions for private and public letters, they could certainly just as easily have appropriated these same norms in the Pastorals.

As such, these literary or, more precisely, rhetorical contexts and the stereotypical forms of the personal details of the Pastorals convey nothing about the letters' historical content. Rather, the credibility of these personalia could be questioned only on empirical-historical grounds, provided that the biographical and geographical details were to stand in blatant contradiction to events otherwise known, as is the case, for instance, with the legends of the apocryphal Acts of the Apostles. But this discrepancy has in no way been demonstrated for the Pastorals.[5]

On the contrary, the biographical and geographical particularities of the Pastorals can be tallied with a whole array of incidents that are known from Acts and the earlier Pauline letters. A congruous picture emerges quite spontaneously, without textual alteration, and even in some of the most inconspicuous details where deliberate harmonizing is inconceivable. This assertion will be demonstrated below for 1 Timothy, Titus, and 2 Timothy. In what follows, "Paul" stands for the person named and active in these letters, whether or not he or someone else is actually responsible for composing the Pastorals.

## 2

(a) According to 1 Timothy, Paul had directed Timothy, his son in the Spirit, to remain in Ephesus when he himself wanted to go to Macedonia (1 Tim. 1:3). This detail corresponds to information in Acts and the Corinthian letters that can be related to events in the years A.D. 56 and 57. In the spring of 56 Timothy, accompanied by Erastus and a few others, had traveled to Corinth by way of Macedonia with the first Corinthian letter (Acts 19:22; 1 Cor. 4:17; 16:10a). In this epistle Paul introduced his youthful helper with expressions suggestive of phrases typical to the letters to Timothy[6] (1 Cor. 16:10b-11a: "for he is doing the work of the Lord just as I am; therefore let no one despise him"; cf. 1 Tim. 1:18: "so that ... you may fight the good fight"; 4:12: "let no one despise your youth"; 2 Tim. 3:17: "equipped for every good work"; 2 Tim. 4:5: "do the work of an evangelist").

Paul urged the Corinthians to receive Timothy hospitably and to send him back as soon as possible to Ephesus where he was waiting impatiently for him, Erastus, and the others (1 Cor. 16:11b: "I am expecting him with the brothers and sisters"). As a faithful co-worker of Paul, it is likely that Timothy carried out this travel plan. To all appearances it seems that he returned to Paul in Ephesus in the summer of 56, although Acts does not mention this explicitly.[7] But this arrival would correspond in 1 Timothy to the presupposed situation for Paul's departure: After Timothy's visit in Corinth, Paul received his trustworthy cohort back again in Ephesus and instructed him to remain there to take over responsibility for the community, while he himself was about to depart for Macedonia.

It should be pointed out that in giving this order Paul did not say that he had already left for Macedonia, but that he was intending, or at the point of going there (1 Tim. 1:3, *poreuomenos* [pres. part.]). This detail allows the possibility of interpreting 1 Timothy as an admonitory speech in Ephesus that can be compared with the situation of Paul's final session before the Ephesian elders in Acts 20:17–35. As a matter of fact, the instructions and admonitions in 1 Timothy are formulated not so much for Paul's most intimate circle of disciples as for a broader public; in other words, they cohere with the assumption that not only Timothy but also the whole congregation and even outsiders were intended to hear the message. The detailed reminiscences of the call of the apostle (1:12), the commission to Timothy (1:18), the directions for organizing community prayer and positions of leadership (2:1–3:13), social life (5:1–22), or the warning against the false teaching (1:6–11; 4:1–5; 6:3–10) were not reserved for the ears of Timothy alone. All of these messages were at one and the same time to serve as teaching for the gathered congregation, as well as information for the

larger community. With this public character of the presentation, the pronounced rhetorical style is in full accord. Paul declares in somewhat solemn
tones: "The saying is sure and worthy of every affirmation" (1 Tim. 1:15);
"This charge I entrust to you, Timothy, my son" (1:18); "In the presence
of God and Jesus Christ and the elect angels, I adjure you to heed this"
(5:21); "But as for you, man of God, shun this and diligently pursue righteousness, godliness, faith, love, patience, humility" (6:11). Paul sees himself
throughout in the role of a speaker who, standing before Timothy and the
assembled community, prepares for his imminent departure by instructing
his youthful replacement and those members of the congregation present (as
Acts 20:1 would also suggest: "When he had called together the disciples
and exhorted [*parakalesas*] them, he bid them farewell and departed for
Macedonia").

Paul's farewell message in Miletus before the Ephesian elders (Acts 20:17–
35) reveals a similar situation and presents a similar rhetoric. Although
the speech has been formulated by Luke, its context clearly assumes that,
during his third missionary journey, Paul delivered a hortatory address to the
Ephesian elders that forms an illuminating analogy to the parenetic setting
of 1 Timothy.

This estimation of 1 Timothy as a community address makes sense
chronologically in so far as the beginning of Timothy's independent duties
as pastor in Ephesus would ensue immediately after his return from Corinth
in the summer of 56. In this way Timothy's activity during Paul's absence
receives sufficient time before Timothy appears together with Paul in Macedonia as the co-sender of 2 Corinthians (2 Cor. 2:2), which is to be dated
one year after 1 Corinthians or in the summer of 57 (2 Cor. 8:11; 9:2: "since
last year"). During this year Paul worked in the vicinity of Troas—that is,
in Mysia—and then journeyed to Macedonia where with great agitation he
awaited news from Titus concerning Corinth (2 Cor. 2:1–2). While still in
Ephesus Paul had only announced his trip to Macedonia (1 Tim. 1:3), but
surprisingly on the way he experienced great response in Troas. He therefore stayed in Mysia longer than anticipated (2 Cor. 2:2) until in a moment
filled with both external and internal tension he crossed over to Macedonia
(2:13; 7:5). He took Timothy along and together they wrote 2 Corinthians
(1:1). Because the "we" form is used throughout this letter—much more frequently in fact than in any other of the Paulines (108 times in 2 Corinthians,
59 times in Romans, and 54 times in 1 Corinthians)[8]—the personal notices
are tied more intimately than usual to both senders, to Paul, and at the same
time to Timothy. This "we" explains why the repeated lists of affliction and
suffering in 2 Corinthians deal with recently experienced and almost un-
bearable persecutions in Asia, even though Paul had departed from Ephesus

a year earlier (2 Cor. 1:8–11: harassment to the point of despair; 4:8–18: always being given up to death; 6:4–10: through great patience defending their credentials as God's servants amidst unheard-of atrocities). Thus when Timothy left with Paul for Macedonia in the summer of 57, it was because the situation in Asia had grown desperate.

As one of the provocators of the persecutions in Asia, a coppersmith by the name of Alexander is mentioned (1 Tim. 1:20; 2 Tim. 4:14). This man is certainly identical with the Jew Alexander who, at the uproar ignited by the Ephesian silversmiths, had attempted to address the crowd (Acts 19:33). It is not purely coincidence that a threefold cluster of detail is common to both texts: the name of the man (1 Tim. 1:20; Acts 19:33); his membership in the smithy guild (2 Tim. 4:14; Acts 19:23–27); and his allegiance to Judaism (according to 1 Tim. 1:7; 4:3, the false teaching consisted above all in judaizing pressures; cf. Acts 19:33).

Yet even apart from Alexander's connection with the Ephesian silversmiths' demonstration, the Pastorals indicate that Timothy had been exposed to peculiarly strident opponents (1 Tim. 1:4, 20; 6:4, 20; 2 Tim. 1:15; 2:16, 23; 3:1–9, 13). Because of these difficulties, Timothy in the following year suspended the activity assigned to him in A.D. 56 (1 Tim. 1:3) in order to be near Paul again (2 Cor. 1:1). And owing to the same exigencies according to Luke in Acts, Paul in 58 waived another trip to Ephesus so that he would not lose too much time on his journey back to Jerusalem (Acts 20:16). Instead, he summoned the Ephesian elders to Miletus (20:17), delivering to them a parting address which invites parallels with 1 Timothy. In Miletus Paul reminds his audience of the plots of the Jews against him (Acts 20:19), confesses his innocence in view of upcoming martyrdoms (20:26), and enjoins them as newly commissioned leaders of the congregation (*episkopoi,* as in 1 Tim. 3:1) to vigilance against rapacious "seducers." To be sure, Luke has given the speech a stylized form, but evidently on the basis of his knowledge of the situation in Ephesus, which, in 1 Timothy, is painted in strikingly similar colors. On the other hand, any attempt to explain 1 Timothy as a fabrication imaginatively derived from the Acts account turns a great deal of straightforward facts into puzzling details and "pulls out of the hat" a master innovator of intriguing antiquities!

(b) According to the letter to Titus, Paul had directed Titus, his son in the Spirit, to remain in Crete in order to appoint elders in the congregations already existing in some of the cities there (Titus 1:5). Paul did not say that he also had worked in Crete, only that he had Titus stay there while he himself continued his activity elsewhere (Titus 1:5: *apelipon se*—"I had you remain," similar to 2 Tim. 4:20: *Trophimon apelipon en Mileto*—"I had Trophimus stay back in Miletus, because he was ill").

In Acts, Luke does not offer any pertinent information regarding this occurrence. The short-lived anchoring of the ship off the south coast of Crete at Fair Havens in the vicinity of Lasea on the way to Rome (Acts 27:8) did not allow Paul, the prisoner, to undertake any mission on the island, and there is no mention of any Titus as a fellow traveler. Furthermore, the letter to Titus does not give the slightest hint of any captivity of the apostle. Consequently, this epistle must be related to a time either before or after Paul's imprisonments in Jerusalem, Caesarea, and Rome, A.D. 58–62 (Acts 21:33–28:31). If the first alternative is preferred, then a lucrative situation opens up in which the various details can be aligned with circumstances and events already known. If the second alternative is maintained, then a rather content-less scheme emerges that is left suspended in a vacuum.

Now if the letter to Titus is placed in the summer of 58 before Paul's arrest in Jerusalem, then the only problem to be addressed is the silence in Acts concerning Titus and the mission in Crete. But this lacuna accords with Luke's silence about Titus throughout his Acts, an odd state of affairs that nevertheless has a 'biographical' explanation. For it is also quite re-markable that Luke knew apparently none of the particulars surrounding Paul's new visit to Corinth at the end of 57 to the beginning of 58, a visit for which Titus had so dutifully prepared (2 Cor. 2:13; 7:6–16; Acts 20:3 mentions summarily only three months in Hellas). But as it turns out, Luke was active in the north, for he was later able to divulge specific informa-tion about Paul's companions on their return through Macedonia (20:4), depicting their continuing journey to Miletus in the "we" style (20:5–15). Luke's own personal situation thus explains why he does not have anything to report about Titus' work in Corinth, A.D. 57–58.

The letter to Titus can be inserted without difficulty into this gap in Acts. In the autumn of A.D. 57, Paul had sent Titus from Corinth to Crete and had him stay there in order to supervise affairs that still needed attention, before the apostle himself a couple of weeks prior to Easter of A.D. 58 set out from Corinth on his return to Jerusalem (Acts 20:3b; cf. "Easter" in v. 6a; Rom. 15:25–26).

This correlation of events is confirmed by comparing 2 Corinthians with Romans. According to the former, Titus had been dispatched in the summer of 57 to work in Corinth on the previously announced collection (2 Cor. 8:17–23); and even after Paul's arrival in Corinth, Titus assisted him for some time with this project. But when Paul wrote Romans from Corinth in the spring of 58 (Rom. 15:26; 16:23), he mentioned Timothy (16:21) and many other collaborators active in Macedonia or Greece—but not Titus. Here Paul's correspondence with his trusted disciple provides the missing historical link. For when Paul was writing Romans, Titus had already parted to pursue his work in Crete in the winter and spring of 57–58. He was simply no longer with Paul at that time in Corinth.

Further corroboration for connecting the letter to Titus with Paul's return journey from Corinth in the spring of 58 can be discovered in the charge to Titus to wait in Crete for the arrival of Artemas or Tychicus before meeting the apostle in Nicopolis (Titus 3:12a). This Artemas is otherwise unknown, but Tychicus was one of the Christians from Asia who accompanied Paul on his return to Jerusalem (Acts 20:3). Among the various towns named "Nicopolis," the one with which Titus would be familiar without further specifics must be meant. The important port of Nicopolis in Epirus south of Dalmatia and Illyricum would meet this criterion, because Paul, after extending his activity as far as the border of Illyricum (Rom. 15:19), would have passed through Epirus when he met Titus again in Corinth (2 Cor. 8:18). Paul wanted to spend the winter in this port city with its vital link to Italy (Titus 3:12b). For after visiting Jerusalem, he had intended to develop his mission in the west to a greater extent beyond the vicinity of Illyricum (Rom. 15:19), taking the gospel from there to Italy and on even as far as Spain (15:20–29). Because of his imprisonment in Jerusalem, Paul did not return to Epirus, although he may have already sent Artemas to Crete, while Tychichus had accompanied Paul to Jerusalem and was later utilized in making journeys to Colossae and Ephesus from Caesarea (Col. 4:7; Eph. 6:21; 2 Tim. 4:12).[9] Now according to 2 Timothy, Titus did in fact make his way to Nicopolis to comply with Paul's earlier request (Titus 3:12), because Titus' activity in Dalmatia (2 Tim. 4:10) presupposes a stop in that city. In turn, this stop can be understood as a fulfillment of Paul's instruction in the letter to Titus. When he did not find Paul there, Titus linked up with the work Paul had already begun in Illyricum and embarked on a mission of his own to Dalmatia. That Titus was to advance to Nicopolis fits entirely with Paul's agenda during the apostle's return through Macedonia and Asia Minor in the spring of 58.

By the same token, if Paul's parting word to Titus at the beginning of his letter is taken to point to the apostle's setting out from Corinth in the spring of 58 (Titus 1:5: "I had you remain in Crete"), the letter to Titus cannot have originated until sometime during Paul's subsequent travels to Jerusalem through Macedonia and Asia Minor. Paul explicitly greeted Titus in the names of all those who were with him at the time (Titus 3:15), referring not to a local congregation but to his traveling companions. It is with such an entourage, to which Tychicus also belonged, that Paul spent a week in Troas shortly after Easter 58 (Acts 20:4–6). And it is in this context at an opportune moment that he wanted to send either Artemas or Tychicus to Crete in order to replace Titus, thus allowing Titus enough time to start out before winter to meet Paul in Nicopolis (Titus 3:12). Paul must have reckoned with sending one of these disciples along the usual maritime route to Crete, that is, launching from Cnidus or Rhodes (Acts 21:1; 27:7). It follows that the letter that outlines this plan must have arisen at a point previously visited, like Troas (Acts 20:6), or, more probably, Miletus (20:15). Because of the relative proximity of Miletus to Crete, the quickest way to send relief for Titus would have been precisely from this juncture. There Paul, a couple of weeks after Easter 58, could also count on completing the proposed itinerary: sending Artemas or Tychicus to Crete by ship from Cnidus or Rhodes; a visit in Jerusalem in time for Pentecost (Acts 20:16); new activity in the west and a meeting with Titus in Nicopolis before winter (Titus 3:13). Moreover, in this ancient center of Ionic philosophy, his quotation from the pre-Socratic philosopher Epimenides would be particularly apropos (Titus 1:12).

Luke's account of Paul's speech in Miletus in Acts 20:17–35 contains parallels not only to the first letter to Timothy but to the letter to Titus as well. In both cases there are elders and pastors (*episkopoi*, Acts 20:17, 28; Titus 1:5, 7); on the other hand, Jewish "troublemakers" (Acts 20:19; Titus 1:10) and deceivers are mentioned who are compared to savage beasts (Acts 20:29; Titus 1:12), and, on account of their perverted teaching, many disciples are being snatched away (Acts 20:3; Titus 1:11). Taken as a whole, the letter to Titus, like 1 Timothy, constitutes more a public address than a private letter. It depicts situations current in Asia Minor, including the organization of community life both within the congregation and in the larger society, as well as the rejection of the gospel by Judaism. Although the letter to Titus was written for the churches at Crete, an isle scarcely known to Paul, the author accommodated his themes as far as possible to the conditions in Asia Minor that he had come to experience firsthand. If the city of Miletus is delineated as the original backdrop for the parenetically shaped message to Titus, then Timothy would have been one of the disciples accompanying the apostle (Acts 20:4). His presence with Paul would then help to clarify why the problems described in this letter to Titus are similar to those of 1 Timothy, although the situation in Crete was most likely not entirely the same as in Ephesus. But the main reason for the resonance of the epistle to Titus with vicissitudes in Asia Minor is its distinct rhetorical character. What the apostle had decided to convey to his useful co-worker in Crete should also be made known to the Asian communities through a public reading of this letter. The congregation in Miletus comes to mind first, where the epistle could have exercised a role similar to the address reproduced by Luke in Acts, before it was forwarded to Crete as well as circulated more widely in the immediate environs.

c) The many personal details notwithstanding, the second letter to Timothy was also patterned essentially for a wider audience. As an example, Timothy did not have to be reminded of the faith that Paul had received from his parents and Timothy himself from his grandmother and mother (2 Tim. 1:3, 5). Such personal allusions were valuable rather as appeals to the readers and hearers of the letter wherever it would be recited. The same holds for all the other persons and personal details in the letter such as the reference to Paul's captivity for the benefit of the elect (2:9–10), the reminder of his trials in Antioch, Iconium, and Lystra (3:11), or the depiction of his abandonment in prison (4:10–11). All these personal particulars can be seen to coincide with both biographical and pedagogical objectives.

The desire to instruct a wider circle of disciples is expressed programmatically by the exhortation in 2 Timothy 2:2: "What you have learned from me, entrust to faithful people who will be able to instruct others as well." The entire structure of the letter underscores this orientation to a more general public. In the first and third sections of the epistle the text alternates between "you" and "I" (1:3 "you" and 1:4 "I"; 2:1 "you" and 2:8 "I"; 3:10 "you" and 4:6 "I"), so that a reciprocal model for disciple and master comes to the forefront.[10] An earnest, if not ceremonious, parenetic tone also pervades these passages, for example, 3:10–11: "But you have followed me in my teaching, conduct, aim in life, faith, patience, love, steadfastness, persecution, suffering." Without doubt, the author of this epistle did not write Timothy to inform him of such autobiographical details or to impress him with literary grandiloquence. Rather, he wanted to teach all the leaders and members of the congregations who would come in contact with the letter about Paul's priorities and of the tasks outlined for his colleague—all for the purpose of fortifying their faith and loyalty while, at the same time, offering them practical pointers for their community life.

This open, homiletical character of 2 Timothy in no way implies that the personalia are to be caricatured as the literary flourish or even fiction of a later forger of Paul. Only if a picture were to emerge that would be historically impossible could such a judgment be warranted. All the personal and geographical terms form within the letter itself a sharp and coherent picture that can be brought into focus with other documents and that tallies with well-known facts from the life of Paul. Even the travel route of the epistle is traceable through a number of themes and issues that were written with certain communities in mind and that would eventually be taken up by those churches, as the bearer of the epistle would pass through their vicinity and read the letter aloud to all those gathered together.

According to statements of 2 Timothy, Mark served as the messenger for the letter and was instructed to seek out Timothy in Mysia (2 Tim. 4:11b).

From there the two of them were to pass through Troas on their way to meet Paul (4:13). Mark and three other companions of the apostle mentioned in 2 Timothy—Demas, Luke, and Tychicus (2 Tim. 4:10–12)—are also referred to in the other captivity epistles Philemon and Colossians (Philem. 24; Col. 4:7, 10, 14), and thus were together with Paul when these letters were written from Caesarea (because according to Philem. 9—"and now also a prisoner of Jesus Christ"—Paul has just entered into a situation new to his career, a period of captivity that can be made to fit only his imprisonment in Caesarea).[11] The rather specific descriptions of the fellow workers in 2 Timothy presuppose that Timothy had been attached to this circle in Caesarea and was now to receive an update on current developments. But such news would have sparked even greater interest for all the Christians along the letter's path who would have the opportunity to read or hear the letter read aloud. The provenance of 2 Timothy is therefore Caesarea, and Mark was to take the letter to Timothy from there by way of the Cilician Gates through Asia Minor. In every detail, all the remaining references to cities and districts in 2 Timothy confirm this route of travel. It follows that the letter must have originated during the two-year captivity of Paul in Caesarea but later than Philemon, Colossians, and Ephesians; that is, in A.D. 59 or 60.

The short notice concerning Onesiphorus' arrival in Rome (2 Tim. 1:16–17) should not be construed as an incarceration of Paul in that city when the apostle was preoccupied with 2 Timothy. To be exact, verses 16b-17 state concerning Onesiphorus: "He was not ashamed of my chains, but having arrived in Rome he conducted a zealous search for me and found me."[12] Onesiphorus did not travel to Rome with great zeal in order to find Paul or to visit him in jail; rather, his zeal began when in Rome he did not encounter Paul as he had anticipated. It is at that point that his earnest searching and his finding the place of Paul's imprisonment are presented as marvelous deeds to be rewarded specially by the Lord at the Day of Judgment (1:18). If it had been a matter of a Roman imprisonment, then no rigorous search would have been necessary, because any person could have shown Onesiphorus the way to the prison, and a visit with the apostle would have been a matter of course—hardly an extraordinary act of love. But when the rest of the topographical details in 2 Timothy are seen to point to Caesarea as the place of custody, then a far less trivial perspective emerges. Now it becomes clear that, without any knowledge about a confinement of Paul, Onesiphorus had expected to see Paul in Rome. He began to search for Paul—which he did fervently—and finally found him in Caesarea. From this perspective his act of compassion appears worthy of Paul's effusive praise. Certainly this explanation requires Onesiphorus to travel exceptionally far to visit Paul. But this type of undertaking would not have been unthinkable for Onesiphorus; he had supported the communities in Ephesus in a particularly effective manner (2 Tim. 1:18), and his home there constituted, like Aquila's and Priscilla's (2 Cor. 16:10), a center for the Christians (2 Tim. 4:19). For that reason and because he is mentioned immediately after Aquila (2 Tim. 4:19), he should be reckoned, like Aquila, an entrepreneur in Ephesus. It should also be noted that if Aquila and Priscilla were able to pursue business alternately in Rome, Corinth, and Ephesus (Acts 18:2, 18, 26; 1 Cor. 16:19; Rom. 16:3; 2 Tim. 4:19), then such entrepreneurial excursions are not inconceivable for Onesiphorus as well.

To summarize, Onesiphorus did not, in the first place, go to Rome to visit Paul. Rather, during his last stay in Ephesus, Paul had mentioned his plans to visit the metropolis (Acts 19:21; cf. Rom. 15:23), and therefore Onesiphorus had expected to see the apostle in Rome when he himself traveled to that city. When he did not find Paul there, Onesiphorus diligently sought him out, eventually finding him as a prisoner in Caesarea. It is only from this perspective that Paul's glowing praise of Onesiphorus in 2 Timothy becomes fully understandable.

The proposed travel route for the letter lends additional support for a Caesarean origin. The main points on this journey can be established from the rhetorically charged messages patterned throughout the epistle and targeted to the particular cities of Asia Minor that Mark himself was to convey as he would pass through (2 Tim. 4:11). Paul had already urged a similar exchange to the congregations at Colossae and Laodicea (Col. 4:16). This plan of producing discrete but open letters, intended as circulars, transforms seemingly unnecessary or even trivial details in 2 Timothy into matters of public consequence as well as practical application.

Already the reference to Paul's religious heritage (2 Tim. 1:3) makes sense when it is kept in mind that from Caesarea Mark was first of all to reach Tarsus. Here in Paul's hometown this open letter would bolster the faith of the Christians. Recalling the traditions of his own family, moreover, would not have been without value in view of the contemporary judaizing current (Hymenaeus and Alexander, 1 Tim. 1:20; 2 Tim. 2:17; 4:14). The same holds for the rather solemn, sermonic appeal to the faith of Lois and Eunice, the grandmother and mother of Timothy. These Jewish women lived in Derbe, Timothy's home (Acts 16:1), and the reference to their genuine Christian faith was meant to make an impact on the believers there. After the visit to Derbe, Mark was to press on to the Christians in Lystra, Iconium, and Antioch in Pisidia. Paul wanted to strengthen the believers' courage by harkening back to his long-suffering in persecution during his first missionary journey there (2 Tim. 3:11). From the epistle to the Colossians, written in Caesarea a few months earlier,[13] it becomes clear that Paul had planned for Mark to make a subsequent trip to Colossae: "When he comes to you, receive him hospitably" (Col. 4:10). Mark is presented to them as a cousin of Barnabas (4:10), because the latter was known in Colossae from the days when he had conducted evangelization in Pisidian Antioch (Acts 13:14)—the stepping-off point for mission in that area (13:49).[14] The prevenient but now revealed mystery of elective grace and the suffering of Paul for the sake of the elect are themes distinctive for Colossians, and they are also found in 2 Timothy (Col. 1:24, 26–27; 2 Tim. 1:9–10; 2:10). As the next stop for Mark, 2 Timothy intimates Ephesus, where Onesiphorus' family could learn of the apostle's gratitude for his loyalty and where the community would be made aware of Paul's concern over the false teaching and for those especially who had fallen away (2 Tim. 1:15; 2:16–39; 4:14). Finally, Mark was supposed to reach Timothy in Mysia and go back with him to Paul after picking up the apostle's coat and some of his books (4:11, 13, 21a). Because the apostle had actually visited Troas in the spring of 58 (Acts 20:6), his request to fetch these items would fit well in the continuing activity of Paul. But there does not appear to be much sense at all in expressing such a request if 2 Timothy is assigned to a period many years later.

In view of Timothy's and Mark's return journey, Paul remarked further that he had sent Tychicus to Ephesus (4:12). As the other captivity epistles indicate, Tychicus had first presented Colossians and Philemon to the Colossian community (Col. 4:7–9) before going ahead through various communities to Ephesus with the Ephesian circular[15] (Eph. 1:1; 6:21). It was here in Ephesus that Timothy was to confer with Tychicus.[16] At the same time, Paul warned Timothy about the coppersmith Alexander in Ephesus (2 Tim. 4:14), who should be identified, as argued above, with the Jewish silversmith of the uproar in Acts 19:33, as well as with the judaizing zealot leader of 1 Timothy 1:20. On the other hand, Paul sent greetings to his friends in Ephesus—namely, Priscilla, Aquila, and the family of Onesiphorus—while Erastus (Acts 19:22) was to remain behind at Corinth (2 Tim. 4:19–20). After the stay in Ephesus, Trophimus could be visited in Miletus, where he had been left behind due to illness (4:20b). From here Timothy should proceed via ship, for it was evidently with an eye to the conditions for sea travel that Paul urged his disciple to come before winter (4:21a).

Paul needed Timothy's as well as Mark's help, because only Luke of the apostle's cohorts stood available at his side (4:11). According to Philemon and Colossians, in *c.* A.D. 59 a number of Jewish and Greek Christians were at the apostle's disposal in Caesarea: Timothy, Tychicus, Epaphras, Aristarchus, Jesus Justus, Mark, Luke, and Demas (Philem. 23–24; Col. 1:1; 4:7, 10, 14). Two of these men who were fellow prisoners, Aristarchus and Epaphras, would not have been of much service (Acts 2:2; Col. 4:10;

Philem. 4). And the Jewish friend, Jesus Justus, though he had aligned himself with Paul (Col. 4:11), probably did not belong to the inner band of associates, and in any case is not mentioned again. With all the rest except Luke, it becomes both implicitly and explicitly clear from 2 Timothy that they had departed for various regions a few months later: Timothy, Tychicus, Mark, Demas, and in addition an otherwise unknown Crescens (2 Tim. 4:10–12). The persons and circumstances detailed in 2 Timothy compose a fully organic relationship with the descriptions of Paul's co-workers in Philemon and Colossians, with only some reserve regarding Jesus Justus, who is not mentioned again.

Is it conceivable that the list of names in 2 Timothy is the result of a literary imitation of the earlier captivity epistles? The predominating interests of the apostolic and postapostolic generations argue against this supposition. For them a rapid spreading of the Word and a stabilization of the church, not biographical artifacts, were of the utmost importance. Certainly legends arose gradually around the apostles and their disciples, but these attached themselves to miraculous episodes. No interest of this kind is displayed in the sober description of 2 Timothy. What is more, in the first and second centuries when the church was fervently engaged in mission, there are no historical indicators that could explain why someone would be motivated to go to such great lengths to pluck out names from the Colossian and even from the very brief Philemon letter to use them in a totally different sequence and context in order simply to effect an air of reality. That anybody should have done this for historically interested readers without recourse to miracles seems itself completely miraculous. On the contrary, the personal statements in Colossians and Philemon and those in 2 Timothy develop quite spontaneously into a fully integrated picture of the interruption and delay in Paul's career of A.D. 59–60, when only Luke was left at his side (2 Tim. 4:11a). It is inconceivable that a member of the ancient church or a representative of the so-called early-catholicism should have adopted historico-critical points of view in order to design from the onomasticon of Colossians and Philemon the coherent portrait known as 2 Timothy.

Even less imaginable is a fabrication or "secondary" production of the itinerary of 2 Timothy that allegedly has no historical points of contact with the mission of Paul but is the creation of a pseudonymous author. Many passages of the letter point both expressly and tacitly to the communities and individuals whom Mark was to encounter along the way. In addition, Timothy's and Mark's return journey is traceable in several instances. A subsequent reworking and interpolation from such partially concealed elements presupposes a refinement for which there is no historical precedent and which would not have had the slightest significance for believers, not to mention disinterested and skeptical parties, during the subapostolic period. But on the other hand, if the itinerary is viewed as primary information stemming from Paul and his circle, then clear agreement results with facts well substantiated from other sources:[17] Second Timothy was written in Caesarea, at some point after Colossians and Philemon but before the winter of 59 or 60.

**3**

A number of arguments against Pauline authorship, or at least against a Pauline chronology of the Pastorals, have been propounded that are not based on the personal details analyzed above, but upon generalized notions of a progressive development of certain aspects of the Pastorals, such as: (a) the structure of their language, (b) their concept of the ministry, and (c) the heresy rejected. It cannot be disputed that significant substantive problems come to the fore here. Nevertheless, the persons and personal circumstances that fit closely into the situation of the apostle carry far more weight than the unavoidably formal schemes that purport to date linguistic and ecclesiastical development.

(a) There is no doubt that stylistic differences exist between the earlier Pauline letters, on the one hand, and the captivity epistles as well as the Pastorals, on the other, even if word statistics do not exhibit much more of a difference between these two groups than between individual examples of Paul's earlier epistles. And yet no one has adduced substantial evidence for the impossibility of a certain flexibility of linguistic style for either the apostle or his assistants. A far more honest approach would take seriously Paul's claim of adapting himself to the particular needs of his readers, whether Jews or Greeks or those weak in faith, so that he could be "all things to all human beings" (1 Cor. 9:19–23). Thus concerning the frequently labeled "deutero-Paulines" or "pseudepigrapha" of Colossians and Ephesians as well as the letters to Timothy and Titus, due attention must be paid to their connection to Asia Minor and their corresponding rhetorical style. These letters represent a florid, heavy baroque rhetoric that calls to mind the rhetorical style of "Asianism," one of whose "school" centers was located in Ephesus. Could not Paul of Tarsus and his literary team have adapted and applied a distinctive epistolary style in their communications with Colossae and Ephesus, as well as to such native inhabitants of Asia Minor as a Timothy or Titus?

(b) The three Pastoral epistles were structured fundamentally as directives to leaders of congregations rather than to believers at large, as is the case for the rest of the Paulines. Accordingly, they contain more instructions for functionaries and communal life than do the rest of Paul's letters. But this distinction has nothing to do with the dating of the Pastorals. It is simply not possible to set up a standard that can measure in advance the speed of developing offices and positions of leadership in the diverse congregations of the Pauline mission. Attempts in modern research to do precisely this often betray an a prioritistic schema that has already determined the results of the investigation.

(c) Furthermore, it should be noted that the false teaching repudiated in the Pastorals does not summon sufficient evidence for a late date. In the first instance, various strains of Jewish nomism and asceticism are denounced (1 Tim. 1:6–10; 4:1–5; Titus 1:10–16), and they are not unlike the judaizing tendencies found in Galatia and Phrygia (Gal. 3:10–15; 5:10–21; Col. 2:16–23). In the second place, the letters reject arrogant reliance on "knowledge" and enthusiastic spiritualization of the resurrection (1 Tim. 6:2; 2 Tim. 2:18), and these motifs directly echo the gnostic tendencies in Corinth (1 Cor. 1:2; 15:12). The same phenomena appear together in Colossians as judaizing, ascetic, and gnostic speculation (Col. 2:8, 16–23). No *terminus a quo* can be established for the emergence of such spiritual tendencies.

On the other hand, a *terminus ante quem* can be determined for the admonitions of the Pastorals to political obedience (Titus 3:1) and even prayer on behalf of Caesar and the ruling authorities (1 Tim. 2:1–4). After the Neronian persecution of A.D. 65, such optimism vis-à-vis the imperial power could no longer represent the sentiments of a Christian writer.

# The Historical Setting of Colossians

## Place and Date

The Place of ancient Colossae was discovered by William J. Hamilton in A.D. 1835,[1] but the city has not yet been excavated. He found a hillock (Turkish *hüyük* "tumulus") with a few traces of the old city on the southern bank of the river Lycus in Phrygia, near the village of Chonai, which is located further south at the foot of Mount Cadmos.[2]

The river Lycus is a southern tributary of the Meander, famous not only for its many curves, which have given an architectural element the name of meander, but also for its fertile valley which opens toward the West coast near Ephesus and produces enormous crops of figs and olives.

In pre-Christian times Colossae was a station on a highway through the Lycus and Meander valleys which connected the cities of Phrygia with Ephesus.[3] Being a southern parallel to the old Persian street which ended at Sardis, it took over much of the international traffic between West and East. This is evident from older itineraries found in the books of Herodotus and Xenophon, who called Colossae an important and flourishing city (Herodotus, *History*, VII, 30; Xenophon, *Anabasis*, I, 2, 6). Colossae was also known for its wool industry. By dying the wool the enterprisers gave it a dark-red color (Strabo, *Geography*, XII, 8, 16) that was generally known as Colossian (Latin *colossinus;* Pliny, *History*, XXI, 51). It is worth noticing that Paul, in his two letters to Colossae, particularly apostrophized local employers and laborers, including Philemon and Onesimus (Col. 3:22–4:1; Phm. 1, 11, 16), and some of them may have been occupied with this color industry.

In the days of the apostles, however, Colossae was no more a big and rich town but had been surpassed by two cities located 17 and 20 kilometers further west and north-west in the same valley; Laodicea south of the river and Hierapolis north of it. They were mentioned by Paul as centers of Christians in close connection with those in Colossae (Col. 2:1; 4:13, 15, 16), and their wealth was based on a textile industry of a similar kind. In his geographical

First published with the same title in *The Review and Expositor* 70 (1973): 429–38; reprinted by permission.

121

survey written about A.D. 18, Strabo said the largest cities of Phrygia were Laodicea and Apamea; further east on the caravan street referred to above, whereas he reserved Colossae for a subsequent list of smaller Phrygian cities (Strabo, *Geography*, XII, 8, 13). The impressive ruins of Laodicea and Hierapolis[4] illustrate their importance during the first post-Christian centuries, a fact to which Colossae does not offer any counterpart.[5]

Concerning the date of the Epistles to the Colossians, it should be observed that Colossae was most probably destroyed in A.D. 61 by a dreadful earthquake which ruined nearby Laodicea, and, in distinction from the latter, Colossae was not said to have been restored. All available historical documents produced after the year 61 contain no concrete remarks on the city of Colossae. Laodicea and Hierapolis were referred to in several texts of the first two centuries, but, with reference to the years after A.D. 61, Colossae was no longer mentioned in connection with them.

Implicitly and explicitly, the following texts will demonstrate that Colossae was destroyed in A.D. 61 and never regained any real importance after this catastrophe:

1. Tacitus, *Annals*, XIV, 27, 1:

In the same year (A.D. 61) one of the famous cities of Asia, Laodicea, was destroyed by an earthquake and restored through its own resources without any contribution from our people (that is, from Nero and the Romans).

Tacitus did not refer to Colossae but only to Laodicea because he found it remarkable how soon this city was built up again, and because this city alone was generally known when he wrote his Chronicle around A.D. 120. Although not mentioned, Colossae was probably damaged on the same occasion because of its situation 17 kilometers higher up in the same valley. Strabo expressly called the whole region a center of repeated earthquakes (Strabo, *Geography*, XII, 8, 16).

2. Pliny, *History*, V, 105:

The very famous city of Laodicea . . . is on the river Lycus, and the Asopus and the Caprus wash its sides. It was first called the City of Zeus, then Rhoas. The rest of the peoples who belong to this jurisdiction, and may be worth mentioning, are the Hydrelitae, Themisones, and Hiera-politae.

The subsequent clause includes a detailed list of peoples belonging to another district. When writing this around A.D. 75, Pliny found no reason to mention Colossae. Later he added it while recording some places of lesser importance known to him from earlier sources (V, 145):

Here (in Phrygia) the cities most widely known, except those already mentioned (V,105), are Ancyra, Andria, Celaenae, Colossae, Carina, Cotyaion, Ceraine, Conium, and Midaium.

But this list was a historical retrospect, including very disparate elements like Ancyra and Iconium, and did not bring any up-to-date information. In another context, in a description of natural miracles, Pliny spoke of petrifications found in the river at Colossae (XXXI, 29). As these passages do not betray a particular knowledge of the city and its people, they enforce the impression that Colossae had lost all importance when Pliny collected his material.

3. Revelation 1:11 and 3:14:

Send the book to Ephesus, Smyrna ... and Laodicea. Write to the angel of the church in Laodicea; This says the Amen, the reliable and truthful martyr, the beginning of God's creation (the last phrase corresponds to Col. 1:15).

It was around A.D. 95 that John received his revelation. The seven churches of Asia to which he was asked to write included Laodicea without any reference to Colossae, which he never mentioned in his book. Certainly the epistle of John to the Laodiceans was introduced by a passage reminiscent of a passage in Paul's epistle to the Colossians (cf. the quotation above), and John may have been influenced by the latter or by Paul's simultaneous epistle to the Laodiceans (mentioned in Col. 4:16). But even so, the book of Revelation has absolutely left out the church of Colossae, and this confirms the supposition that Colossae had no importance after the catastrophe and reconstruction of Laodicea in A.D. 61 as reported by Tacitus (see above).

4. The *Sibylline Oracles*, III, 471, with reference to the emperor Nero (A.D. 54–68):

After this, Laodicea, you will be thrown headlong down, you splendid city of the Carians on the marvellous water of the Lycus.

The same *Oracles*, IV, 106:

My poor Laodicea, once an earthquake will overturn and destroy you, but you will set up a city again with broad streets.

Shorter lamentations on the catastrophe of Laodicea are found in V, 290; VII, 22; XIV, 85. In XII, 286 a similar lamentation refers to Laodicea and Hierapolis as going to be destroyed together, but nothing is said about Colossae. The fictitious prophecies found in these Jewish and partly Christian oracles, actually composed in the first Christian centuries, were based on a vague historical knowledge of the events described. It is remarkable that Colossae never interested the authors, for the references are only to Laodicea, in one case also to Hierapolis. This can be explained by the distance in time between the catastrophe and the prophecy. When the oracles were produced, Colossae had been for a long time without the importance which it had in the days of Paul, so that a proclamation of its destruction was not interesting.

5. Eusebius, *Chronicle*, ed. R. Helm, p. 183, 1.21f., concerning A.D. 62:

> In Asia (Minor) three cities were overthrown by an earthquake, namely Laodicea, Hierapolis, and Colossae.

The date given here is A.D. 62, one year later than in the report of Tacitus quoted above, and Eusebius wrote his *Chronicle* nearly two hundred years after that of Tacitus. But he used different sources, and together with the remarkable silence on Colossae found in the other documents here quoted, the explicit notice of Eusebius may be used as an argument to confirm the assumption that Colossae was destroyed simultaneously with Laodicea, according to Tacitus in A.D. 61, according to Eusebius in A.D. 62.

A series of literary documents thus indicate that Colossae had no importance during the years which followed the catastrophe of Laodicea in A.D. 61 or 62. This in turn implies that the Epistle to the Colossians must have been written before A.D. 61 or 62. If it had been written later by a disciple or a forger in the name of Paul—several experts propose a date between A.D. 80 and 100—the author would not have been so thoughtless as to address himself to a city and a church which hardly existed or had at least conveyed their importance to Laodicea some twenty or forty years earlier.

## The Church of Colossae

The church of Colossae was not founded by Paul; at least there is no indication of this in Acts or Colossians. Probably some people were converted in Colossae after the first missionary journey of Paul in the years 45–48, which did not bring Barnabas and Paul to Colossae but as far as Pisidian Antioch, 200 kilometers east of it (Acts 13:14). In this important Hellenistic center and modern Roman colony they had a great success among Jewish proselytes and Gentiles (13:43, 48), which even led to a spread of the gospel "in the whole country" (13:49). Augustus, who made efforts to develop Pisidian Antioch had improved the above-mentioned street which connected the eastern and western parts of southern Anatolia;[6] so there was an excellent connection between Pisidian Antioch, Apamea, Colossae, Laodicea, and the Meander valley. On this highway the gospel may very well have been spread

from Antioch to Colossae, when it was promulgated in the whole neighbor-
hood. It is a probability which is confirmed by the way Paul prepared the
Colossians on the visit of Mark (Col. 4:10); by introducing Mark as the
cousin of Barnabas, the apostle implied that his readers were familiar with
this leader of the Gospel campaign in Pisidian Antioch.

Several circumstances make it evident that Paul had come to Colossae and
the other cities of the Lycus valley in connection with his third missionary
journey *c*. A.D. 55:

1. One reason is the itinerary displayed by Luke in two separate passages. After visiting Galatia and Phrygia (Acts 18:23), the apostle was said
to have passed "the upper parts" or the inland regions before coming to
Ephesus (19:1). Luke reported this in order to illustrate the background
of Paul's extensive activity in Ephesus, a topic which dominates the whole
context (18:24–27; 19:1–40). From the horizon of Ephesus, "Phrygia" and
"the inland regions" were in the first instance understood as the Lycus and
Meander valleys accessible by that Augustean highway which came from Pisidian Antioch, Apamea, Colossae, and Laodicea. And when Luke recalled
a journey of the apostle through Galatia and Phrygia in this general manner
and without specific details, he probably indicated a visit to groups of believers already existing. Since the oldest traces of Christians in Phrygia are
found exactly in the New Testament letters supposed to be read by people in
Colossae, Laodicea and Hierapolis (Phm. 1–2; Col. 1:2; 4:13, 16; Rev. 1:11;
3:14), it must be assumed that Paul visited these cities on his third journey.

2. Furthermore, the letters to Philemon and the Colossians imply that
Paul had older connections with Colossae and Laodicea. In the first instance
there were his friend Philemon, who had been converted by the apostle (Phm.
19), and his fellow-worker Epaphras, who came to visit Paul in his captivity
(Col. 1:8; 4:12). There were also people like Nympha, who led a house
community in Laodicea (Col. 4:15), and Archippus, who had just taken
over some ministry in Colossae (Phm. 2; Col. 4:17). It is not impossible that
Paul had met them in other contexts, but it seems most likely that he knew
them from a visit to Colossae and Laodicea.

3. Beside these individual acquaintances one has to consider the general
affection of the Colossians toward Paul of which Epaphras had informed
him (Col. 1:8), as well as the present exertions of Paul for the sake of the
churches in Colossae, Laodicea, and Hierapolis of which he assured them
(2:1), and his additional greetings to the brethren in Laodicea, including
Nympha (Col. 4:15).

Paul had not met every member of these churches, for his admonitions
were also extended to neophytes in Colossae and Laodicea who had never
seen his face (Col. 2:1) but mainly been converted and instructed by Epa-

phras (1:7). Nevertheless the numerous indications of personal relationships to Paul found in Philemon and Colossians imply that leading and older elements of the churches in question knew the apostle from an earlier stay among them. There is no reason to regard this implication as literary fiction, and it corresponds to what Acts can tell us about Paul's third journey.

## The Recipients and the Setting

In the Letter to Philemon and the Epistle to the Colossians the persons mentioned and the situation presupposed are practically the same. Both writings present themselves as written or rather dictated (Col. 4:18) by Paul in captivity (Phm. 1, 10, 13, 23; Col. 1:24; 4:18). They were sent to friends of his in Colossae, which is also true of Philemon because Archippus and Onesimus were at home there (Phm. 2, 10; Col. 4:9, 16). The task of bringing Onesimus to Colossae (Phm. 12; Col. 4:9), and with him the letters to Philemon and the Colossians, was given to Paul's friend Tychicus (Col. 4:7–8), a Christian from Asia (Acts 20:4). Greetings were conveyed from and to nearly the same persons in both letters, but their names were by no means given in the same order so that any hypothesis of dependence can be plausible (Phm. 1–2, 23–24; Col. 1:7; 4:7–19). In particular, the fact that Epaphras of Colossae appears in both writings, though in different contexts (Phm. 23; Col. 1:7; 4:9), is a remarkable evidence of a common background. Philemon and Colossians contain numerous indications of having been created as parallels, dictated and delivered at the same time, with the inclusion of the same persons in a coherent situation. This complex of relations cannot be understood as the result of artificial imitation.

With regard to such names included and the situation presupposed, two other captivity epistles may be compared with Philemon and Colossians, namely Ephesians and Second Timothy (the latter being called so without any chronological subordination to First Timothy). Here the author is said to be Paul while still in prison (Eph. 1:1; 3:1; 4:1; 2 Tim. 1:1, 8; 2:9), whereas Timothy no longer appears together with Paul as sender. In the situation presupposed by Ephesians, Timothy seems to have left for some other place, and the state of things presupposed by Second Timothy implies that he was active somewhere near Troas in Mysia northwest of Ephesus (2 Tim. 4:13), where Paul had preached when he returned from this third journey (Acts 20:4–12). The list of names found in Ephesians and Second Timothy is also comparable with that of Philemon and Colossians, and not even here can a deliberate imitation be made probable. Demas, Luke, and Mark are named by three of the letters in different contexts (Phm. 24; Col. 4:10, 14; 2 Tim. 4:10–11). And whereas Tychicus was supposed to deliver the letters to Philemon, to the Colossians, and to the Ephesians in the hands of their recipients (Tychicus is mentioned in Col. 4:7 together with Onesimus who is the subject of Phm., and alone in Eph. 6:21), the letter called Second Timothy referred back to his visit to Ephesus (2 Tim. 4:12). The actual situation of these disciples can be restored on the basis of the details and the picture is coherent with that found in Philemon and Colossians.

Although the literary background of Ephesians and Second Timothy is a much debated problem, the biographical material they contain, whether primary or not, has to be studied in connection with Philemon and Colossians, to which Ephesians and Second Timothy bring additional information.

Philippians will not be considered here, for it does not represent the same list of names[7]—not even the similarity between the names of Epaphras and Epaphroditus is an exception, as the former was from Colossae (Phm. 23; Col. 1:7; 4:12), the latter from Philippi (Phil. 2:25; 4:18). This fact, together with the different character of the captivity presupposed, proves that Philippians belongs to another context.[8]

The first question will be what Philemon and Colossians have to say about the situation of Paul and his friends while Timothy was still together with the apostle (Phm. 1; Col. 1:1), and the second question will be what Ephesians and Second Timothy want to say about the situation when Paul had let Timothy leave for Mysia (Eph. 1:1; 2 Tim. 1:1; 4:13).

1. Fundamental is the information given by the letter to Philemon, which is generally regarded as Paul's personal writing. Attention has to be drawn to Philemon 9b:1[9] "I appeal to you, being myself like the old Paul, but now also the prisoner of Christ Jesus." Because of the expression "now also" there is no doubt that Paul had quite recently been arrested, so that his captivity meant a new situation to him. According to earlier statements (2 Cor. 6:5; 11:23; Rom. 16:7) he had not seldom been in jail (*phylakē*), but in these cases he referred to shorter arrests like the one in Philippi (Acts 16:23–26). The captivity mentioned in Philemon and the other epistles was no temporary experience only but a state of things expected to be of long duration, though it had just begun. Earlier the apostle had been occasionally in jail, but not permanently in chains for the sake of Christ. Now he knew that he was a prisoner in chains (*désmios*), and even felt proud of it (Phm. 9, "now also"; Col. 1:24, "I rejoice in my sufferings").

Philemon and Colossians had often been connected with the persecution arranged by the silversmiths of Ephesus in A.D. 56 (Acts 19:23–40a), but this attack ended within a short time and without any imprisonment (19:40b—20:1). The apostle called it a fight with animals in a figurative sense (1 Cor. 15:32; *katà ánthropon*, "on a human level"). It is pure imagination to speak of any captivity in Ephesus.

The only period of Paul's life when he was laid in chains for any longer time was his public arrest in Jerusalem and Caesarea from A.D. 58 to 60 (Acts 21:37–26:32), continued by his private arrest in Rome from 60 to 62 (Acts 28:16–31). It was only at Caesarea that he was able to announce that he was "now also a prisoner of Christ Jesus" (Phm. 9). The captivity referred to in Philemon must have been that in Caesarea, and the same observation is applicable to Colossians.[10] A necessary conclusion is that Philemon and Colossians were sent from Caesarea to Colossae *c.* A.D. 59.[11]

From this captivity Paul let his disciple Tychicus go to Colossae with Onesimus and the writings to Philemon and the Christians there (Col. 4:7–9). Tychicus had been among the numerous collaborators from Macedonia and Asia who followed Paul when he, like a victor, returned from his collection journey and came to Jerusalem at Pentecost in A.D. 58 (Acts 20:4f., 16). It was the presence of these Hellenists in Jerusalem that irritated the Jews from Asia who had seen Trophimus from Ephesus, the compatriot of Tychicus (Acts 20:4), in the city and said that Paul had brought Gentiles into the Temple so that he ought to be killed (21:28f.; 24:19). The background of Paul's captivity in Caesarea was this Jewish zeal against his connections with Hellenists, and he also referred to it when speaking of his troubles for the sake of the churches in Colossae and Laodicea (Col. 1:24; 2:1). When he was in prison at Caesarea, some of the disciples from Macedonia and Asia were still with him. This is evident from the fact that Aristarchus of Thessalonica accompanied Paul on his return to Jerusalem (Acts 20:4), then was in prison together with Paul (Phm. 24; Col. 4:10), and followed him on the ship which brought the apostle to Rome (Acts 27:2). Among the disciples who surrounded Paul, according to Philemon and Colossians, there were several people from Asia, in the first instance Timothy and Tychicus (Phm. 1; Col. 1:1; 4:7), who had followed him already when he left Macedonia and Asia (Acts 20:4); in the second instance Epaphras and Onesimus who had come later from Colossae to join him (Phm. 10, 23; Col. 1:7f; 4:12f.), which they could do as pedestrians if they wanted to see Paul in Caesarea. The task of delivering the letters to Philemon and the Colossians in Colossae was given to Tychicus in this situation at Caesarea *c.* A.D. 59 (Col. 4:7f), and he was at the same time made responsible for the return of Onesimus to his master Philemon (4:9).

2. When he wrote Colossians, Paul was also planning some further journeys of Tychicus, Timothy, and Mark which are reflected in Ephesians and Second Timothy. If these captivity epistles are studied together with Colossians and without any dogmatic theories about their authenticity, a picture of the different journeys emerges which is historically consistent.[12]

Tychicus was not only supposed to deliver the writings to Philemon and the Colossians in the hands of their readers. It is also probable that he was sent away with that no longer extant epistle which Paul wanted to be read in Laodicea and then in Colossae (mentioned in Col. 4:16). After this Tychicus was obviously supposed to extend his journey to Ephesus in order to present the believers with the epistle known to us as Ephesians (Eph. 6:21). It is uncertain whether this epistle was only written for the Ephesians, since in the introduction some manuscripts do not include the words "in Ephesus."[13] However, the words at issue are found in most documents and Tychicus was probably at home in Ephesus like his countryman Trophimus (Acts 20:4; 21:29). For these reasons, the epistle seems to have been mainly referred to Ephesus, and the sending of Tychicus to Ephesus is also mentioned in the next captivity epistle (2 Tim. 4:12). Although the letter called Ephesians may have been written for baptismal gatherings of different churches in Asia, its ultimate relation to Ephesus is confirmed by Second Timothy. One and the same journey of Tychicus is thus reflected by the four captivity epistles in question, implying that he started from Caesarea *c.* A.D. 59, then passed through Colossae, Laodicea, and the Meander valley and came to Ephesus, where he was known by many.

Timothy was not mentioned in the writing to Ephesus, so he seems to have left Caesarea before Paul sent Tychicus with this epistle. According to Second Timothy, Paul had in the meantime sent Timothy to Mysia in northwestern Asia Minor, where he was supposed to reestablish Paul's and his own connections with the church in Troas (Acts 20:4–12; 2 Tim. 4:13). The silence of Ephesians with regard to Timothy is thus explained in the same natural way.

In his writing to the Colossians, Paul also prepared the readers for a visit of his friend Mark (Col. 4:10). Second Timothy shows what his intention was: Mark was sent to Colossae and further westwards in order to bring the epistle called Second Timothy to Paul's delegate Timothy in Mysia, and Paul wanted the latter to return with Mark before the winter began (2 Tim. 4:9, 11, 21). The names and places quoted in Second Timothy reflect this journey of Mark from Caesarea, through Lyconia and Phrygia to Mysia in northwestern Asia Minor. One should not be misled by the reference to Rome from whence Paul's friend Onesiphorus had come to visit him (2 Tim. 1:17). All other names and places mentioned in Second Timothy are in harmony with that intention of his to send Mark from Caesarea to Colossae and further on, as indicated by Colossians.[14] Since the visit of Mark in Colossae was announced in an epistle written at Caesarea around A.D. 59, and since Second Timothy implied that Mark should meet Timothy in Mysia, where he was asked to fetch the cloak and the books left by Paul at Troas in A.D. 58 (Acts 20:6; 2 Tim. 4:13), and then return with Mark to Paul before the winter, the situation presupposed by the epistle called Second Timothy indicates an origin in the autumn of the same or the following year, c. A.D. 59 or 60.

The reason why reflections of Mark's itinerary are found in Second Timothy is that Paul or his amanuensis, perhaps Luke (2 Tim. 4:11),[15] wanted this epistle to be read in each church which Mark visited on his way to Timothy. Every believer should have a chance to be comforted and strengthened by the admonitions of Paul addressed to his friend Timothy.

Because of this public character of the epistle, a reference to the belief found in Timothy's mother and grandmother was inserted (2 Tim. 1:5), for they lived in the city of Derbe (Acts 16:1), through which Mark had to pass on his way from Caesarea to Colossae (Col. 4:10). For the same reason the Christians, to whom Mark would come in other cities of Lyconia, were reminded of Paul's earlier troubles in Antioch, Iconium, and Lystra (2 Tim. 3:11). After the visit to Colossae (Col. 4:10), Mark was expected to make the Christians of Ephesus familiar with the epistle to Timothy. He should especially let the house of Onesiphorus know about Paul's appreciation of this man (2 Tim. 1:16–18; 4:19) and make sure that people in Asia realized the danger of the new heresy (1:15; 2:16–3:9). After this it was planned that Mark should meet Timothy in Mysia (4:11) and go back with him via Troas (4:13). Paul needed their help since his only collaborator was presently Luke (4:11). Among the other friends who had left him, Paul mentioned Demas and Tychicus (4:9, 12), and they were, besides Luke, exactly the men who had been with Paul when he wrote the previous captivity epistles (Phm. 24; Col. 4:7, 14). Thus the itinerary and the list of names found in Second Timothy correspond to what Colossians and the other relevant documents tell about Paul's activity during an imprisonment that must be referred to Caesarea and the years 58–60. It is questionable whether any member of the early church would have found it worthwhile to restore or construct such antiquities in a later situation.

The four relevant captivity epistles, Philemon and Colossians, Ephesians and Second Timothy, were meant to be read by Christians in Phrygia and Asia. With the exception of Philemon which had only a private character their vocabulary and theology were adapted to audiences living in these countries. Therefore their style took over elements of Asianist rhetoric, whereas their message was formed out in opposition to Jewish, Gnostic, and other tendencies found in the environment of the readers. Such aspects must also be considered when the historical setting of Colossians is to be established. Nevertheless, a historical orientation should not start with stylistic and theological combinations, but with an objective analysis of names involved and events alluded to. This was the intention of the present study.[16]

# Caesarea, Rome,
# and the Captivity Epistles

*Translated by Manfred Kwiran and W. Ward Gasque*

Students of the history of the New Testament literature should not assume *a priori* that Paul's imprisonment presupposed by Philemon, Colossians, Ephesians, and Philippians refers to the same location. When the Book of Acts reports an imprisonment in Caesarea (*c.* A.D. 58–60) and in Rome (*c.* 60–62), the possibility that Philemon, Colossians, and Ephesians—whether "genuine" or not—may presuppose one location, and Philippians a different one, must be considered.

In point of fact, references contained in the two groups of letters which convey information concerning the sender and recipients are quite different. The assumption that we are dealing with two different situations is, therefore, not unwarranted.

## I

Certainly, as far as personalia are concerned, Philemon, Colossians, and Ephesians[1] form a group by themselves. The popular question concerning the Pauline or non-Pauline origin and contents of Colossians and Ephesians in no way influences this factor. We have as a starting-point the "genuineness" of Philemon, a fact which is recognized by contemporary scholarship in general. Whether Colossians and Ephesians are regarded as having been written by Paul or are believed to be forgeries, it is in any case necessary to find out what these related epistles tell us about the situation of the apostle, his fellow workers, and the correspondents. It is also noteworthy that Philemon and Colossians show no literary dependence on one another, and yet they contain similar personal references. Greetings are sent from practically the same people (Phm. 23; Col. 1:7; 4:12–19), and they were to be delivered

First published with the same title in *Apostolic History and the Gospel. Biblical and Historical Essays presented to F. F. Bruce on his 60th Birthday,* ed. W. W. Gasque and R. P. Martin (Exeter: Paternoster, 1970), 277–86; reprinted by permission.

(evidently at the same time) to the recipients by one Tychicus, who is accompanied by Onesimus (Phm. 2, 12; Col. 4:7–9). Ephesians, which is closely related to Colossians (regardless of the question whether it was written by Paul or by one of his disciples), also assumes that Tychicus was to bring this epistle (Eph. 6:21ff.) to his fellow countrymen in the province of Asia (Acts 20:4). Since this Tychicus can be assumed to be an Ephesian (after the analogy of his companion, Trophimus, in Acts 21:29), the readers who know him are to be sought first in Ephesus (so Eph. 1:1, majority reading). These references concerning the situation of the epistles, even if the situation was for some unknown reason invented, indicate that Tychicus first came to the Lycus River valley with the letters to Philemon and the Colossians and then went on to Ephesus through the Meander valley with the Ephesian letter (cf. 2 Tim. 4:12); or, alternatively, one could imagine the same route in reverse, depending on whether the letters originated in Caesarea or in Rome. At any rate, one has here a natural, uniform and straightforward description of the situation. Furthermore, the personal as well as the topographical circumstances clearly bind the three letters together; even on the assumption that Colossians and Ephesians are spurious, it would be necessary to take notice of the description of the situation.

On the other hand, Philippians[2] stands by itself. The only thing this epistle has in common with the others is the cooperation of Timothy (Phm. 1; Col. 1:1; Phil. 1:1). All the rest of the personalia are different. Epaphras and Epaphroditus are not to be identified: the former is in Colossae, while the latter is at home in Philippi. The suggestion that the prison epistles of Asia Minor and the epistle to the Philippians could have been dispatched in connexion with one another is made difficult by the geographical situation. In fact, however, there is no reason to assume that these three epistles were written during the same imprisonment of the apostle as Philippians. On the contrary, the differences between the two groups of letters suggest different occasions.[3]

# II

First, the background of Philemon, Colossians, and Ephesians needs to be discussed. (The conclusion that only Caesarea fits the references in question may be mentioned at the start.)

Since the beginning of the present century, a number of authors have held the view that Ephesus was the place of origin for the prison epistles, even though the New Testament contains not the slightest reference to any such imprisonment for Paul. Paul mentions repeated arrests (2 Cor. 6:5; 11:23; Rom. 16:7), but he does not locate any of these in Ephesus. Luke gives the exact opposite impression: he tells how (*c.* A.D. 56) the uproar of the silversmiths (Acts 19:23–34) was stopped by the officials (19:35–40; 21:1). Paul recalls the same dreadful encounter in 1 Corinthians 15:32 (*etheriomachesa*: to be understood figuratively; a real fight with animals would have left other traces in literature). The hypothetical imprisonment in Ephesus is conceivable as the occasion for the "Epistle to the Ephesians" only on the basis of the assumption that the epistle was a circular letter (since "in Ephesus" is omitted from some manuscripts); but the strong reading includes the words "in Ephesus." In the case of Philemon and Colossians, as well as Philippians, the theory of an Ephesian imprisonment is saddled with contradictions to the narrative of Acts. These three letters refer to Timothy as co-sender (Phlm. 1; Col. 1:1; Phil. 1:1); however, shortly prior to the riot in Ephesus, Timothy was to have gone to Macedonia (Acts 19:22). Mark and Luke are near the imprisoned Paul (Phm. 24; Col. 4:10, 14); yet Mark had not accompanied Paul to Asia Minor; and Luke, insofar as the "we"- references of Acts say anything about him, makes no mention of the arrest in Ephesus and was not there at that time. Thus the theory of an Ephesian imprisonment can neither be substantiated by any New Testament references, nor can it be brought into harmony with such.

On the other hand, the imprisonment of Paul in Caesarea at about A.D. 58–60 (Acts 23:33–26:32) fits quite well as background for the prison epistles addressed to Asia Minor.

As far as chronology is concerned, what Paul tells Philemon in Colossae about his situation (Phm. 9b) is extremely important: "I, Paul, [appeal to you] by the fact that I am such an old man, and now also a prisoner for Christ Jesus." According to the context (v. 8) Paul believes that he could claim his authority as an apostle. But he appeals rather to the sympathy of Philemon (*agape,* 7, 9a) and simply presents the following petition on behalf of Onesimus as an older man (*presbutes,* one who is over fifty years of age), and as a prisoner. There is no doubt that the wording "*now* also a prisoner" indicates that Paul has been arrested only shortly before, and that he considers his imprisonment to be a new situation and an honour. This fits only an imprisonment in Jerusalem and Caesarea (*c.* A.D. 58–60). Therefore, in the case of Philemon an ideal possibility of dating and locating the origin of the letter has been suggested: Paul wrote the epistle most probably at *c.* A.D. 59 in Caesarea.

In the case of Colossians and Ephesians, many experts are again concerned with the question of authenticity; it is doubted whether the theology and ecclesiology of these epistles make such an early date possible. However, one should also be critical enough to see the questionable nature of all systematized explanations concerning the stages of doctrinal development.

In the religious world development does not run in one continuous line, but the thoughts flow rather differently according to the nature of the soil. On the personal and topographical level, Philemon, Colossians, and Ephesians demonstrate such complete agreement that they appear either to have originated in the same connexion or are the work of an editor who surreptitiously attempts to give the impression that they were written at the same time. In the latter case it would be useful to know how it occurred to later forgers to make use of some of the older names and dates contained in the brief letter to Philemon in order to legitimize Colossians or Ephesians, even when it must have been obvious to such forgers that the introduction of current problems and circumstances would have been more profitable than the search for such antiquities. This much is clear: the statements in Colossians and Ephesians agree with those of Philemon and indicate an origin at the same time, *viz.* A.D. 59 in Caesarea. Either rigid conceptions concerning the development of theology must be modified, or the present correspondence of personalia in the three letters have been deliberate.

On the geographical side, the simplest picture of the trips which are mentioned or presupposed is gained by assuming that the three epistles originated in Caesarea. Paul is accompanied by several Hellenistic Christians (Phm. 23f.; Col. 1:7; 4:7–14). According to Luke, such Hellenistic-Jewish and Greek followers were present at Paul's return from the collection journey prior to Pentecost in A.D. 58 (Acts 20:16) and were the occasion (unjustly, according to Luke) for the tumultuous attack on Paul in Jerusalem (20:4; 21:28f.; 24:19). Three persons who are mentioned in these epistles have a part in the account of this journey in Acts: Tychicus, Aristarchus, and Luke (the latter is included on the assumption that the "we"—passages include him [Acts 20:5, etc.]). It is possible that Tychicus, as well as his fellow countryman Trophimus, followed Paul to Jerusalem (Acts 21:29) and then also to Caesarea; however, he is no longer listed among the companions of Paul on his trip to Rome. The assumption that Tychicus, starting out on his trip from Caesarea, was to deliver the three letters to Asia (two to Colossae, one to Ephesus) leads to an uncomplicated and satisfying picture of the circumstances behind the sending of the letters. Moreover, Aristarchus conveys a greeting (Phm. 24) as a fellow prisoner of Paul (Col. 4:10) and as such takes part in the journey to Rome (Acts 27:2). Luke gives a similar greeting (Phm. 24; Col. 4:14) and the "we"-passages seem to indicate that he took part in the trip to Rome as well. It is possible to interpret these greetings from Aristarchus and Luke as coming either from Caesarea or from Rome; however, the numerous other names in the table of greetings encourages one to favour Caesarea as the place of origin, and it seems improbable that so many disciples of Paul shared his voyage by ship to Rome.

Epaphras (Phm. 23), who had recently arrived from Colossae (Col. 1:7f; 4:12), is among the other of Paul's fellow prisoners who send greetings. One can easily imagine him among the other Hellenistic companions of the apostle (some of whom were arrested in Palestine). Against the suggestion of his participation in Paul's trip to Rome is the fact that there is no evidence to suggest this; in addition, an arrest in Rome would not fit the description which Acts gives concerning the mild treatment which Paul received there. Furthermore, the geographical circumstances allow for the assumption that the runaway slave, Onesimus of Colossae, had come to Palestine on foot, had asked for Paul's protection in Caesarea, and was sent back to Colossae with Tychicus (Phm. 12; Col. 4:7-9), again on foot. It is more difficult to imagine that this young slave journeyed to Rome by sea and then back again. In addition to providing a simpler explanation of the geographical data, the presence of the group of Hellenistic Christians, to whom attention has already been drawn, with Paul on his trip to Palestine following his third missionary journey may have prepared the way psychologically for Onesimus to confide in Paul.

It was especially during his imprisonment in Caesarea that Paul could have expected that he would be sent across Asia on his way to Rome, and thus he would be able to visit Colossae (Phm. 2). He might then go from Ephesus to Italy and eventually, having been acquitted, reach Spain (Rom. 15:3f., 28). If, on the other hand, he wrote the three epistles in Rome, then the plans for a trip to Spain have to be dismissed as having been no more than a passing thought. However, in Rome, Paul would not have set his eyes on little Colossae as goal for a trip following the journey to Spain.

Politically oriented concepts in Ephesians suggest that Caesarea fits best as the background for this letter (whether it was written by Paul or by a disciple). While in Jerusalem in A.D. 58, Paul himself experienced the animosity which the majority of the people there had for Greeks. The occasion was the claim that he had brought Greeks into the sanctuary (Acts 21:28f.).[4] On the wall between the court of the Gentiles and the court of the women, where the so-called Holy Place started,[5] there were inscriptions containing restrictions which encouraged the division of mankind into Gentiles and Jews. A transgression of this line of demarcation by the uncircumcised meant the death penalty for the transgressor (Josephus, *Bell.* V.193f.; *Ant.* XV.417). Fragments of these inscriptions are today located in Istanbul and Jerusalem.[6]

Paul was taken in protective custody to Caesarea, to keep him safe from the Zealots and their hatred of foreigners. There the oral accusations of the Sanhedrin were brought forward (Acts 24:1-9). According to Josephus, at this particular time the animosity between Jews and Gentiles was even worse in Caesarea than in Jerusalem. Greeks (according to Josephus, they were Syrians) and Jews threw stones at one another. Each party denied the other the right of citizenship (*isopoliteia*). The street battles spread even to Jerusalem after a new high priest by the name of Ishmael ben Phabi had come to power (in A.D. 59). The two parties in Caesarea appealed to the emperor; and, as one would expect, Burrus and Nero (in A.D. 61) declared the Greeks to be lawful citizens in Caesarea (Josephus, *Ant.* XX. 173–84). Similar riots in the year 66 in Caesarea ignited the Jewish War (Josephus, *Bell.* I. 284–92). During his imprisonment in Caesarea (A.D. 58–60) Paul would have had special reason to think about (a) the dividing wall in Jerusalem, (b) the animosity between Jews and Greeks, and (c) the disputation concerning the right of citizenship. It is no accident, therefore, that these topics of political concern influence the theological language of Ephesians: Paul speaks of (a) the ethnic dividing wall (Eph 2:14 b), which has been removed in Christ, and the new temple (2:20); (b) the animosity between Jews and Gentiles (2:14c, 16b; cf. Col. 1:21), which has been changed into peace through Christ (2:15b, 17); (c) the divine citizenship (2:19), which in Christ belongs also to the Gentiles (3:6), as well as the fact that every nationality (*patria*) on earth has its origin in God the Father (3:15; cf. Col. 3:11). These politically oriented terms in Ephesians fit the situation of Paul in Caesarea so exactly that this city alone is suitable as a background for the epistle. This would be true regardless of whether the epistle was written by Paul or by one or his co-workers. (If the epistle is a forgery, then the author had unusually accurate information to hand.) The reason that such political images are found useful in the case of Ephesians, but not so much in the case of Colossians, is due to the situation of the readers in Asia: In Ephesus, municipal citizenship had been granted to the Jews,[7] while in Colossae this privilege was not of immediate interest.

## III

Other factors need to be considered in the attempt to locate the Pauline imprisonment lying behind the Philippian letter (cf. the reference to "chains," Phil. 1:7, 13, 14, 17).

The specific references in the epistle point toward Rome and thus to the years *c.* A.D. 60–62 (Acts 28:16, 30), as it was generally assumed by the older criticism. It will be made clear by what follows that the attempts to locate the place of origin of this epistle in other places rest on unwarranted conclusions and partly on historical misinterpretations.

The total lack of evidence for a Pauline imprisonment in Ephesus speaks against this theory (cf. above). Some have interpreted the expression, "praetorium" (Phil. 1:13) as referring to the residence of the governor (as in the gospels). Paul states that his imprisonment is now common knowledge "to the entire praetorium and all the others." Here he thinks of a body of people and other individuals, not an official residence. At any rate, the word was not used for the personnel of a governor either in Greek or in Latin;[8] it is also noteworthy that the governor of Ephesus was not a propraetor, but rather a proconsul. Thus the use of the word "praetorium" in Philippians for a group of persons can only mean the imperial bodyguard which is designated by this loan-word from Latin in several Greek inscriptions (cf., among others, L. Huezey and H. Daumet, *Mission archéologique* [1876], Nr. 130–131; *Inscriptiones graecae* 14 [1890], Nr. 911; W. Dittenberger, *Orientis graeci inscriptiones* 2 [1905], Nr. 707); the term in Latin was the normal expression for the well-known guard (Pliny, *Hist.* XXV, 6:17; Suetonius, *Ner.* IX:2; Tacitus, *Hist.* 1:20, etc.).

Tiberius had placed this elite guard near the Porta Nomentana in Rome. During the first Christian centuries these praetorian cohorts remained stationed in the metropolis, although at times sections of the guard accompanied the emperor into the field of action. Inscriptions found in other areas (as already mentioned) deal only with some veterans who previously had been praetorians. Representatives of the Ephesus theory believe, erroneously, that a few inscriptions found near a road close to Ephesus suggest that a local detachment of the imperial body was located there (*CIL*, 6085, 7135, and 7136). In fact, however, these inscriptions deal with a retired praetorian who after his service with the guard was assigned the position of gendarme (*stationarius*) on that highway. One can hardly create an entire force out of one policeman! The active praetorians had the responsibility of protecting the emperor and the capital city; the deployment of the group throughout the provinces during Paul's time would have been impossible militarily. Besides this, Asia was a senatorial province and was therefore ruled by civil authority; for this reason, no troops were stationed there.

The conclusion that the praetorium is to be understood as a body of persons also rules out Caesarea as the place of origin of Philippians. Auxiliary troops under the supervision of the procurator were stationed here, but none of the elite soldiers of the praetorium. Since the details of Philemon, Colossians, and Ephesians which have been discussed earlier in the present essay point to Caesarea, the very different statements of Philippians appear to suggest another locality. Only Rome, therefore, is entirely suitable as the location for the writing of Philippians.

As far as matters of chronology are concerned, it is to be observed that Paul no longer refers to his imprisonment as a new condition (as in Phm. 9). He no longer speaks emphatically concerning his sufferings as a prisoner in chains (Phm. 1, 9f., 13; Col. 1:24; 4:18; Eph. 3:1, 13; 4:1; 6:20), but only makes vague references to "chains" (Phil. 1:7, 13f., 17) in the sense of a limitation of his freedom. Furthermore, Paul no longer speaks of fellow prisoners (cf. Phm. 23; Col. 4:10), but only of fellow workers whom he is able to meet and send out at will (Phil. 2:19, 25, 28; 4:18). He is able to thank the recipients for sending a contribution for his support (2:25, 30; 4:10–18). This fits Paul's situation in Rome exactly. Here he was permitted to live in a rented room under the surveillance of a guard (Acts 28:16, 23, 30). In Philippians the apostle speaks of his legal standing (*ta kat' eme*, Col. 4:7; Eph. 6:21; Phil. 1:12) in an entirely new way: his defence of the gospel (Phil. 1:7, 16) has been effective (1:12), and he hopes that the legal procedures will soon be over (1:19–26; 2:24).

In terms of geography, the distance between Rome and Philippi causes no difficulty, even though some scholars consider it a problem because of the number of trips which are presupposed by the letter. Granted, the distance is about twice as long as the one between Ephesus and Philippi; but it is not as far as the one from Caesarea to the recipients. Moreover, the epistle presupposes only two journeys: (1) Epaphroditus has come from Philippi with a contribution for Paul (Phil. 4:18); and (2) a companion has reported to the people in Philippi concerning an illness which befell their envoy (Phil. 2:26, 30). Paul did not have to wait for confirmation of their having received this news, but rather counted on the speedy circulation of such news by faithful brethren. Neither did he wait for the return of Epaphroditus to Philippi before he wrote the epistle, but, rather, he had Epaphroditus take the completed letter along with him (2:25). Only a few months would be needed for Epaphroditus to make the journey, with the contribution from Philippi, to Rome and for Paul to send information to the Philippians by a companion. Good connections between Philippi and Rome existed in the Via Egnatia and the Via Appia. If the weather was not wholly unfavourable, a ship could make the passage from Greece to Italy in about a week (Pliny, *Hist.* XIX. 19:3f. speaks of the stretch between Puteoli and Corinth as a record of five days and thereby gives us a picture of the possibilities).[9] Since Paul lived for two whole years in his rented room in Rome (Acts 28:30), there was ample time for the trips referred to in Philippians. The trip to Spain (Rom. 15:24, 28), which has been mentioned previously, is not in contradiction to his intended visit to Philippi (Phil. 1:26), if one locates the Epistle to the Philippians in Rome, since in the capital it would have been possible for Paul to think of a journey to the West and then hope for a new visit to the East, where Philippi was an important centre.

It is of primary political importance that Philippi was a Roman colony settled by veterans (Acts 16:13). For those who had full privileges of citizenship in Philippi, military hierarchy and Roman citizenship were fundamental concepts of life. For this reason, it would also have been of interest to Paul to refer to the praetorium in the sense of the imperial bodyguard (Phil. 1:13). In Philippi, his readers knew Roman veterans, and the Roman praetorium was to them very well-known. This fact bolsters the apostle's report that practically the entire guard and others have come to realize that his imprisonment is the result of his proclamation of the gospel. Of course, Paul did not make a careful investigation in order to determine whether or not all the praetorians knew him; but he had the impression that in the barracks they spoke of him in a generally positive way.

A politically accused prisoner like Paul was guarded by a soldier (Acts 28:16) who was of the barracks of the praetorians. Josephus verifies this in his account of the arrest of Agrippa in Rome (*Ant.* XVIII.186–204). Of the two prefects of the bodyguard, one of them was responsible for the guarding of this kind of prisoner. During the Roman imprisonment of Paul and up to the year A.D. 62, the clever politician, Burrus, alone held this honour. Tacitus reports incidents at which Burrus used his guards as policemen, at times in opposition to Nero's cruel intentions (Tacitus, *Ann.* XIII. 48; XIV. 7–10; etc.). A prisoner who was accused of a foreign teaching could, occasionally, arouse the sympathy of the praetorian prefect. This, in fact, did occur between the oriental philosopher, Apollonius of Tyana, and the prefect, Aelianus (Philostratus, *Life of Apoll.* VII. 16–28). Although the account is highly imaginative, the dialogue between the philosopher and the prefect can clarify how the apostle was led to his optimistic report concerning the entire praetorium. Because of his discussions with the praetorians, he was convinced that the religious reason for his accusation was now known to the entire bodyguard.[10]

The Roman capital also provides the background for those images used by Paul in Philippians which refer to the political realm. This is true in the case of the exhortation to a worthy evangelical behaviour as a citizen (*politeuesthe*, Phil. 1:27), as well as of the reference concerning the true, heavenly commonwealth (*politeuma*, 3:20).

It was impossible for the readers to misunderstand the reference to Rome and Nero's clients in the greeting from "those *of Caesar's household*" (Phil. 4:22). Clients and servants of the emperor lived in several places, but primarily in Rome. Here there also existed a Jewish synagogue of the Augustenses, the imperial freedmen (J. Frey, *Corpus inscriptionum judaicarum* I [Rome, 1936], p. LXXIIIf.); and it was here also that Poppaea, in the year 62, protected the interests of the Jewish community (Josephus, *Ant.* XX.195; *Vit.* 16). It is not surprising that the Christian proclamation found at that time a hearing in the imperial court with the imperial clients. Paul is happy to be able to extend greetings from clients of the imperial house to the readers in Philippi. This fine point is lost if one does not accept Rome as the place where Paul had such success in important circles (Phil. 1:12) and from where he writes to encourage the Philippian Christians to share in his joy (2:18, etc.).

# *Appendix 1*

# Synopsis of
# the Pauline Chronology

*This synopsis by the editors presents the results of the conclusions reached for each of the individual letters.*

*Early Palestinian Jewish–Jewish Christian Tension*

1. 2 Thessalonians (A.D. 52, summer)

2. 1 Thessalonians (A.D. 52/53)

*Rising Zealotism*

3. Galatians (A.D. 55)

4. 1 Corinthians (A.D. 56, spring)

5. 1 Timothy (A.D. 56, summer/fall)

6. 2 Corinthians (A.D. 57, summer)

7. Romans (A.D. 58, early)

8. Titus (A.D. 58)

*Paul's Captivity*

9. Philemon (A.D. 59)

10. Colossians (A.D. 59)

11. Ephesians (A.D. 59)

12. 2 Timothy (A.D. 60)

13. Philippians (A.D. 61/62)

*Appendix 2*

# A Biographical Sketch of Bo Reicke

Bo Ivar Reicke was born July 31, 1914, in Stockholm, Sweden, son of the furniture merchant Ivar Reicke and his wife, Esther, née Danielsson. He attended school in Stockholm, completing "gymnasium" (high school) in 1933. After compulsory military service, he entered the Faculty of Arts of the University of Stockholm in September of 1933 and transferred two years later to the Faculty of Arts of the University of Uppsala. He graduated from there in 1937 with a B.A. in the History of Religions, Classical Greek, and Philosophy.

In 1938 he matriculated in the Faculty of Theology of the University of Uppsala, completing the B.D. in 1941 and, subsequently, a one-semester course in Practical Theology. He was ordained a minister of the Lutheran Church of Sweden in December of 1941.

The year 1942 saw the beginning of his studies leading to the Doctor of Theology degree. In May of 1946 his dissertation was published, and he successfully performed the public defense ("The Spirits in Prison and the Descent into Hell: A Study of I Pet. 3.19 [Copenhagen: Munksgaard, 1946]). For his thesis and its defense, Reicke was awarded a teaching position in the Faculty of Theology, University of Uppsala; he taught there from September of 1946 to June of 1953.

In 1953 Reicke was invited to fill the Chair of New Testament of the University of Basel, Switzerland. He taught in that position from October of 1953 until his retirement in July of 1984. During his tenure there, Reicke served as "Doctoral Father," or doctoral supervisor, for more than forty international students, more than half of whom came from the United States.

Guest professorships included the University of Vienna, Austria, and Union Theological Seminary of Virginia, and he lectured frequently in distinguished lectureships in Europe, North America, and South Africa.

Reicke was a member of the international Society of New Testament Studies (SNTS) from its postwar rebirth in 1947 until the time of his death. In 1982 he was honored as the society's president. Additional academic societies included Nathan Söderblom-Sälilskapet (Uppsala) from 1947 (corresponding member 1953–1987) and the Académie Internationale des Sciences Réligieuses (Bruxelles) from 1972; he served as the society's vice president, 1986–87.

Reicke's many books, scholarly and ecclesiastical articles, and sermons are published in Swedish, German, French, and English. He was married to Ingalisa Reicke, née Åhström, M.A., 1941, with children Agnes (bank lawyer in Zürich) and Daniel, Dr.phil. (art historian in Basel).

Professor Reicke passed away at his home in Basel, May 17, 1987.

From his retirement in 1984 until his death in May 1987 Professor Reicke continued his scholarly endeavors. Foremost among his publications was his major study of the origins and relations among the Synoptic Gospels, *The Roots of the Synoptic Gospels* (Philadelphia: Fortress Press, 1986). His work also included the publication of sermons as well as scholarly articles in journals, encyclopedias, and Festschriften.

The manuscript on the history of the Pauline correspondence was finished just before his death; it is published here as Part II. Five essays on related topics dating from 1953 to 1983 form Parts I and III of the volume. It was Professor Reicke's plan to publish a volume, "The Apostle Paul and Pauline Theology," which should include his "History of the Pauline Correspondence," the five essays included here, and several other essays specifically on Paul's theology. We list the titles on Pauline theology here to illustrate Reicke's lifelong occupation with the full range of the apostle's life and impact:

"The New Testament Conception of Reward," in *Aux sources de la tradition chrétienne: Mélanges offerts à M. Goguel* (Neuchâtel/Paris: Delachaux et Niestlé, 1950), 195–206.
"The Law and This World According to Paul: Some Thoughts Concerning Gal. 4:1–11," *JBL* 70 (1951): 259–76.
"Zum sprachlichen Verständnis von Kol. 2,23," *Studia Theologica* 6 (Lund: Gleerup, 1953), 39–53.
"Syneideis in Röm. 2,15," *TZ* 12 (1956): 157–61.
"Natürliche Theologie nach Paulus," in *SEÅ* 22–23 (1958): 154–67.
"Unité chrétienne et diaconie, Phil. 1,1–11" in *Neotestamentica et patristica, Oscar Cullmann zum 60. Geburtstag* (Leiden: Brill, 1962), 203–12.
"Paul's Understanding of Righteousness," in *Soli Deo Gloria, in Honor of W. C. Robinson* (Richmond: J. Knox, 1968), 37–49.
"Paulus über das Gesetz," *TZ* 41 (1985): 237–57.
"Homiletisch orientierte Auslegung von 1.Thess. 5:1–11," *TZ* 44 (1988): 91–96.

—I. Reicke

*Appendix 3*

# Biographical and Bibliographical Notes

## Festschriften and Biographical Sketches of the Life and Work of Bo Reicke

*The New Testament Age: Essays in Honor of Bo Reicke*, 2 vols., ed. W. C. Weinrich (Macon: Mercer University Press, 1984). A dedication by Oscar Cullmann opens the first of two volumes of 42 essays in over 570 pages contributed by an international group of scholars. A bibliography of Bo Reicke's works up to 1983 (sermons and reviews excepted) completes volume 2 (books and articles, 1942–1983, pp. 553–60).

*Good News in History: Essays in Honor of Bo Reicke*, ed. Ed L. Miller (Atlanta: Scholars Press, 1993), 206pp. This volume is a tribute to Professor Reicke from his many doctoral students. On the occasion of the SNTS meeting in Atlanta, Georgia, 1986, a dinner was hosted in his honor during which essays in typescript from a larger number of his students were presented to him. In 1993 ten of the essays from this larger collection, as well as a biographical tribute to Professor Reicke by Bruce N. Kaye, were published in the Scholars Press Homage series (see "Professor Bo Reicke: A Biographical Appreciation," pp. 193–200, reprinted in *TZ* 50 [1994]: 295–307). In addition, this volume makes available in English (pp. 173–92, trans. Ed L. Miller) an article by Professor Reicke published some years earlier as "Einheit und Vielfalt in der neutestamentlichen Theologie," in *Lutherische Kirche in der Welt: Jahrbuch des Martin Luther-Bundes* 35 (1988): 14–35 (see bibliog. below).

"Professor Bo Reicke zum Gedenken." By Oscar Cullmann in *Uni Nova* 47 (1987): 17–18 (summary of Reicke's life and work).

"Reicke, Bo Ivar." By D. P. Moessner in *Dictionary of Biblical Interpretation*, 2 vols. (Nashville: Abingdon Press, 1999), 2.380 (surveys three of Reicke's major works).

# Completed Bibliography of the Works of Bo Reicke (1983–1999)

## Books

*The Roots of the Synoptic Gospels* (Philadelphia: Fortress Press, 1986).

## Pamphlets

*Alte Luther-Drucke in Basel: Ausstellung zum Luther-Jubiläum 1983 in der Basler Universitätsbibliothek* (Basel: Univ.-Bibliothek, 1983).

## Articles

"Aus der Geschichte der Theologischen Fakultät der Universität Basel," *Uni Nova* 26 (1983): 12–14.

"Die Entstehungsverhältnisse der synoptischen Evangelien," in *Aufstieg und Niedergang der römischen Welt* II,25,2 (Berlin: de Gruyter, 1984), 1758–91; ET, "The History of the Synoptic Discussion," in *The Interrelations of the Gospels: A Symposium,* ed. D. Dungan; Bibl. Ephem. Lov. 95 (Leuven: University Press & Peeters, 1990), 291–316.

"Paulus über das Gesetz," *Festschrift für Markus Barth zum 70. Geburtstag, TZ* 41 (1985): 237–57.

"The Universality of Salvation According to the New Testament," in *Salut universel et regard pluraliste: Colloque de l'Acad. Internat. des sciences relig. 1984* (Paris: Desclée, 1986), 25–37.

"Sosiale faktorer i Bibelns verden," in *Nye Store Bibelleksikon,* vol. 1 (Oslo: Norröna Forlag, 1986), 45–54.

"Religioner i Bibelns omgivning," in *Nye Store Bibelleksikon,* vol. 2 (Oslo: Norröna Forlag, 1986), 9–37.

"From Strauss to Holtzmann and Meijboom: Synoptic Theories Advanced during the Consolidation of Germany 1839–1870," *NovT* 29 (1987) 1–21.

"Positive and Negative Aspects of the World in the New Testament," *Westminster Theological Journal* 49 (1987): 351–69.

"The Historical Setting of John's Baptism," in *Jesus, the Gospels, and the Church: Essays in Honor of W. R. Farmer,* ed. E. P. Sanders (Macon: Mercer University Press, 1987), 209–24).

"Einheit und Vielfalt in der neutestamentlichen Theologie," in *Lutherische Kirche in der Welt: Jahrbuch des Martin Luther-Bundes* 35 (1988): 14–35; ET, "Unity and Diversity in New Testament Theology," in *Good News in History: Essays in Honor of Bo Reicke,* ed. Ed L. Miller (Atlanta: Scholars Press, 1993), 173–92.

"Homiletisch orientierte Auslegung von 1.Thess. 5:1–11," *TZ* 44 (1988): 91–96.

"Christ et le Temps," in *Temps et eschatologie: Données bibliques et problématiques contemporaines,* ed. J.-L. Leuba (Paris: Ed. du Cerf, 1994), 65–86.

## Encyclopedia Articles

"Philippians," in *International Standard Bible Encyclopaedia* 3 (1986): 836–41.

"G. A. Jülicher," in *Dictionary of Biblical Interpretation,* ed. J. H. Hayes (Nashville: Abingdon Press, 1999), 1:650–51.

"The Synoptic Problem," in ibid., 2:517–24.

"Descent into Hell," in *Oxford Companion to the Bible* (New York: Oxford University Press, 1993), 163.

"Gehenna," in ibid., 243.

"Hell," in ibid., 277–79.

"Early Christian Chronology," in ibid., 119–21.

## Sermons

"Das leere Grab (Matt. 28,1–8). Ostersonntag 1987," *Theologische Beiträge* 19,2 (1988): 58–60.

Sermon in the Notre Dame of Jerusalem Chapel, Easter Day, April 22, 1984, in *The Interrelations of the Gospels: A Symposium,* ed. D. Dungan; Bibl. Ephem. Lov. 95 (Leuven: University Press & Peeters, 1990), 610–13.

# Endnotes

## Foreword

1. Bo Reicke's well-known commentary *The Epistles of James, Peter, and Jude* (AB 37 [1964]) is the English translation of the Swedish manuscript that had been completed already in 1954 but, for technical reasons, was not published until 1968.

2. For more biographical data about Bo Reicke's life, see Appendixes 2 and 3 at the end of this volume, and also Bruce N. Kaye, "Professor Bo Reicke: A Biographical Appreciation," in Ed L. Miller, ed., *Good News in History: Essays in Honor of Bo Reicke* (Atlanta: Scholars Press, 1993), 193–200 (see listing below in Appendix 3).

For a bibliography of Bo Reicke's published works up to 1983, see "Reicke Bibliography," in *The New Testament Age: Essays in Honor of Bo Reicke*, 2 vols., ed. W. C. Weinrich (Macon: Mercer University Press, 1984), 2:553–60. For a complete list of Reicke's publications subsequent to 1983, see Appendix 3 below.

## Introduction

1. R. E. Brown, *An Introduction to the New Testament* (ABRL; New York: Doubleday, 1997) 672.

2. *Neutestamentliche Zeitgeschichte. Die biblische Welt von 500 v. Chr. bis 100 n. Chr.*; Dritte, verbesserte Auflage (Berlin: W. de Gruyter, 1982), 253. The English edition, *The New Testament Era* (Philadelphia: Fortress Press, 1968), is translated from the second German edition of 1964 (cf. ET, p. 306, on the Pastorals as exhortations to "political and social solidarity" during the time of Vespasian). Reicke's desire to write a NT introduction before revising the chronology of the Pastorals is indicative of the way he wanted to present the larger picture as the key to solving the "problem" of the Pastorals, rather than defending their "Pauline" authorship per se.

3. "Caesarea, Rome, and the Captivity Epistles," see below, pp. 131–40.

4. 2 Cor. 11:23; Reicke cites Rom. 16:7 as referring also to short-term imprisonment; see, e.g., p. 73.

5. "Caesarea, Rome, and the Captivity Epistles," see below, p. 137; see esp. below, pp. 136–40.

6. For example, see 2 Cor. 1:8; cf. Acts 20:18–19, 31. Even Paul's comment in 1 Cor. 15:32, which some exegetes understand as an allusion to incarceration—"I fought with wild beasts in Ephesus, figuratively speaking (*kata anthropon*)"—Reicke argued could not be so understood because of the idiom "in a figure of [human] speech"/"so to speak." Paul's combat had to be taken metaphorically as fighting his enemies rather than literally of direct confinement, perhaps including some form of exposure to wild animals (see his discussion below of 1 Corinthians, Part II, "The History of the Pauline Correspondence").

7. Acts 20:1; cf. 19:8–10, 17–20, 23–41.

8. See esp. Brown, *An Introduction to the New Testament*, Chapter 25, "Pseudo-nymity and the Deuteropauline Writings," 585–89.

9. Reicke did, of course, devote much of his study to Paul's theology, includ-ing comparisons and contrasts with other NT and early Christian writers; see, e.g., "Paulus über das Gesetz," *TZ* 41 (1985): 237–57 [Festschrift, Markus Barth], and see Appendix 3 of this volume.

10. For Part II, the placing of all thirteen Paulines into three qualitatively distinct, historical periods (see Table of Contents and Appendix 1) is not part of the original draft and is an attempt by the editors to draw attention to Reicke's general conclu-sions, without suggesting any limits on the hermeneutical scope and impact of the letters themselves.

## Judeo-Christianity and the Jewish Establishment

1. J. C. O'Neill, 'The Charge of Blasphemy at Jesus' Trial before the Sanhedrin,' in E. Bammel (ed.), *The Trial of Jesus. Cambridge Studies in Honour of C. F. D. Moule* (London, 1970), 72–77.

2. B. Reicke, *Glaube und Leben der Urgemeinde* (Zürich, 1957), 55–114.

3. Seeing that James, the son of Zebedee, was reported to have been killed "by the sword" (Acts 12:2), S. G. F. Brandon has concluded that Agrippa I was also concerned about the seditious aspect of Christianity: *The Trial of Jesus* (London, 1968), 48. But in connection with this persecution, *c.* A.D. 42, the king's concern was expressly said to be to please the Jews (12:3), and his general ambition to strengthen Pharisaism was emphasised by Josephus. There was no reason for any Jewish opposition to Rome under the glorious King Agrippa, and there is no reason to believe that James and his fellow Christians had ever appeared to be a danger to the empire.

4. B. Reicke, *Neutestamentliche Zeitgeschichte*, 3rd edn. (Berlin, 1982), 191ff, 238ff (ET *The New Testament Era* [London, 1968], 188–224, 237–510).

5. M. Smith, 'Zealots and Sicarii: Their Origins and Relation,' *HThR*, 64 (1971). 1–19, wants to find three stages in the development of zealotism: (1) several repre-sentatives of 'zeal' in the sense of resistance to direct Roman government (p. 18); (2) the rise of the *sicarii* A.D. 54 (pp. 13, 18); (3) the organisation of the Zealots, A.D. 67 (p. 19). The impetus given by the *sicarii* was in any case important for the further development of the resistance movement.

## The Historical Background of the Apostolic Council and the Episode in Antioch

1. The author used the original German edition of H. Schlier (*Der Brief an die Galater* [1949]), 33, 37, 41. [In rendering the German, *Novum Testamentum Graece* (27th ed.; Deutsche Bibelgesellschaft) was consulted as well as the RSV and NRSV —ed.]

2. Already in the ancient church this historical problem was noticed: L. Cerfaux, "Le chapitre XVe du Livre des Actes à la lumière de la littérature ancienne," *Studi e testi* 121 (1946): 107–26.

3. Cf. the analyses, e.g., by H. Schlier (*Der Brief an die Galater* [1949]: 66–78); O. Linton ("En dementi och dess öde," *SEÅ* 12 [1947]: 203–19); idem ("The Third

Aspect," *StTh* 3/1 [1950]: 79–95); J. Dupont (*Les problèmes du Livre des Actes* [1950]: 51–70); S. Giet ("L'assemblée apostolique et le décret de Jérusalem," *RSR* 39: [1951]: 203–20); O. Cullmann (*Petrus* [1952]:47ff).

4. Cf. the summary by Dupont [*Les problèmes*], 57–61.

5. Cf. ibid., 61–67. Acts 11:27–30 has been the subject recently of a special investigation by S. Giet ("Le second voyage de S. Paul à Jerusalem," *RSR* 25 [1951]: 265–69).

6. Cullmann, *Petrus*, 39ff.

7. See n. 1.

8. J. de Zwaan, "Gallio, Paulus' rechter," in *Jezus, Paulus en Rome* (1927): 94–111; W. Rees, "Gallio, the Proconsul of Achaia," *Scripture* 4 (1949): 11–20.

9. P. Gaechter ("Petrus in Antiochia (Gal. 2.11–14)," *ZKTh* 72 [1950]: 177–212) has also touched upon the external political developments (p. 185); but he stresses mainly personal circumstances.

10. B. Reicke, "Den äldsta jerusalemsförsamlingens liv enligt tvenne parallella traditioner (Apg. 2:42–4:32 och 4:42–5:42)," *Svenska Jerusalemsföreningens Tidskrift* [*Journal of the Swedish Jerusalem Society*] 48 (1949): 37–42; 67–79; 100–16.

11. B. Reicke, "Sionisternas angrepp på Stefanus. Bidrag till den historiska förståelsen av Apg. 6"; ibid., *Svenska Jerusalemsföreningens Tidskrift* 50 (1949): 4–26. [As the secretary of the Swedish Jerusalem Society and editor of its quarterly review, Reicke published the above-mentioned articles on Acts in Swedish. The material was later used in his book *Glaube und Leben der Urgemeinde*; ATANT 21 (Zürich: Zwingli Verlag, 1957).—I. Reicke]

12. Jos. *Ant.* XIX,6–7 (292–334); *Mishna Bikk.* III,4; *Sot.*VII,8; E. Schürer, *Geschichte des jüdischen Volkes* 3 (4th ed. 1901): 553–62; R. H. Pfeiffer, *History of New Testament Times* (1949), 37f.

13. E. Schürer, *Geschichte des jüdischen Volkes*, 571.

14. P. *Lond.* 1912. H. I. Bell, *Jews and Christians in Egypt* (1924): 23–37; S. Loesch, *Epistula Claudiana* (1930): 8–11; M. P. Charlesworth, *Documents Illustrating the Reign of Claudius and Nero* (1939; Nr. 1–2); V. M. Scramuzza, *The Emperor Claudius* (1940): 64–79.

15. The conflict broke out again under Isidorus and Lampo, but not until A.D. 53 (see Bell, *Jews and Christians*, 19ff; Scramuzza, *The Emperor Claudius*, 78, 256).

16. For various reasons, this identification is regarded by some scholars as the only feasible one to hold. I will mention only a few of more recent authors: A. Oepke, *Der Brief des Paulus an die Galater* (1937): 39f; O. Bauernfeind, *Die Apostelgeschichte* (1939), 186; M. Dibelius, "Das Apostelkonzil," *TLZ* 72 (1947): 193–98; W. Kümmel, "Das Urchristentum, III," *TR* N.F. 17 (1948): 28–33; H. Schlier, *Der Brief an die Galater* (1949): 76; Linton, (see n. 3).

17. Jos. *Ant.* XX,5,2 (101); Tac. *Ann.* XII, 43; Eus. *Chron.* II (ed. Schoene, 152f); Oros. VII, 6, 17.

18. Joach. Jeremias, "Sabbathjahr und neutestamentliche Chronologie," *ZNW* 27 (1928): 98–103.

19. Moreover, it cannot be denied that, at the same time, concern for the unity of the church can also have contributed to the mutual understanding (cf. Ch. de Beus, "De positie van de gemeente te Jerusalem in de oudchristelijke kerk, in het licht van Gal. 2:6," *NedThT* 7 [1952]: 1–18).

20. Jos. *Ant.* XX,8,5ff (160ff); idem, *Bell.* II,13,3 (254ff); Tac. *Ann.* XII, 54.
21. Eus. *Hist. eccl.* II, 23.
22. Jos. *Ant.* XX,9,1 (200).
23. Concerning James, the brother of the Lord, see H. Leclercq ("Jacques le Mineur," *Dict. d'archéol. chrét.* 7,2 (1927): cols. 2109–16 (Hegesippus' information about James is regarded as essentially reliable [col. 2110]). More critical is H. von Campenhausen ("Die Nachfolge des Jakobus," *Zeitschrift für Kirchengeschichte* 63/2 [1951]: 133ff), whereas E. Stauffer ("Zum Kalifat des Jakobus," *Zeitschrift für Religions-und Geistesgeschichte* 4/3 [1952]) comes to the conclusion (p. 206): "From the perspectives of tradition criticism and the history of ideas when investigating the extra-canonical James traditions, one can hardly proceed carefully enough." But what is being presented above is simply the Jewish-Christian sentiment of James, and this basic orientation can hardly be contested.

## Philippians

1. On the authorship of Acts, see also Bo Reicke's *The Roots of the Synoptic Gospels* (Philadelphia: Fortress Press, 1986), 166–74.
2. The archaeology and topography of Philippi are known through French and Greek excavations (P. Collart, P. Lemerle and D. Lazarides, *Philippe et la Macédoine orientale à l'époque chrétienne et byzantine* [Paris, 1945]).
3. See above, "Judeo-Christianity and the Jewish Establishment, A.D. 33–66," pp. 9–15.
4. See esp. below, "Caesarea, Rome, and the Captivity Epistles," pp. 131–40.
5. Cf. the author's article in *The International Standard Bible Encyclopedia* 3 (1986): 838–39; B. Van Elderen, ibid., 929. A few inscriptions from the area around Ephesus, often cited as evidence of the letter's Ephesian origin, refer not to the imperial bodyguard but to a retired veteran of the praetorium who was active in the area as a rural constable.
6. Reicke (*International Standard* [n. 5]), and also below, "Caesarea, Rome, and the Captivity Epistles," pp. 131–40.
7. J. Frey, *Corpus inscriptionum judaicarum* 1 (1936): 72f.
8. Because this Epaphroditus acted on behalf of the Philippian congregation ("your messenger and minister," Phil. 2:25), he is not to be confused, despite the similar name, with the Epaphras, who came to Paul from Colossae ("who is one of yourselves," Col. 1:7 and 4:12).
9. 1 Thess. 1:1–2:16 to the congregation; 2:17–3:13 on Paul; 4:1–5:26 to the congregation; Phil. 1:1–26 on Paul; 1:27–2:16 to the congregation; 2:17–30 on Paul; 3:1–4:9 to the congregation; 4:23 on Paul.
10. Starting with 2 Thessalonians, this is Paul's standard greeting of peace through the rest of his epistles (with the possible exceptions of the shorter variant readings for 1 Thess. 1:1 and Col. 1:2).

## The Chronology of the Pastoral Epistles

1. H. Koskenniemi, *Studien zur Idee und Phraseologie des griechischen Briefes* (1956), 201–05.
2. Ibid., 91: "When we investigate actual private correspondence, especially papyrus letters, we can perceive a broad spectrum from the most intensely personal all

the way to the stodgiest impersonableness conceivable." Conversely, Koskenniemi states (p. 91): "It can be considered from the outset as certain, that in a purely fictitious epistle, where a strong, personal vitality is connected with the fiction of an intimate relationship between the correspondents, much more 'naturalness' and 'freshness' can be discovered than in a purely matter-of-fact or objectively 'real' letter." In other words, a stylistic criterion is unsatisfactory in distinguishing between factual and fabricated letters.

3. NRSV; for the Greek text, consult the German original, p. 83 [ed.].

4. Koskenniemi, *Studien*, 147: "One has every reason to suppose that for the apostle these expressions depend on the general stylistic customs known to him, whereby this usage would turn out to be common Greek." The Pauline letters thus supplement the material preserved elsewhere, mainly in the Egyptian papyri.

5. If one proceeds axiomatically from the unauthenticity of the Pastorals, the circular deduction alluded to above emerges. N. Brox perpetrates this in his "Zu den persönlichen Notizen der Pastoralbriefe" (*BZ* 13 [1969]: 76–94). He plays down the biographical descriptions of the Pastorals as literary tricks and in so doing appeals to Koskenniemi (see nn. 1, 2, 4), without paying attention to the cross-fertilization established by the philologist between popular folk letters and literary epistolary productions.

6. NRSV; for the Greek text, consult the German original, p. 84 [ed.].

7. This connection was drawn to the author's attention through a private correspondence of Bishop J. A. T. Robinson.

8. R. Morgenthaler, *Statistik* (1958): 104.

9. B. Reicke, "The Historical Setting of Colossians," *Review and Expositor* 70 (1973): 429–38.

10. H. Maehlum, *Die Vollmacht des Timotheus nach den Pastoralbriefen* (Basel: F. Reinhardt Verlag, 1969), 53–67.

11. B. Reicke, "Caesarea, Rome, and the Captivity Epistles," *Apostolic History and the Gospel. Biblical and Historical Essays Presented to F. F. Bruce*, ed. W. W. Gasque and Ralph P. Martin (Grand Rapids: Eerdmans, 1970), 275–86. See below, pp. 131–40.

12. For the Greek text, consult the German original, p. 90 [ed.].

13. Reicke, "The Historical Setting," 437; see also below, pp. 121–30. Reicke, "Caesarea, Rome, and the Captivity," 279–82; see also below, pp. 131–40.

14. Reicke, "The Historical Setting," 432; see also below, pp. 121–30.

15. Ibid., 436–37; see also below, pp. 121–30.

16. As Eph. 6:21 implies [ed.].

17. [Editor's note:] Cf., e.g., the remark by John Knox: "It must be recognized that the ties binding Colossians to Philemon are far stronger than any bonds with Ephesians—ties so strong and intricate, so very improbable as the inventions of even the cleverest pseudepigrapher as to render it virtually impossible to decide that Colossians is not a genuine Pauline letter, as Philemon undoubtedly is" ("On the Pauline Chronology: Buck—Taylor—Hurd Revisited," *The Conversation Continues: Studies in Paul & John. In Honor of J. Louis Martyn*, ed. R. Fortna and B. Gaventa [Nashville: Abingdon Press, 1990], 264–65).

## The Historical Setting of Colossians

1. W. J. Hamilton, *Researches in Asia Minor, Pontus, and Armenia* (London: J. Murray, 1842), 506–13.

2. W. M. Ramsay, *The Cities and Bishoprics of Phrygia* (Oxford: Clarendon Press, 1895–97), I:208–16; P. Benoit, "Paul, Epître aux Colossiens," *Dictionnaire de la Bible* Suppl. 7 (1961), col. 157.

3. Ramsay, *op. cit.*, 208, 217–21.

4. C. Humann, C. Cichorius, W. Judeich, and F. Winter, *Altertümer von Hierapolis* (Berlin: G. Reimer, 1898), 42–47, on paganism, Judaism, and Christianity.

5. A few inscriptions are from the necropolis of Colossae but more from Laodicea and other places in the Lycus valley. See Ramsay, *op. cit.*, II:542–53; W. H. Buckler and W. M. Calder (eds.), *Monuments and Documents from Phrygia and Caria*, "Monumenta Asiae Minoris Antiqua," (1939), VI: Xf., 1–18.

6. M. J. Mellink, "Antioch of Pisidia," *The Interpreter's Dictionary of the Bible*, (1962) I:144 (the number 6 in the order of the footnotes was inadvertently left out in the original publication [ed.]).

7. J. B. Lightfoot, *Saint Paul's Epistle to the Philippians* (London: Macmillan & Co., 1868; reprinted), 31–45, 99–104, 171–78.

8. B. Reicke, "Caesarea, Rome, and the Captivity Epistles," *Apostolic History and the Gospel*, ed. W. W. Gasque and Ralph P. Martin (Grand Rapids: Eerdmans, 1970), 278, 282–86.

9. Ibid., 279.

10. H. A. W. Meyer, *Kritisch-exegetischer Handbuch über die Briefe Pauli an die Philipper, Kolosser und an Philemon* (4. Aufl.; Göttingen: Vandenhoeck and Ruprecht, 1874), pp. 210f.; E. Lohmeyer, *Die Briefe an die Philipper, an die Kolosser und an Philemon*, "Kritisch-exegetischer Kommentar über das Neue Testament," ed. H. A. W. Meyer (9. Aufl.; Göttingen: Vandenhoeck and Ruprecht, 1953), 24.

11. Reicke, *op. cit.*, 278–82.

12. Ibid.

13. J. Gnilka, *Der Epheserbrief*, "Herders theologischer Kommentar zum Neuen Testament" (Freiburg: Herder, 1971), 1–7.

14. M. Dibelius, *Die Pastoralbriefe*, "Handbuch zum Neuen Testament" (3. Aufl.: Tübingen: Mohr, 1955), 95f.

15. C. F. D. Moule, "The Problem of the Pastoral Epistles," *Bulletin of the John Rylands Library*, 47:430–52, 1965.

16. Therefore, modern theological expositions of Colossians and the other Epistles were not quoted above. Besides the documents, attention was rather drawn to older studies occupied with the fundamental historical evidence.

## Caesarea, Rome, and the Captivity Epistles

1. See literature cited in W. G. Kümmel, *Einleitung in das Neue Testament* (Heidelberg: Quelle & Meyer, 1973), 241–64, 409f., 412 (=ET, 237–58, 382f., 397).

2. See Kümmel (p. 277, n. 1) for the literature, 229–41, 409 [=ET, 226–37, 389].

3. The commentary which is still the most useful for introductory matters is J. B. Lightfoot, *St. Paul's Epistle to the Philippians* (London & New York: Macmillan, 1868, 1st ed; reprinted: Grand Rapids, MI: Zondervan, 1963).

4. Concerning the gates of the temple, cf. E. Stauffer, "Das Tor des Nikanor," *ZNW* 44 (1952/53), 44–66.

5. The inner courts made up the "sanctuary" in the narrow sense of the word (*to hieron:* Acts 21:28; Josephus, *Ant.* XV.419). Therefore, Luke's expression is not wrong (so H. Conzelmann, *Die Apostelgeschichte* (Tübingen: Mohr [Siebeck] 1963), 30f., 123).

6. C. Clermont-Ganneau, "Une stèle du temple de Jérusalem," *Revue archéologique,* nouv. ser. 23 (1872): 214ff.; W. Dittenberger, *Orientis graeci inscriptiones selectae* 2 (1905): Nr. 598; Strack-Billerbeck II (1924): 761f.; J. H. Iliffe, "The *Thanatos* Inscription from Herod's Temple: Fragment of a Second Copy," *The Quarterly of the Department of Antiquities in Palestine* 6 (1936): 1–3; I. I. E. Hondius, *Supplementum epigraphicum graecum* 8, 1 (1937): Nr. 169; E. J. Bickerman, "The Warning Inscriptions of Herod's Temple," *JQR* 37 (1947): 387ff.; B. Reicke, "Hedningarnas begränsade tillträde till Herodes' tempel," *Svenska Jerusalemsföreningens tidskrift* 46 (1947): 116–24; J. Finegan, *Light from the Ancient Past* (Princeton: Princeton University Press, 1959), fig. 118 (following p. 282), also 325–26; J. Frey, *Corpus inscriptionum judaicarum* 2 (1952), Nr. 1400.

7. B. Reicke, *Neutestamentliche Zeitgeschichte* (Berlin: de Gruyter, 1964), 212 [=ET, *The New Testament Era* (Philadelphia: Fortress Press, 1968), 287].

8. G. S. Duncan, *St. Paul's Ephesian Ministry* (London, 1929), 109: *Praetorium* "must be taken not of the place as a building but of the people who are associated with it." The negative remark is correct, but the positive conclusion does not fit the lexical finding.

9. E. Hilgert, "Schiffahrt," *BHH* 3 (1966): col. 1696.

10. Concerning the bodyguard, similarly F. F. Bruce, "Praetorium," *BHH* 3 (1966): col. 1482.

# Index of Ancient Sources

# Index of Modern Authors

CPSIA information can be obtained at www.ICGtesting.com
Printed in the USA
BVOW021555210911

271769BV00003B/253/P